Every Little Thing About You

Every
Little Thing
About You

LORI WICK

HARVEST HOUSE PUBLISHERS
Eugene, Oregon 97402

Scripture references are taken from the King James Version of the Bible.

Cover design by Terry Dugan Design, Minneapolis, Minnesota

Cover photo courtesy of the East Texas Research Center photograph collection

EVERY LITTLE THING ABOUT YOU
Copyright © 1999 Lori Wick
Published by Harvest House Publishers
Eugene, Oregon 97402

ISBN: 0-7394-0465-2

Printed in the United States of America.

Books by Lori Wick

A Place Called Home Series
A Place Called Home
A Song for Silas
The Long Road Home
A Gathering of Memories

The Californians
Whatever Tomorrow Brings
As Time Goes By
Sean Donovan
Donavan's Daughter

Kensington Chronicles
The Hawk and the Jewel
Wings of the Morning
Who Brings Forth the Wind
The Knight and the Dove

Rocky Mountain Memories
Where the Wild Rose Blooms
Whispers of Moonlight
To Know Her by Name
Promise Me Tomorrow

The Yellow Rose Trilogy
Every Little Thing About You

Contemporary Fiction
Sophie's Heart
Beyond the Picket Fence (Short Stories)
Pretense
The Princess

Acknowledgments

What a time it's been. This book has been with me for literally years. I was ready to begin writing in 1992, but the Kensington Chronicles came along. They in turn led to other works, so Texas was shelved for a time. But because of that, the Yellow Rose Trilogy has taken on better form and dimension, and I think the books might be better than the first drafts in my mind.

All this to say, I'm so excited to finally put this first book down on paper. The people I need to acknowledge have patiently helped me come to this point. A huge thank-you goes to:

Phil Caminiti. Your wisdom as we walk through the book of Mark has been invaluable to me. Thank you for your insight, love of the Word, and humble desire to be more like Jesus Christ. Thank you for teaching the student, not the lesson. My world is a bigger place because of you.

Denise Caminiti. The time in your Bible study has been a joy and a delight. I love your honest approach and easy agenda. Thank you for your patience with me and for never failing to show me love and acceptance. I consider you a friend so dear.

The women from Bible study. If I try to name all of you, I will be sure to miss someone. Please allow me to thank all of you for your love and kindness. I learn so much from you and Thursday mornings are a highlight of the week for me.

The elders' wives at BECC. Thank you for what you've shared and taught me. I am privileged beyond measure to know and fellowship with you. Thank you for your hunger and humility and the way you bring glory to God.

My own precious Bob. You hung in there, Wickie! This book was put on the back burner so many times, and still you waited in silence. Thank you for being patient and for cheering the loudest along the way.

Did I laugh before you were born?
Not quite so often, I'm sure.
Did I know about a mother's love before you?
Not by half.
Keep growing, keep trusting,
and never forget that I love you.
For my Tin Man.

Prologue

September 1881
Austin, Texas

THE MIDAFTERNOON SUN beat down unmercifully as the cowboy, a Texas Ranger, rode into town. Heat waves shimmered on the horizon, and the blowing dust caused the horse's eyes to squint as Slater Rawlings tethered the dark roan animal to the hitching post. Other than seeing that the horse could reach the water trough, Slater gave little heed to Arrow's comfort. For weeks the rider had been working on the courage to tell his boss about his decision, and now it was time to do the job. It was a relief to arrive at the Austin office and walk in the door.

❧·❧·❧

"Why can't you do both, Slate?" Marty Bracewell asked one of his best rangers just 15 minutes later. "Why does this faith thing mean you have to leave?"

"It's not my faith—just as it is, Brace," the younger man tried to explain. "And it's not the job itself. It's the travel. I'm tired of tracking and being out on the trail. I want to settle in someplace for the winter, possibly longer." What Slater Rawlings didn't try to explain was the need to get to church on Sundays—the ache inside of him for fellowship. Brace, whose life was the Rangers, would never have understood.

"You'll be back," Brace said with confidence, the desk chair creaking as he leaned back with ease. "It's in your blood, just like it's in Dakota's. You'll be back."

Slater didn't even reply. He stood, lifting his hat to his head.

"Take care, Brace."

"I'll do that. You do the same. I want you coming back fit."

Not only did Slater not reply to this, he didn't even look back as he placed his badge on the desk. With a hand to the doorknob, he quietly let himself out. Just moments later he was back astride Arrow and headed out of town. With a thought of how cool the hills would be, he headed west.

One

October 1881
Shotgun, Texas

FRIDAY AFTERNOONS WERE normally quiet. Saturday nights were a little more rambunctious, but most days and evenings in Shotgun were peaceful. It was for this reason that Liberty Drake was surprised to be needed. Being called out of the sheriff's office to one of the saloons was the last thing she expected, but Shotgun had laws about carrying firearms into the saloons or after sunset, so she had a job to do. She strapped on her holster and followed Jep, the saloon owner's 11-year-old son, down the street. The boy ran, but Liberty walked, not apathetic, but not certain she needed to be out of breath when she arrived.

And indeed, things were quiet when she pushed through the swinging doors of the Brass Spittoon. Jep's father, Gordie, nodded his head to a table in the corner. Liberty took in three men. Two were daytime regulars, but the blond was a stranger. There wasn't even a drink in front of him, but Liberty had no choice.

"Excuse me," Liberty began politely, waiting for the man to look at her. "I need you to surrender your firearm to me. Shotgun has outlawed firearms in the saloons and after dark."

Slater looked up at the woman beside him. She was dressed in baggy men's clothes, which did nothing to hide her gender, and he could only stare. *Was that really a sheriff's badge on her vest?* His hesitation cost him. With a move so fast and smooth that Slater blinked, the woman's gun cleared leather as swiftly as she lifted his own gun from the holster at his hip.

"You'll need to come with me, sir," Liberty said calmly.

"What?" Slater returned, finally uttering his first word.

Liberty gestured with the gun and moved so he could stand. "This way, please," she ordered congenially but watching every move as he slowly rose. One of the other men handed saddlebags to Liberty, and after she'd thanked him and draped them over her arm, she moved Slater again with the motion of her gun.

As though he'd been frozen from the cold, Slater moved very slowly as he walked through the saloon. At the table he had stopped just short of reaching for his pocket to show his Ranger's badge when he remembered it wasn't there. He also remembered what such a move would look like. He didn't want to run the risk of having this woman shoot him. She had cleared leather very smoothly, but that didn't mean she could shoot straight. Barely managing to keep his amazement concealed, he walked ahead of her and out onto the street. He made the mistake of turning to her as soon as he was outside and felt cold steel press into his ribs.

"Just turn back around," she said evenly, "and lead the way straight up the walk."

Now seething inside, Slater turned and obeyed. He didn't know when he'd been so angry. At six foot, he was not a huge man, but this small woman with the badge, clearly too full of herself, had him at her mercy. With a prayer for calm that was slow in coming, Slater did as he was told. They hadn't walked for a minute when she spoke.

"In here," she directed, and Slater, already aware of the location, went through the door of the sheriff's office. He heard the door shut behind him and turned.

"Empty your pockets onto the desk, please," Liberty ordered, all business, as she put the saddlebags out of reach on the floor. "Nice and slow will do fine."

Slater did so without ever taking his eyes from her, which meant he couldn't miss the way she watched him in return. She was calm; he had to give her that. As he looked into her eyes, he knew with a bone-chilling certainty that she would shoot if she felt she had to.

"Now your boots," she instructed.

Slater hesitated and heard the gun cock.

"All right," he said smoothly. "I'll just tell you, though, I do have a knife in my boot. I won't use it—I just wanted you to know."

"Put the knife on the desk," Liberty said, taking a second to eye the Bowie knife that appeared. Not a heartbeat later her eyes were back on her prisoner, who was removing his boots with slow, measured movements.

"Your belt now," Liberty said as soon as he stood back to full height. He was a taller man than she liked to deal with, but she didn't think he was going to threaten her. She couldn't, however, take any chances.

"Turn around," was the next order, once all of Slater's belongings were on the desk. "Head into the cell."

Slater did so, the feeling of unreality washing over him again. He turned as soon as he was inside and watched as the door was shut and locked. He also watched as Liberty holstered her gun, set his on the desk, and began to speak.

"Dinner comes at 6:00 this evening, and breakfast tomorrow at 7:00. You're expected to be neat and quiet. Unless you're wanted for something, the charge to get out is ten dollars."

"*Ten dollars!*" Slater growled in outrage. "You can't be serious."

Liberty shrugged. "We need a new jail, and this seems like the most obvious way to come up with the money."

Slater's mouth fell open. He couldn't believe what he had just heard. How in the world had he thought this was a nice little town?

"I don't suppose you have it," Liberty said now, her voice resigned as she studied him.

"Why would you say that?" Slater was just irritated enough to ask.

Liberty's brows rose. "You can't even afford a haircut and a shave." There was no censure in her voice, only calm reason. Slater swallowed his rage as she turned away. He turned his back on the bars. The cell was standard fare, but he saw what she meant—repairs were needed.

With a sigh that he made no attempt to hide, Slater walked to the bed and collapsed on the straw mattress, which sent up a musty odor. He leaned against the wall and tried to stay calm. Nothing worked. Wrong as it was, he was furious, and for right now he was going to stay that way.

Ten dollars, he thought once again. *That'll be the day.*

🌿 🌿 🌿

"How'd it go?" Griffin Drake asked the moment he stepped into the sheriff's office—his office.

"Just a newcomer in town. He wouldn't give up his gun."

Griffin's eyes went to the cell, where he could see long legs stretched out from the bunk but no body or face.

"Did he give you any trouble?"

"No, but he's bigger than I like to deal with."

Griffin smiled. Liberty was always honest.

Brother and sister both heard movement in the cell just then and turned to see the prisoner coming to stand at the bars.

"I'm Griffin Drake," Liberty's brother volunteered, "sheriff here in Shotgun. What's your name?"

"Slater Rawlings," the prisoner said, his eyes going between them. "You're the sheriff?"

"Yes."

"And you want ten dollars from me?"

"Unless you're wanted, and then no amount will gain your release."

"How was I supposed to know about guns in the saloon?"

"It's posted above the bar," Griffin told him calmly.

"I didn't go to the bar. I don't even drink."

"Then what were you doing in the saloon?"

I can't spend all my money on the luxury of a hotel room, and there's no place else to go in this town after you've slept out in the woods, Slated thought to himself, but he wasn't about to admit that to them.

Griffin waited calmly for an answer, but the man turned away. Griffin and Liberty exchanged a glance.

"He doesn't like you, big brother," Liberty said, her voice low but her eyes lit with a smile. "He was much nicer for me."

Griffin smiled back. "Let me guess, Lib. You were holding your gun."

Liberty laughed a little and stood. "I'd better get home so I can help Mam with dinner."

"All right," Griffin said as he walked Liberty outside. "Thanks for your help." There was no missing the contentment in his voice as he looked up and down the street and even back at the sheriff's office, not new by any stretch of the imagination.

Liberty said her own goodbyes, thinking not for the first time that her brother was the perfect man to act as sheriff in Shotgun. He loved this town, believed in it, and trusted the people who helped run it.

❧ ❧ ❧

When Griffin moved back inside to his desk, he saw that his prisoner had returned to stand at the bars.

"Don't tell me you let your sister walk the streets alone." Slater's voice was mildly sarcastic. "It's getting dark. She might be harmed."

Griffin did not rise to the bait. On the way to the desk, he said, "Not my sister. She's the fastest gun in town."

Slater shook his head in disgust. Was the man a fool? He certainly didn't look tough enough to be the sheriff. He wasn't small, but he had the face of a boy—merry eyes, smooth cheeks, and all.

"I don't suppose you want to tell me if you're wanted anywhere," Griffin commented as he lifted a stack of wanted posters and flyers onto the desktop from a drawer. "It might save me some time."

"I'm not wanted," Slater said coldly, knowing the lawman would have to check anyway. Slater watched him start on the stack. Twice Griffin rose to hold a picture up to the fading light at the window and then look toward the bars. But he only went back to the desk.

"So tell me," Griffin began after a good ten minutes. "Why didn't you just give up your gun?"

Slater sighed. "You wouldn't believe me."

"Try me."

"I was stunned. I honestly didn't think she could be serious."

"I believe you," Griffin said conversationally. "It's happened before." This said, Griffin reached for the wallet Slater had been commanded to put on the desk. He could see a few bills without even opening it. "If I don't find you in this stack, it looks like you could pay your way out of here."

"Don't count on it." Slater's voice was decidedly cool. "Ten dollars is robbery, and we both know it."

Griffin shrugged. "The food's not bad, and it doesn't get noisy until Saturday night."

Slater didn't reply. Neither did Griffin. It would be easier for the sheriff not to have a man locked up, but he would leave it up to him.

The stack was still rather high when Griffin needed to move around a bit. He scooped up Slater's belongings and took them to the safe in the corner. There wasn't much inside, but the wallet, knife, timepiece, papers, belt, and saddlebags just about filled it. He then checked the boots for weapons and set them by the bars.

"What time is it?" Slater asked.

"Coming onto 6:00. Supper will be here soon."

"I can't say as I'm very hungry."

"Suit yourself," Griffin replied in his calm way, and Slater knew a moment of respect. One of the hallmarks of a good Ranger was calmness. Another was politeness, and he knew he'd failed there. But this was so irritating, and at the moment he couldn't think why God would put him in this place. He had fought the Lord for weeks about leaving the Rangers, and now that he'd talked with Brace, he found himself in jail.

Slater shook his head as he went back to the bunk. He could well imagine Brace's face if that man could see where he was, not to mention his brother Dakota's. Slater made himself sit back against the wall before he tried praying again.

🍃 🍃 🍃

"All right, Libby," Kate Peterson, Liberty's mother, said as she adjusted the candles on the table and moved the basket full of biscuits. "I think that just about does it. Duffy is carving the meat."

"I'll put the gravy in the blue boat just before we sit down."

"Good. Where are Zach and Laura?"

"You sent them out to wash."

"Oh, that's right. Some days I think my head has rolled off my shoulders and I haven't noticed."

"It's still there, Mam," Liberty smilingly told her.

Kate smiled back and said, "I think I'll have you run a plate of food over to your brother."

"He's at the jail with a prisoner."

"Oh, who did he bring in?"

"I brought him in, and his name is Slater Rawlings."

Kate was instantly alert. Since Griffin's deputy had moved across state a month back, Liberty had been filling in. It was not the first time, nor was it an ideal situation, but at times a matter of life and death.

"Everything all right?" Kate asked her daughter.

"Yes. He's new to town and didn't know the rules. He hesitated, and I felt I had no choice but to lift his weapon."

Kate nodded. She didn't fear Liberty's being shot—the younger woman was very competent with a firearm—it was more the things men said to her that Kate objected to. No mother wanted vulgar things said to her children, but when the child was a young, unmarried woman, it was all the harder. At times Kate wanted a different life for her daughter, a life without Griffin's refitted pants or a gun. Kate honestly believed that would be best, but for the moment, this was where God had them.

"I washed," five-year-old Laura announced as she came to the dining room doorway.

"Thank you, dear. Please tell your father we're all ready in here."

"Papa!" Laura dashed from the room on that note, and both women turned as Zach entered. He was a serious six-year-old with a heart of gold.

"Are you washed, Zach?" Liberty asked her young half-brother.

"Yes, but I got my shirt a little wet."

"It will dry," Liberty said kindly as she touched his fair head.

"Laura says we're ready!" Duffy Peterson, one of Shotgun's doctors and Kate's second husband, said as he came on the scene just then, a platter of roast pork in his hands. He added it to the table, and in his warm, wonderful way invited everyone to sit down. He then asked them to bow in prayer.

"Family is so special, Lord," he said reverently, "and we thank You for the ones You've gathered here. Thank You for the sweet fellowship we have in You. Thank You for this food, and for the strong bodies You've given to us. Help us to be filled without being greedy, and to remember that every bite is from Your hand. In Jesus Christ's name I pray. Amen."

The meal began on that good note and only got better. Duffy had been called upon that day to deliver twins—always fun news. He was peppered with questions for a good ten minutes; questions he patiently answered.

"Boys or girls?"

"One of each."

"Who was born first?"

"The boy. I think they're calling him John after his father."

"Did they cry hard?"

"Yes, but we kept them warm, and they settled right down for their mother."

"Is their mother all right?"

"She's doing very well."

"Will you see her again this week?"

"If they call me, yes."

"We'll have to get over with a basket of baked goods," Kate suggested in an effort to stem the tide.

"The pantry's full right now, so that shouldn't be a problem," Liberty said as she remembered she had not brought in the gravy. She rose to do this, giving husband and wife a moment to speak.

"She brought a man in today," Kate said for her husband's ears alone.

"Did it go all right?"

"She said it did. Griffin is still at the jail with him."

"I can bake," Laura put in suddenly.

"What's that, honey?" her mother asked, needing to let the other conversation drop. Her husband watched her for a moment.

"I can bake for the babies too."

"Yes, you can, and we'll just do that. All right?"

Laura nodded, looking pleased.

"Tell me, Zach," his father said conversationally, "what was the funnest thing that happened in school today?"

"We got to read outside."

"Oh, that is fun. Did you all have books, or did Mrs. Murch read to you?"

"She read to us first, but then the older kids took turns."

"Very good. You'll be having your turn before you know it."

Zach smiled up at his father, his favorite person in the world. While other boys wanted to chase after frogs and go fishing, Zach Peterson wanted to sit with a book and read. Some of the children at school had said that such things were sissy, but not Zach's father. Duffy had told him that reading was wonderful and that he should never feel ashamed of his love for it. Right after that, Zach had found himself very interested in fishing, and he tried it with his father, who made it the greatest outing of the entire summer.

"I'm sorry about this gravy," Liberty apologized as she returned with the dark blue gravy boat and set it on the table. "I'm going to start parroting you, Mam, about my head falling off."

"Did you help Griff today?" Zach suddenly asked.

"Yes, I did. I was there for a few hours."

"Did you put someone in jail?" This came from Laura, and Liberty nodded.

"Did you need your gun?"

"Yes. The man waited a little too long to do as I asked, and I couldn't take any chances."

"Is Griff with him now?"

Again Liberty nodded. "That was the plan."

Kate was thankful that the subject was dropped after that. They finished the meal on another topic, and she wasn't forced to keep her feelings hidden. Thoughts of Liberty helping Griffin played in her mind the entire evening, but she prayed and worked to give her two oldest children to the Lord. It was a huge relief, however, when it was time for her younger children to go to bed. She kissed Liberty goodnight and finally gained the privacy of her bedroom. Duffy wasn't far behind her. He found his wife sitting on the edge of the bed, facing away from the door. Duffy slipped his shoes off and climbed onto the mattress. With gentle fingers he unbuttoned the back of her dress and then softly kissed her neck.

"Are you all right?"

"I think so," Kate answered honestly as she slipped from her cotton dress and sat back down in her petticoat and chemise, turning a little so she could look at her husband. "She's so calm, Duffy."

"She has to be, Kate. You don't want her carrying her emotions on her sleeve when she has to pull that gun."

Kate's breath caught in her throat, and Duffy pulled her into his arms and held her close. Kate clung to him. She didn't want to cry, but she felt a desperate need to be held. Duffy was only too happy to oblige.

He hadn't seen her coming. He hadn't known she was going to walk into his life when she did. They had known each other for years, lived in the same town, and gone to the same church, but he hadn't noticed her until almost a year after Thomas Drake died. Kate had been teaching school in those days—the town's sheriff had not been able to leave a huge legacy behind—and still trying to do her job as a mother to Griffin and Liberty, the only two of her five children to make it past infancy. Then she had taken ill.

Duffy would never forget Liberty's pale face as she came to his office.

"Mam is sick," the slim 12-year-old had said.

"Who is sick?" Duffy questioned her.

"Mam. She's hot and quiet."

Duffy had finally figured out that Liberty was referring to her mother. He had hung a sign on his door and followed her home. And Kate had been sick—very sick. Duffy still remembered asking God if He would take the children's mother as well as their father.

Some days passed before he felt she was out of the woods, and even then she wasn't back in the schoolhouse for more than two weeks. And that first day when school dismissed, Duffy was there. He used her health as an excuse for a long time but eventually gained the courage to ask if he could court her. He thought his heart would burst when she said yes.

"I was married to Thomas and had two babies by the time I was Libby's age," Kate said suddenly; Liberty was not long past her twenty-first birthday. "I don't want Libby to marry for anything but love, Duffy, but I find myself wishing she would show more interest in some of the young men who like her."

"Kate," Duffy said seriously, waiting for her to look at him, "you're trying to change circumstances that are out of your control rather than serving God in the midst of them. And you're worrying."

Kate looked up into his wonderful face. Older than she was by ten years, he'd never planned to marry. But he had suddenly found himself in love with her, and in time, Kate had loved him back. The day she married him was one of the happiest of her life. And his faith was so alive. He had been busy as a doctor, but not having a wife or children for so many years had left him with great amounts of time for Bible study and prayer. She learned something from him every week.

"You're right. I need to give her back to the Lord."

"And you need to keep asking God, in His will, to bring someone into her life. You've been happily married, you've seen Libby with people, and you naturally think she would flourish in marriage and parenthood. I do too. So we both need to keep going to God about this."

"She is special, isn't she, Duff?"

"Very. And although some of the men here are fine young men, I think it's going to take someone just as special as she is, someone who understands how multifaceted she is, to claim her heart."

Kate nodded, thinking not for the first time that it was wonderful to know he loved Griffin and Liberty as he did Zach and Laura. She kissed him and thanked him before rising to ready for bed. The week had been long, and she was weary. Thirty minutes later, her husband beside her, she drifted off to sleep, but not before asking God to help her take Duffy's advice: Serve God where you are; don't ask Him to take you elsewhere before you obey. She had made it flowery—that was more her way—but the meaning was still clear.

Two

LIBERTY'S NEAT HAND MOVED across the paper, her head bent as she filled out a report on Slater Rawlings' arrest. There wasn't much to tell, but Griffin was particular about details. He had been ready to do the report himself until he remembered that Liberty was coming in because he had a meeting with the mayor and two members of the town council. He had nearly dragged his sister outside before he left.

"Lunch will be coming while I'm gone, so you be careful."

"I will, Griff, but he doesn't seem that dangerous to me."

"I don't know," Griffin replied with a small shake of his head. "He's probably not, but there's something about this guy, some kind of inner turmoil. I can see it in his eyes. He's angry about being in there, but I know he could pay his way out. He wasn't all too happy this morning when I gave him breakfast, so just be on guard."

Liberty had nodded. "I'll watch myself—him too."

"All right. Thanks, and be sure to thank Mam for those sweet-rolls."

"I'll do it. Hey," Liberty called to him before he could get far. "What about tomorrow?"

"If he hasn't paid his way out, I'll bring him along."

Liberty smiled. "Let's hope you have a quiet night tonight."

Griffin only waved and continued down the street. Liberty went back inside to start the paperwork and give the office a complete dusting. She knew that the prisoner stood at the bars for a while and watched her, but she didn't speak to him or even look in his direction.

"I need something out of my saddlebags," Slater suddenly said.

"You'll have to wait for the sheriff to get back for that," Liberty told him, not bothering to raise her head.

"When will that be?"

"I'm not sure."

"What do I call you, by the way?"

"Deputy."

"What's the matter with this town that a woman has to act as deputy?" Slater muttered, but the woman at the desk just kept writing. Feeling even more irate, he watched her, but in the corner of his mind knew that he was being unjust. He was a prisoner, which meant he had few rights. If she didn't want to talk with him, it was her privilege. Slater let his head rest against the bars and was still in that position when the door opened.

"Oh, Liberty, it's you!" a female voice exclaimed.

Slater watched the woman at the desk laugh.

"It's nice to see you too, Tess."

"I'm sorry." Tess Locken was contrite as she came to stand before the desk. "I was so hoping to find Griff."

"I can't imagine why," Liberty teased. "I'm more fun than he is."

"You are fun, Lib," Tess said sincerely, "but," and here she sighed a little, "I'm not in love with you."

"Oh, well," Liberty shrugged as if the loss were hers. "Can I do anything for you?"

"Only if you know whether Griff is free for dinner Monday night."

Again Liberty shrugged. "I wish I could help."

"Well, I'll just—oh!"

Liberty followed Tess' gaze, knowing she'd just spotted their guest. Slater was still standing, his hands protruding through the bars so his forearms could rest comfortably, his look expressionless as he stared out at them.

"Is he dangerous?" the other woman asked, her voice dropping to a stage whisper.

"He hasn't been so far."

"Did you bring him in?" Tess' voice had risen, but she moved closer to Liberty.

"Yesterday."

Liberty's friend lowered her brow. "He needs a haircut."

The deputy's eyes sparkled as her hand came to her mouth, a movement Slater couldn't miss. He stood very still, doing everything he could not to glare at them. To be talked about as if he wasn't there was maddening.

"Well, I'd better scoot," Tess said quietly. "Tell Griff hello."

"Do you want me to mention Monday night?"

Tess' head cocked to the side in a way that made her look like a scatterbrained female, something she was not. It didn't help that her blue eyes were as innocent as a child's.

"I guess you can go ahead and tell him, but also say that I'll check back with him. Mother said to be sure and tell him to come even if he can only make it for dessert."

Liberty smiled at her. Tess' expression had turned so hopeful.

"I'll relay all of it, Tess."

"Thanks, Libby."

The other woman left on that note, but not before taking one more look at the man behind the bars. The fear in her eyes was not comfortable to Slater, but as he'd been doing for almost 24 hours, he hardened his heart.

"When's lunch?" he asked rudely.

"As soon as it arrives."

Liberty had gone back to the paperwork, and Slater saw that he would get nothing more. Ignoring the voice that reminded him he knew better than to act this way, he stretched out on the bunk and lay still until the noon meal arrived.

❧ ❧ ❧

"I'm headed to church this morning," Griffin said to Slater as he gave him breakfast on Sunday morning. "I'll have to cuff you, but you can join me if you've a mind to."

Slater thought fast; two nights on that bunk was having an effect. Nevertheless, he still said, "I'm not very fresh for church."

"I'll get some extra water to you."

"I'd need my saddlebags."

"I can get out what you need."

Slater saw it for the olive branch it was. There was no denying that this man had been more than fair. Slater knew he was being stubborn about paying.

"I'd appreciate that" was all Slater said before turning to the bunk to eat the food and drink the coffee that arrived on the tray.

"I'll be back in about an hour," Griffin said as he went out the door. Not anticipating trouble, he certainly hoped to learn a little more about the man who at present was quite the mystery. Griffin guessed Slater to be in his midtwenties, but there was a worldliness about him that made the sheriff think he knew his way around. That wasn't all. From time to time Griffin also saw regret in Slater's light blue eyes and wondered what plagued him. He hadn't honestly thought Slater would accept the offer to attend church—not many did when they learned they had to be cuffed—but Griffin was pleased nonetheless.

Riding home, Griffin let himself in the back door of his own house and began to ready himself for the day. He never relished wearing his guns with a suit, so he opted for clean denim pants, a nice shirt, and a narrow tie. He shaved carefully, looking forward to the service but also to possibly catching sight of Tess. He was sorry he'd missed her the day before. He didn't know if going to her house for dinner was wise, but saying no to the invitation would have been easier if he could have spent a few minutes with her. Now he found himself wanting to accept the invitation just to see her.

His heart sighed with the quandary of it all even as he moved through the house to leave. Having someone love him had never been part of his plan; loving her back was even less so. With a prayer for continued wisdom and kindness, he mounted his horse, Tess on his mind until he arrived back at the jailhouse to help Slater with his saddle-bags.

🌿 🌿 🌿

Griffin watched Slater take his Bible in cuffed hands. The sheriff nearly shook his head in wonder as he directed Slater out the jailhouse door. A little more of the mystery was solved. Whether or not this man had accepted the words of Scripture and claimed them for his own, he was clearly under some type of conviction. *No wonder he was so angry*, Griffin thought as he waited until the service started and then escorted his prisoner to the corner of a rear pew. The congregation was on their feet joined in prayer, which allowed Griffin to bring Slater in unobtrusively.

The men sat down with the rest of the worshipers when the pastor closed the prayer, and Griffin saw Liberty rise from the other side of the church to head to the piano. He glanced at the man beside him and saw that he'd noticed as well. A mischievous thought passed through Griffin's mind, a hunch he had to try out. He spoke when Slater glanced at him.

"She looks different in a dress, doesn't she?"

For several heartbeats Slater frowned at the sheriff in confusion before his eyes flew back to the woman at the piano. He stared in disbelief. *Could that actually be the deputy?* Slater had all he could do to keep his mouth closed.

Looking utterly feminine in a bright yellow dress, Liberty readied herself at the keys, completely unaware of Slater's scrutiny. That man took in the way she'd swept her hair off her neck, thinking he'd never seen her without a hat. The dress had long, fitted sleeves, and Slater was surprised by how small her arms and shoulders were; there was never a hint of form in the baggy clothes she wore. The neckline of the dress was rounded with white lace, and it looked as though she had a locket at her throat. Slater had to tear his eyes away when Griffin handed him the hymnal. He didn't know the song at all but did his best. Anything to keep his mind on why he was there.

Slater suddenly gave up and began to pray the way he should have prayed two days before. He stopped trying to sing and poured his heart out to God, confessing his pride and anger. He knew when the song ended but was not quite ready to open his eyes. Not until Griffin leaned over and asked if he was all right did he open his eyes, his heart feeling pounds lighter with the load lifted.

Why do I fight everything You want me to do? Slater asked the Lord when three other people stood and moved to the front, not toward the piano, but toward the pastor. Slater thought they were going to sing until he saw that Liberty had left the piano bench.

"We have a little skit for you this morning," Pastor Ross Caron told the congregation as his wife, Felicia, their daughter, Mayann, and their son, Tanner, came forward. Pastor Caron had a way with drama, and his parishioners were accustomed to his putting a Bible passage or an illustration into skit form.

Tanner and Mayann went off to the right side of the church, but Felicia stood right in front of the pulpit, a mixing bowl and spoon in her hands. Ross came onto the scene from the side.

"Felicia, have you seen Mayann? I asked her to bring me those notes I have upstairs. She's been gone for 20 minutes."

Felicia shook her head, her arm cradling the bowl as she stirred. "I asked her to bring the clothes in off the line, but when I looked out a minute ago, nothing had been done."

Ross walked away shaking his head. Felicia kept up her stirring for a moment and then set the bowl aside. "I guess I'll have to do it myself," she said as she walked to the side of the room.

Ross came back to the center now, and on his way, he stumbled and righted himself.

"What in the world? Mayann, where are you? I just tripped over your skates. You left them right in the hall. Mayann!" he tried again, but when he received no answer, he shook his head and went back the other way.

As soon as he was gone, Mayann and Tanner walked slowly across the front.

"You mean it?" Mayann asked. "You want me to be in charge of the money?"

"Yes," Tanner told her. "You're good with numbers, and we want to be sure that all the proceeds go to the new hymnals."

"I'd love to do it. I can't wait to tell my folks."

Ross and Felicia came back to the middle then, and Mayann wasn't long in joining them.

"You'll never believe what happened!" Mayann nearly shouted. "I've been asked to be in charge of the hymnal money. Isn't that great?"

"The hymnal money?" Ross said with surprise. "That fund is growing fast, Mayann. That's a large responsibility. I'm not sure you can do it."

"Yes, I can," she told her parents. "I've always been good with numbers."

"But there's more to it than that, Mayann," her mother put in. "You've got to be responsible with the account book and all the receipts."

"I will be," the girl assured her parents, who looked at her for a moment.

"Where are the sermon notes I asked you to get me?" Ross finally questioned her.

Mayann's hand came to her mouth.

"Did you fold the laundry when you got it off the line, Mayann, or just throw it in the basket?"

"Oh, no!" she said. "I forgot all about that."

"You also forgot where your skates belong. I tripped on them."

Mayann hung her head. Ross ended the skit by saying, "We've got some work to do."

Slater took in the words of each actor, impressed with the idea and point that was made. He was staring straight at the pastor when that man stepped behind the pulpit and asked, "How good is your reputation? Mayann's wasn't very good with her parents, was it? That wasn't a complicated skit. Anyone could figure it out. But the message needs to hold a lot of weight with all of us. How good is your reputation? How good is *my* reputation? Can the people of this congregation come to me if they feel I'm wrong, or do they fear I'll be angry and send them away? Can I come to you and know that you'll listen to me? Is your reputation that good?

"As we look again in our Bibles at the life of Nehemiah, we see that his reputation was excellent. Let me give you just a few examples. Nehemiah is saddened by sin as we see in chapter 1, verse 4, and his first response is to pray and recognize God's greatness, verse 5. He's humble, verse 6; repentant, verse 7; and he claims God's redemption, verse 10. Go to chapter 2 and see that he's bold, a trusted worker, organized, discreet, tactful, and gives credit where credit is due."

Pastor Caron looked up from his Bible and notes. "I don't know about you, but I can learn from this man."

So can I, Slater thought. He realized he'd never even read the book of Nehemiah. The Texas Ranger who had led him to the Lord had urged him to study in the New Testament. Beyond that, Slater had spent so little time in church that his training had been very limited. This was one of the reasons he'd walked away from his job.

Slater had let his mind wander further than he intended. Surprised when everyone stood for the closing prayer, he didn't have a chance to bow his head. Since the sheriff was already leading him outside, he had all he could do not to drop his Bible with cuffed hands. He looked forward to getting back to the jail and paying his way out. He was surprised again when Sheriff Drake did not return him to the jail.

☙ ☙ ☙

"Then what did you do?" Liberty asked Laura, their faces close as the little girl sat in her sister's lap.

"I just looked away," Laura told her, working not to let her voice quiver.

"You did well," Kate inserted from her seat nearby. "I'm glad you didn't pinch back."

Laura nodded and looked down at the dark bruise on her arm. One of the other children at church had pinched her.

"I didn't cry," Laura told them, "but I think Zach wanted to."

"Zach loves you," Liberty put in. "He hurts when you hurt."

"I love Zach too."

Liberty kissed her sister's soft temple and hugged her close. Laura had always treated Liberty like another mother—both children did—and their mother had never done anything to alter that.

"All right, Laura," Kate instructed after she kissed her youngest daughter too. "Will you please help me get things ready for dinner?"

Laura nodded.

"Please take your dolls off that chair. Your brother brought a guest today."

"Who is it?"

"You'll meet him when he gets here. Where is Zach?"

"I think he's outside."

"Please go tell him we're almost ready to eat."

Griffin and Slater, both sitting in the parlor, listened to this last sentence in silence. Slater had not uttered a word since Griffin had led him from the church, and Griffin had done little more than lead him up the street, into the front door of a two-story home, and to a satin-covered chair in a very comfortable room, where he now sat.

Not thinking that the sheriff was inclined to visit, Slater let his eyes roam the walls. Clearly a woman lived here. Family pictures were displayed on tables and walls; lace curtains graced windows and doilies sat on the arms of upholstered furniture. And everything was freshly dusted.

"We're ready," a female voice called from the other room.

Griffin stood and approached Slater. "This is my family," he told the prisoner. "I think you'd be more comfortable without the cuffs, and I think I can trust you, but if I'm wrong, I won't hesitate to take you out."

Slater nodded, knowing the man had no choice. Slater only wished he had his wallet so he could lose the cuffs for good. It was a relief to rub his wrists once they were gone, and his enjoyment of that caused him to forget that he might see the sheriff's sister. When he walked into the dining room and saw her, he had all he could do not to gawk. If he'd thought her lovely across the church, he didn't know what to think now. Why hadn't he noticed before the deep hazel of her eyes or the red highlights in her hair?

"Duffy—" Griffin's voice brought Slater back. "This is Slater Rawlings. He's a guest of the jailhouse right now."

"Hello, Slater." Duffy shook his hand and took over. "This is my wife, Kate, my daughter Liberty, my son Zach, and my younger daughter, Laura."

"Thank you for letting me join you," Slater said quietly, taking the chair Griffin indicated. Heads bowed and Duffy prayed. Slater looked up after the close, an ache in his throat for his own family. He was glad that the bowls of food were immediately passed.

"Will she go to hell?" Laura suddenly asked.

"What?" Her father turned to her, a spoonful of mashed potatoes frozen in his hand as he looked at her in astonishment.

"We didn't explain to you, Duffy," Kate put in, not looking at Liberty, who had her hand over her mouth, her eyes brimming with merriment. "Someone pinched Laura at church."

"I see," Duffy said quietly, now in the same state as his stepdaughter. He made himself finish with the potatoes and pass them on, then turned to Laura, all the while working to keep a straight face.

"Did you say it was another girl?" Duffy clarified.

Laura nodded. "I can't tell names unless you tell me to, or it's gossip."

"All right," Duffy nodded over being reminded of his own rule. "This little girl might be lost, Laura, but not because she pinched you. It was wrong of her to pinch you, but she would only go to hell if she never accepted Christ's forgiveness in her life. Do you understand?"

Laura nodded again, and Duffy went back to his food.

Slater glanced around the table and noticed the way all the other adults were busy with their plates as well. He watched Liberty and Griffin share a glance, but other than Liberty's eyes sparkling, she gave nothing away. He wished he could keep watching her. From where he sat, she and Zach were very clear.

Griffin spoke up with a tidbit of news that Zach thoroughly enjoyed, and that seemed to get the conversation ball rolling. Slater remained very quiet and forced himself not to stare or wolf down the delicious food, both of which were strong temptations.

"Who's for pie?" Kate asked after a time.

No one declined. An apple pie came to the table that was so mounded with fruit that it had a hump in the middle. Slater had decided not to speak, but after tasting this pie, he could not contain himself; it was the best he'd ever had.

"This is excellent," he said quietly.

"Libby made it," Kate said, smiling down the table at her.

Slater welcomed a reason to look at her, but she was not looking his way. He stared for several bites of pie, and she eventually looked up, but he couldn't read her expression. Regret knifed through him. She wouldn't see him as anything more than a two-bit drifter, and he had no one to thank but himself. It was almost a relief to have the meal end and Griffin tell him they had to be on their way.

⁍ ⁍ ⁍

"If you'll give me my wallet, I'll get the ten dollars for you."

Griffin looked at the man he'd just uncuffed and nodded. He went to the safe, opened it, and removed the rest of Slater's things. The moment Slater had his wallet, he settled things with Shotgun's sheriff. He then began to fill his pockets with his possessions.

"Where will you head from here?" Griffin asked after he'd sat on the desk, his legs dangling down the side.

Slater looked to the window. "I don't know. I like Shotgun, especially the church. Maybe I'll stick around."

Griffin nodded. "What took you so long to decide?"

Slater shook his head. "Stubborn-mule pride, and I just quit my job. Ten bucks is a lot of money."

"What do you do?"

Slater looked him in the eye. "I was a Texas Ranger until last month."

Griffin's brows rose as a dozen more questions rolled through his mind. When did a man question and when did a man leave a person his privacy? Griffin thought of one safe inquiry.

"Did the church service this morning have anything to do with your decision?"

"It had a lot to do with it. There's nothing like hearing about Nehemiah's qualities to make me see how short I am."

"I felt that same way."

Slater threw his saddlebags over one shoulder and started to say thank you. Griffin cut him off.

"Have you got a place to sleep tonight?"

Slater's mouth quirked. "You mean other than the woods?"

Griffin smiled. "I live next door to my mother and Duffy. You're welcome to one of the bedrooms."

Slater nodded. "Thank you."

"If I'm not there when you get in, use the back door and take any bedroom upstairs."

"I'll plan on that."

"One more thing," Griffin said. "The hotel gives a full plate of food for 15 cents. It's not fancy, but it's always hot and filling."

Slater's hand came out. "Thank you, sheriff."

"You can call me Griffin."

Slater nodded, shook the man's hand, and went to the door. It was a quiet Sunday afternoon, the sun shining, but the breeze was cool as he walked down the street. Slater held his expectations at bay, but on the way to church that morning he thought he'd spotted a bathhouse. It might not be open, but he had to give it a try. If that didn't work, he'd get Arrow from the livery and ride out until he found a deep spot in the creek.

Three

"THAT YOU, SLATER?" GRIFFIN CALLED when he heard the back door open after 8:00 that night.

"Yeah. I couldn't tell if you were here or not."

Griffin appeared at the doorway, a lantern in his hand. He set it on the kitchen table, noticed Slater's slicked-back hair, and grinned.

"If I'd known you were looking for a bath, I'd have told you to use my tub."

Slater shook his head. "The bathhouse was closed, and I couldn't find any privacy on the creek. I had to wait until after dark. That water is cold."

"Come on through here," Griffin invited. He led the way to the living room where he'd been cleaning a gun. This room had gas lighting that cast a warm glow to every corner but didn't penetrate the dark curtains over the windows. The house had looked dark and deserted when Slater rode up. He had taken the liberty of stabling his horse in the back and letting himself in.

"How far did you ride up the creek?"

"About a mile. It's pretty country."

"I think so. Did you get some supper?"

"The hotel. I'm not crazy about lamb, but I've had worse. By the way, do you live alone? Should I be watching not to scare the life out of someone?"

"No, I'm on my own. This was Duffy's mother's house. I moved over when she died."

"Duffy's not your father?"

"No. My father died when I was a kid. Mam married Duff about two years later."

"And had Zach and Laura."

"Yeah," Griffin smiled. There was little that got to his heart faster than his little brother and sister. He suddenly remembered Laura's question at the table and chuckled.

Slater had thought of it too. "Unless I miss my guess, she's something of a character."

"Laura? Yes. She makes me laugh every time I talk to her."

"I thought your sister would choke."

"Libby's like another mother to Laura but with very little discipline; Mam and Duffy see to that. It's the same with Zach."

"He seems like a bright young man."

"He's better read than some adults my age. He has a sensitive heart too."

Slater wanted to ask if Griffin would marry and have his own brood, but he knew it wasn't his affair. The pretty blonde who had come into the jailhouse was clearly willing. Slater wondered if Shotgun's sheriff was holding back for some reason.

"I was in bed late and up early," Griffin suddenly said, finishing his work and putting it aside. "I hope you won't mind if I turn in."

"Not at all. I was hoping to turn in soon."

The men said their goodnights, but Griffin ended up showing Slater to the most comfortable room. He told him to come downstairs if he needed anything and left him alone with the lantern. Slater climbed into bed, intent on reading the whole book of Nehemiah. But he only got halfway through. He was asleep just five seconds after turning down the lantern.

❧ ❧ ❧

Pulling the belt on her dressing gown tightly around her, Liberty slipped out of the house on Monday morning and dashed across to Griffin's house. She had left her revolver in his kitchen—he had volunteered to clean it for her—but she didn't know if he'd gotten to it or not. She was headed to the office this morning and didn't want to forget.

Liberty slipped in the back door and groped around until she had the lantern lit. Griffin was a fairly light sleeper, and Liberty hoped she could get out without disturbing him. She was still looking for the gun when she heard him at the door.

"Sorry, Griff," Liberty spoke while facing the counter. "I just thought I'd better get my gun before I head downtown."

"Why would you leave your gun here?" Slater asked before he thought.

Liberty had only just laid her hands on the weapon. She spun so fast that Slater blinked. The gun was up and aimed at his chest.

"When did you get out?"

"Yesterday, right after lunch."

"What are you doing here?" Her voice was deadly calm, the gun completely steady.

"I just got up." Slater was a little sleepy but waking fast.

"Where's my brother?"

"Probably asleep."

"If you've hurt him—" Liberty began, but Slater cut her off, having just remembered the night before.

"You'll what?" he asked mildly. "Shoot me with a gun that has no bullets?"

"How do you know whether or not it has bullets?" Liberty asked, still not dropping her guard or the weapon.

"Because that's the gun I watched your brother clean last night, and somehow I don't think he loaded it."

Liberty didn't answer. He was probably right, but until she saw Griffin...

"What's up, Libby?" the man of her worries asked as he came in behind Slater. He summed up the scene in a moment, leaning against the opposite wall to address her. "I asked him to spend the night."

Liberty slowly lowered the gun, feeling foolish.

"Fix your robe, Lib," Griffin said softly, and Liberty fell completely apart. She nearly dropped the gun as she set it aside, only to scoop it up the moment she'd drawn the front of her dressing gown back together. She was on the verge of leaving when she realized what she'd done. Liberty made herself turn back and meet Slater's eyes.

"I'm sorry."

He was not given a chance to reply. Liberty quietly thanked Griffin for cleaning the gun and hurried back out the door.

The kitchen was very quiet on her exit. Slater had his eyes on the door but looked over to see Griffin staring at him, his expression one of complete puzzlement.

"I've never seen her so rattled," he said, almost to himself.

"She must have been embarrassed." Slater's hand went to his bare chest. "It never occurred to me that you might have company this early in the morning, or I'd have stayed in my room."

"Well," Griffin shrugged, "she lives next door, and we all kind of come and go as we please." Griffin paused and looked at his guest. This man was nothing like he had first figured. The line about being a Texas Ranger could all be a farce, but Griffin didn't think so. Something inside of him wanted to reach out. "If you find work, Slater, and want to live here, you're welcome. If that ends up being the case, I'll warn the family."

Slater, who had been praying about that very thing, nodded his head and thanked Griffin.

"How did you sleep?" the law officer wished to know.

"Very well. The bed and room are comfortable. Can we set up some type of rent system if I find work here in town?"

"That would be fine, but I'm not worried about it right now."

Slater nodded, taking him at his word on that subject but quite certain there was something else on the man's mind. Slater felt it was best to leave him with his thoughts.

"I'll clean up now," the visitor said.

"Sure. There's water in the bucket there."

Slater used the pitcher that sat close by, filled it, and exited the room. He wasn't gone a second before his head came back around the door frame.

"*You* clean Liberty's gun?"

Griffin laughed before he said, "It's my own fault. I did it for her once, and she liked it so well, I've been roped into it ever since. She's the fast hand and I'm the gunsmith."

"Where did she learn to draw?" Slater couldn't help asking.

"Our father. He worked with both of us from the time we were small, but Liberty was different. She took to handling weapons like a kitten takes to its mother. For as long as I can remember, it's been as natural as breathing for her."

Slater suddenly felt out of words. After a look at his host to see if he expected a reply, Slater turned and made his way upstairs. This was a most unusual situation, and he didn't know how he felt about it. The family he'd met yesterday had been warm and caring. But if they cared, how could they put one of their women in such a dangerous position? Slater did not understand. It made him uncomfortable, but at the same time he wanted to know them better. He wished to be invited into their home as a guest, not a prisoner. For this reason alone, he held his tongue about the things that confused him. Maybe in time it would be clear.

Slater stepped in front of the mirror, the one that sat over the washbowl in his room. He scowled at his reflection. His desire to grow a beard was waning. His hair was just light enough that the attempt only made him look unkempt. Knowing he needed a trip to the barber anyway, he opted to leave the beard until he got downtown.

A shave and a haircut, and then off to find work.

🌂 🌂 🌂

Liberty stood in her bedroom, her brow drawn into serious contemplation. At the moment she wondered if she would ever comfortably walk into her brother's house again. She shook her head, thinking she had never been so surprised. The sheriff's office, the saloons, and even the streets of Shotgun were places she had to be on guard— never here at home and never at Griffin's. Now all that felt as though it had changed. Liberty worked at not being angry at her brother or the blond cowboy who had wandered into town.

"Libby," her mother called from down the stairs, "should I put some pancakes on for you?"

"Yes, please," Liberty called back. She hurried to button the baggy shirt she'd put on before placing the vest over the top. She didn't bother to look in the mirror; it was easier that way.

Oh, stop it! she chided herself. *What do you care what you look like right now? You have a job to do! People are counting on you.* But it wasn't quite that simple. For some reason the blond cowboy's eyes kept coming to mind. He had looked at her when she arrested him, and even in the jail, but the eyes he'd turned on her at the dinner table the day before had been entirely different.

"It's just that it's never happened before," she said softly, her feet leaving the last step and turning toward the dining room. "Everyone else in town is used to seeing you both ways."

"Were you talking to us, dear?" her mother asked.

"No, just to myself."

Kate took in Liberty's face and felt concern. Duffy must have seen something too because he asked from his place at the table, "Are you all right, Lib?"

Liberty thought of the way she'd held a gun on her brother's houseguest that morning. It would have been easy to say no, she wasn't all right, but she wasn't up to explaining right then.

"I'm just thinking," Liberty told them.

Kate and Duffy let it go, but both were watchful.

"Can I go to work with you today, Libby?" Laura asked.

"Don't talk with food in your mouth," her mother corrected.

Laura swallowed with great show and asked again.

"Not today, Laura. If Griffin is with me you might come sometime, but if I'm on my own and needed, you'd be left by yourself."

"I could sit at the desk."

"That's true, but I would want someone with you."

"Zach has a desk at school, and Mam has one in the kitchen."

Liberty only smiled at her before looking at her parents, who had been taking in the whole exchange. Zach's going off to school had been very hard for Laura, and the year had just begun. Duffy and Kate had been talking about getting her a small desk for Christmas, and it seemed that might still be a good idea.

Liberty tucked into her food, all the while listening to Zach tell about the book he was reading. Liberty remembered reading that very book when she was about his age and almost shook her head at the difference. Zach was most impressed with the way the boy had worked to earn money to buy his teacher a present; Liberty remembered little but the girl in the story and the way she took care of her baby sister. She chalked it up to the difference between the genders and then remembered the incident from the morning.

"We're still quite far apart," she mumbled to herself as she headed out the door for work.

❧ ❧ ❧

"Shave and a haircut?" the barber asked solicitously, now that Slater was in the chair.

"Yes, please."

"You're a polite one," the man with the razor commented as he laid Slater back and began to lather his face.

"Why wouldn't I be?"

"No reason, but I don't often see young cowboys stopping to help ladies with their bags or children when their dog runs off."

Slater's eyes went to the large windows that overlooked Main Street.

"You don't miss much, do you?"

The barber grinned unrepentantly. "Nope."

Little more was said as the barber got down to business. Slater had slept well but felt himself relaxing under the man's capable hands. He still had gainful employment on his mind and suddenly realized whom he could talk to.

"Any work to be had in town?" Slater asked as the barber started on his hair.

"What do you do?"

"A little of everything, I guess."

The barber looked at him in the mirror for a moment.

"Hank Hathaway's boy just left for the bright lights of Austin. Hank builds houses. He might be looking for a hand."

Slater's brows rose. It had been a while since he'd worked with a hammer, but he didn't think he'd forgotten any of the basics.

"Do you know where I might find him?"

"A few blocks over. He's puttin' a covered porch on the back of Mrs. Tobler's house. Should have done it years ago; nothing but west sun for hours every day."

Slater smiled a little. If he'd wanted information, he'd come to the right place.

🌹 🌹 🌹

"You ever even held a hammer?" the scruffy-looking old man asked Slater about 15 minutes after he left the barbershop.

"Yes, sir. I've done some building."

"You won't get rich," Hank said.

"I didn't plan on it. Some food and covering the rent would be nice, maybe a new shirt now and again."

Still Hank weighed him. He wasn't as big as his son, but then not many men were. He was polite enough; Hank had to give him that.

"I'll give you a try and pay you when you work, but if I say you're gone, you're gone."

"Yes, sir."

"You can start by lifting the other end of that board and holding it in place. Hold it steady now."

Slater immediately bent to the task, glad he'd seen fit to return his horse to the stable at Griffin's. He'd asked God to help him find work. He now asked His help in not shrinking from any task.

🌹 🌹 🌹

Griffin came in reading the mail. He stood a few feet from the desk, his mind otherwise occupied, so it took several minutes for him to realize his sister was staring at him from the desk chair.

"What's up?" he asked.

"Whatever compelled you to ask him to spend the night at your house?"

Remembering how embarrassed she'd been, Griffin put the mail aside.

"He's not a bad guy, Lib. I was really impressed with the way he wanted to go to church and the way he followed along in his Bible. He found the book of Nehemiah without a bit of help from me."

"He agreed to go to church with you yesterday?"

"Yes, we sat in the back."

This gave Liberty pause; she had not expected this. Griffin often asked prisoners to join him in church, but few accepted.

"I feel worse now," Liberty admitted.

"Why?"

"While he was still behind bars, he wanted something from his saddlebags. I told him he'd have to wait for you, and then I never told you. He probably wanted his Bible."

"Don't be too hard on yourself, Lib. He admitted to me that he was being stubborn about paying the fine. If he'd wanted out enough to get his Bible, he could have paid the ten dollars at any time."

Liberty was thankful for her brother's understanding but still felt uncomfortable about that whole ordeal. *Ah, well, he'll be miles from here in no time. I'll just have to put it from my mind.*

"Were things quiet this morning?" Griffin asked, the other subject slipping from his mind.

"No trouble, but Maddie Flowers stopped to say that her neighbors were on a drunken binge all weekend. She said they've been making their own brew and that we'd do well to burn down that barn of theirs, since that's where the trouble always starts."

Griffin shook his head. "And of course Maddie's brew is only for medicinal purposes, so we should leave her still alone."

Liberty grinned.

"Let's go out in the morning," Griffin suggested. "You'll be in?"

"Midmorning. Right after Bible study."

"All right. I'll see you then."

Liberty left the jailhouse and sheriff's office, thinking it was a nice day for a walk. She untied her horse's reins but didn't climb into the saddle. She even went the long way home. She worked on Monday and Tuesday mornings, and at odd times when Griffin needed her. So far Griffin had not met anyone he felt qualified for the job. The town was getting big enough to consider more law enforcement, but that didn't mean men were available.

"Libby! Is that you?"

Liberty looked over to see old Mrs. Tobler waving a dishtowel in her direction.

"Hi, Mrs. Tobler."

"Come in here!" the old gal demanded. "I can't find my needle. Come in and look for it."

Liberty changed directions without hesitation. Mrs. Tobler was a dear old thing, if a little bossy. It never occurred to her to ask for anything—it was always demanded—but beyond that, she was kindness itself.

"It's slipped down the cushion, I'm sure!" Mrs. Tobler informed Liberty as she neared. "I don't know how I'm supposed to get anything done without my needle."

"What are you working on right now?"

"Pillow slips! And Christmas right around the corner."

Liberty hid a smile as she went in the old woman's front door. Not for anything would she have mentioned that Christmas was well over two months away or that Mrs. Tobler's closet was so full of things she'd made that she probably could give up sewing for the rest of her life.

"All right," Liberty said, standing in the overcrowded living room. "Where were you sitting?"

"Right here. I like to keep an eye on the work out back, so I moved my chair."

"What's going on out back?" Liberty asked as she dropped to her knees and began to search.

"A covered porch," Mrs. Tobler said absently, having moved to the window to peer out. "No, no!" the older woman suddenly exclaimed and dashed out of the room.

Liberty could hear the side door bang and Mrs. Tobler's voice raised in irritation. Shotgun's deputy only shook her head and kept searching. She pulled the cushion from the chair, but that only produced some popcorn kernels and a button. The floor was next.

Liberty was searching, her nose nearly on the rug, when she spotted them. Liberty stared at the cowboy boots in confusion, until she realized someone was wearing them. She tipped her head back and literally gawked into the face of Slater Rawlings. With his haircut and beard gone, he was a different man.

"Aren't you going to pull your gun?" he asked quietly.

Liberty blinked before saying, "Why should I do that?"

"That's what you've done every time you've seen me, so I thought you might have gotten into the habit."

Liberty bit her lip but it didn't work; a smile peeked through, and then a laugh. She moved to get up, and Slater's hand was suddenly right there to help her.

"I really am sorry about this morning."

"It's all right," Slater said. Having seen the way she looked without the men's clothes, he could now see the real Liberty Drake, even in this outfit. She had the most amazing hazel eyes, more gold than anything else. And that hair! Slater wanted to stare and stare.

"You're very understanding."

"And you're looking for something. What is it?"

"A needle."

Comprehension dawned on Slater's face. "That's what she sent me in to do—look for a needle with you."

Liberty frowned. "How do you know Mrs. Tobler?"

"I'm working on her porch with Hank Hathaway."

Liberty's eyes went to the window and back to Slater.

"You're working here in town?"

"Yep." Slater's thumbs went to his belt loops, and he rocked back on his heels. "Hired just four hours ago. I'm the town's newest carpenter."

Liberty found him so cute that she couldn't stop her second smile.

"And why" she asked now, a smile still in her voice, "did Mrs. Tobler think I needed help with the needle?"

"Well, I didn't understand it at the time, but I realize now that she said, 'You might as well help Lib find the needle. I've got to set this old man straight.'"

Hand to her mouth, Liberty dissolved into laughter, and without thinking, she collapsed into the chair, a position that lasted for only a second before she was on her feet again.

"I found it!" she gasped, just stopping short of clutching her stinging backside.

Slater's eyes flew to the seat and there it was, protruding point-side up. It wasn't hard to imagine why Liberty had not stayed in the chair. Slater bent to retrieve it just as Mrs. Tobler came in the door.

"You've found it," she said matter-of-factly. "I knew Liberty could do it with some help." With that the old woman plucked the needle from Slater's fingers. "Now get back out there and keep an eye on him. He knows what he's supposed to do, but you'd better watch him.

"Libby! You come with me. I want you to see that new quilt I put on my bed."

Liberty nodded and even smiled. She followed Mrs. Tobler with a wave at Slater. Slater waved back before moving to exit the room. Before he left, however, he looked back to see Liberty following their hostess, her hand now reaching back to rub the pin hole. Slater stopped for a moment, his heart wrung with tenderness. Even as he proceeded back out to work, the scene remained on his mind along with another emotion, one he couldn't quite define.

Four

"THANK YOU, MRS. LOCKEN," Griffin said kindly on Monday evening. "Everything was great."

"You're welcome, Griffin. Would you like some coffee on the porch?"

Griffin looked at Tess, and she nodded.

"I'll help you, Mama," Tess offered.

"I'm fine, dear. If I need help, I'll ask your father. You go ahead."

Tess led the way but wished she didn't have to. She never wanted it to look as if she'd conspired to get Griffin alone. For this reason she took a chair that sat off on its own when she reached the front porch.

Griffin noticed and even understood why. Tess had never pushed herself at him. This, along with dozens of other facts about this woman, made his feelings even harder to accept. He hadn't planned to love anyone. And he certainly hadn't planned on a sweet, godly woman loving him.

"Was it busy today?" Tess asked, always interested in his work.

"Pretty quiet. Lib was in this morning, but she said it was quiet too."

Tess smiled. "I like Libby so much. She's so fun and smart."

"You're smart too, Tess," Griffin said. He knew she struggled with her self-image. She was a very beautiful woman, with pale blonde hair, skin like cream, and huge blue eyes. And since most people thought that was all there was to her, she had begun to believe it. It didn't help that her father and older brothers were men who had little time for family. Making money was their main concern.

"That's what Libby always says, but when you're with someone as capable as Libby, it's hard to believe."

Griffin didn't answer. Tess hadn't been looking directly at him, so when it got quiet she looked up to find his eyes on her. His face looked boyish, as it often did. It made Tess smile.

"You don't look tough enough to be the sheriff."

"And you're too wonderful to be in love with an old hound dog like me."

"Oh, Griff," Tess said softly.

Griffin watched her look away, her eyes filling. He had talked with Duffy and Pastor Caron, and they had asked him if he was trusting God. He thought that he was, but did trust mean being blind to the facts? When a man had his type of job—the type of job that had killed his father—did he go into marriage without a backward glance? And what if they had children? He would not only leave Tess alone, but his kids too.

Griffin looked out over the quiet street the Lockens lived on. He had been happy to be single, but then Tess moved into town a year ago and came to church with her mother. At first he thought there wasn't much under those pale blonde curls or behind that ready smile, but then she'd visited Mam and Duffy's house at Liberty's invitation, and Griffin learned otherwise. She was a woman whose faith in God was genuine and whose courage was deep.

"Here's coffee," Mrs. Locken said as she used her hip to push open the screen door, the tray in her hands. Griffin rose to take it from her.

"If you don't mind, I think I'll go in and have mine with Albert. Call if you need something."

"Thank you, Mrs. Locken."

Tess rose to pour the coffee and offered him a cup. She fixed it just the way he liked. The light was fading, but when she sat with her own cup, Griffin could see that Tess' eyes were still moist.

"Maybe I shouldn't stay, Tess," Griffin forced himself to say.

"You don't have to if you don't want to," she said to him, and Griffin had to close his eyes. She was so special.

"What do you want me to do?" he finally asked.

Tess took a big breath. "I want you to play me in checkers. You beat me the last two times, and I want a rematch."

For a long moment the sheriff could only look at her. Not able to help himself and not willing to try, Griffin reached over and let one finger slide down her soft cheek.

"I'll get the board."

Tess' eyes closed the moment he stood, her heart wondering how she would make it. Every moment with him was sweet torture. She wanted to sob her eyes out but heard him coming back through the house.

If he isn't for me, Lord, please work a miracle in my heart so it doesn't break in two.

🌹 🌹 🌹

"A shave *and* a haircut," Griffin said when he got home that night and found Slater in the living room. "Did you go for a job or courtin'?"

Slater laughed. "I didn't think it would hurt to look my best."

"Where'd you go—the bank?"

Slater's look was smug. "You happen to be looking at Shotgun's newest contractor."

Griffin was not long in catching on. "I'd heard that Price Hathaway headed to Austin. You must have taken his job. How do you like working for Hank?"

Slater's eyes grew comically. "He knows what he's doing, and he knows what he wants me to do; it's just a matter of getting him to remember that he thought about the order but didn't tell me. I think I know why Price left town."

"Hank's a case, but you're right, he does know how to build. Are you by any chance at Mrs. Tobler's right now?"

"That's the place. She wants a covered porch on the back side of her house. It's only going to shade two windows, but she wants it."

"She's got a big heart but also a mind of her own. Libby went there as a little girl for sewing lessons."

"She was there today."

"For sewing lessons?"

"No. Mrs. Tobler lost her needle and expected your sister to find it."

"Did she?"

"Not until after she sat on it."

Griffin's brow lowered. "Is she all right?"

"That's not a question I could really ask her. I think it smarted, but she might have been more surprised than anything."

"How did you learn about the needle?"

Slater gave Griffin a rundown and that man's face became very thoughtful.

"Did I say something wrong?" Slater had been watching him closely.

"No, not at all," Griffin told him honestly but knew that the rest of his thoughts would have to stay inside. Slater wouldn't thank him and neither would Liberty. *Not to mention the fact that you can't figure out what you're doing in your own relationship, Griffin, let alone getting involved in someone else's.*

"How do you think you'll like a hammer and nails after law enforcement?" Griffin asked in an effort to shift his thoughts.

Slater thought for a moment, his head leaning back against the softly padded chair; it was a question he'd been asking himself all day.

"It's going to take some getting used to," Slater finally admitted.

Griffin nodded but still didn't ask the question that had come to his mind the moment he'd learned this man was a Texas Ranger. That question might take some time or turn out to be one he could never ask.

"There's a church picnic this Sunday afternoon," Griffin told him instead. His mother had let him know that day. "We must have come in after it was announced."

"Right after church?"

"Yes, at the Millers', on the creek."

"Do we bring something?"

"My mother and Libby usually take pity on me and bring enough for a threshing crew. Unless you're in the mood to cook, don't worry about it."

"My skills in the kitchen can't compare to your mother's. I wouldn't starve, but a home-cooked meal always tastes like a feast."

Griffin laughed, but such words made him think of Tess. She was a great cook. With sudden clarity he realized something that had never been evident to him. In the last two months, when Tess' feelings and his own had become clear, he'd talked to Pastor Caron and Duffy. They had been very helpful, but he'd never spoken to his mother—the woman who had been widowed because she'd been married to the town's sheriff.

Sitting across the room, Slater watched the emotions chase across Griffin's face but kept silent. Clearly the man had much on his mind. If memory served him correctly, this was the night the blonde woman had wanted him to come for dinner. Had Liberty called her Tess? Is that where he'd been when Slater found the house empty? Much as Slater wondered, he knew he would never ask.

"I'm for bed," Slater said instead, wanting to give this man who had offered him a home even more privacy.

"I'll bet you are. Waking up to have a gun pointed at you takes it out of a man."

Slater laughed. "When I saw your sister today, I asked her why she didn't draw."

"Did she blush or laugh?"

"A little of both, I guess." Slater stood. "Good night, Griffin."

"Good night, Slater."

Griffin watched him walk from the room, reminding himself that it was way too early to take a full measure of this man, but the temptation to let his mind wander was strong. Liberty needed someone special. The thought no more formed than Griffin's mouth quirked. What brother didn't feel that way? That Tess' brothers might not care suddenly came to mind. As Griffin was coming to expect, it didn't take much to make him think of that woman.

❧ ❧ ❧

"Do you have to work?" Laura asked Liberty the next day. Bible study had just ended.

"Yes. Griffin and I have to check on something."

"Can you give Griff a hug for me?"

"I certainly can. Is there some special reason?"

Laura only shook her head no, seeming in no hurry to leave her sister's lap. Their mother was sitting beside Liberty, and the younger woman decided to question her if she had a chance. The opportunity came a few minutes later. Their hostess, Mrs. Caron, offered cookies to the children, and Laura, looking only mildly interested, left her sister's lap.

"Did you hear what she said?" Liberty asked quietly.

"About the hug? Yes. She's been so clingy, Lib. I think she's coming down with something. She cried this morning when she got juice on her hand."

Liberty's eyes widened in surprise. Her little sister was a very plucky gal. Spilled juice would not normally get her down.

"You look tired, Mam." Liberty had just seen it. "Maybe the two of you have a little bug going."

"Maybe."

"I think you should see the doctor," Liberty said, her eyes sparkling a little. "I hear he gives very personal service."

Kate laughed and put a hand on her daughter's arm. *If she was coming down with something, just talking to Liberty would make her feel better.*

"I'll think about your advice."

"All right. I'd better go. Griff and I have a case to check on. I won't stay any longer than I have to in case Laura gets worse."

"Thank you, dear. Don't forget to eat lunch."

Liberty thanked their hostess and went out front to where she had tethered Morton. Already dressed for work, she swung easily into the saddle. Mrs. Tobler's house was close enough that Liberty could hear the hammers pounding, but she made herself ride for downtown.

Why would you stop, Libby? She couldn't have lost another needle, and there's no other reason to go there right now.

This was all the further Liberty would allow these thoughts to roam. Knowing that she had to go with Griffin to confront the Potters, a consistently risky event, Liberty forced her mind to concentrate on her job. A good thing too. As soon as Griffin spotted her, he exited the office and climbed into the saddle of his own mount, Benny.

"Has there been more word?" Liberty asked, after telling Griffin that Laura had sent him a hug.

"Yes. Mrs. Flowers was back in this morning. The party was still going on last night."

"Ned Potter was nothing short of belligerent the last time I saw him."

"When was this?"

"About two weeks back. He was giving Miss Amy a hard time over the price of eggs and looked mad enough to kill when I stepped in."

"Why didn't you tell me?"

Liberty shrugged. "I forgot about it until just now."

"Well, I hope he remembers."

"Why?"

"Because this is just the first. Ned and his boys have thought themselves above the law just one time too many. I won't take action today, and maybe not even this year, but this is the beginning of the end. I'm going to put enough pressure on to make them uncomfortable."

Liberty agreed with the action but couldn't help wondering what they'd be letting themselves in for.

"Will we see Maddie Flowers too?"

"Yep. She's a little too self-righteous for my comfort. I want her to know that I'm aware of what she's up to, and that just because she doesn't have drunken binges does not make her judge and jury."

They fell silent for the rest of the ride. The Potters lived a ways outside of town. Their place was large and run down, a marked contrast to Mrs. Flowers' spotless paint and yard. They had to pass Mrs. Flowers' house on the way, and both officers caught the way she smugly watched them from the window, but neither sibling waved or acknowledged her call.

Things were quiet at the Potter house. A dog as old and broken-down as most of the rusty farm equipment in the yard barked a hoarse yap at them, but he didn't have enough ambition to move from his place under the porch, not even when Griffin went up the steps and pounded on the door. It was answered by Critter, the youngest of three sons.

"Pa's not here," the teen scowled at him, his eyes squinting against the sun.

"Mind if I come in and look?"

"Yeah, I do!" Critter growled, but Griffin's hand had already pushed the door wide. Liberty was right behind him.

"Get out," Critter said. The officers ignored him. He started a string of curses but stopped when he realized no one was listening. The house was in awful shape, and Liberty couldn't help but wonder how they all stood the smell and the filth. She had never needed to come in here before, but Griffin seemed to know his way around.

"What'd ya want?" Critter tried again as Griffin slipped upstairs, but again no one paid him any heed.

Still taking in the broken furniture, stained walls, and liquor bottles, Liberty thought she and Critter couldn't be too many years apart in age, but their lives had been lived in separate worlds.

"I think I'll have a look at the barn," Griffin said casually as he came slowly back down the stairs.

It wasn't lost on either sibling the way Critter came to attention.

"Pa don't like anybody nosin' out there."

"Well, come with us," Griffin offered mildly. "Give us the grand tour."

Critter seemed at a momentary loss before turning to the door, his body saying very clearly that the law in Shotgun was unjust.

As always, Liberty kept to the rear. More than once she had protected her brother's back, and as Griffin swung the barn door open, hinges howling, she took her standard position. Critter was mutinously silent. He walked in behind the sheriff, not seeming to notice the way Liberty hung back.

"What's in here?" Griffin asked as he approached a wagon covered by a tarpaulin. Without permission, Griffin untied the edge and threw it back.

"Nice load of corn, Critter. It's a little late in the year for planting."

The eyes that followed him were dark with rage. Watching him, Liberty thought he might still be a little done-in from the night before, which would slow his reaction time. His reputation, however, did not lead to trust.

She watched while Griffin came from the stall, his head tipped back inspecting the rafters. With a move that gave nothing away, he approached Critter.

"The shinin's going to stop, Critter. I just want you to know that." Griffin walked as he talked, and the youngest Potter, against his will, was backed up to the wall. "You give your Pa and brothers a message from me: I'm going to shut you down. I can't have you out here gettin' drunk, lightin' fires, and shootin' off shotguns all night. It's gotta stop."

Griffin had Critter flat against the wall now, his eyes hard and serious. Critter's own gaze was no more friendly, and when he suddenly felt a sickle on the wall, he started to reach for it. He had barely moved when the wood near his fingers splintered from a bullet. Critter froze. He'd completely forgotten the deputy. He could have lost part of his hand!

"Have I made myself clear?" Griffin asked.

"You wouldn't be so tough if Pa was here!" Critter spat. The fear had swiftly left, and he was angry again. "He won't be too pleased to know you were here nosin' around."

"He's welcome to come by the jailhouse and lodge a complaint." This said, Griffin held the younger man's eyes for several seconds and then pushed away from the wall. He walked from the barn, Liberty having already moved ahead of him this time, her eyes watching Critter. She was satisfied when he took his eyes from them. Critter's hand went to the back of his neck, and he leaned against the wall with a shake of his head. Liberty had already holstered her gun but now felt free to turn and mount her horse.

Griffin had been watching as well and climbed into his own saddle after Liberty was settled. They turned and rode from the Potters' yard, the dog letting out a few more obligatory woofs.

"Why now, Griff?" Liberty asked as they rode back up the road toward Maddie Flowers'. "You've been sheriff for three years. Why are you putting the pressure on the Potters now?"

"Because Shotgun is growing. I've not wanted to disturb the waters since they've always lived so far out, but the town is moving out here fast. I can't have townspeople in danger because of the Potters' moonshine."

Liberty nodded but still worried. What would old man Potter do when he discovered Griffin had been out? She found herself praying for their safety and also that God would bring a peaceful end to this. Never once did she pray for patience, something she desperately needed once they entered Maddie Flowers' house and were forced for the next hour to listen to her excuses about making moonshine.

🌿 🌿 🌿

"I thought you said you weren't any good in the kitchen?" Griffin accused Slater on Thursday evening.

Slater laughed. "Spoken like a hungry man."

"No, Slater, I mean it. It was very good."

Slater inclined his head modestly and rose to clear the table. Griffin started peeling a bar of soap into a basin of hot water, thinking that Slater was as easy to live with as any man could be. He was quiet, polite, clean, generous with the rent money and food he bought, and pulled his weight in the kitchen. But one question still lingered in Griffin's mind: Why had he left the Rangers? For some odd reason Griffin was hesitant to ask, fearing the answer would be very personal. But he genuinely liked the man. For this reason he extended the invitation.

"I'm headed next door tonight. Mam and Laura are under the weather, and Laura needs a little cheering up. Would you like to come?"

"If you're sure I won't be in the way."

"Not at all. We'll go right after cleanup."

Which is precisely what they did. Slater had offered to cook that evening. He'd been overrun with homesickness that day and wanted to make a beef dish that his family often had on the ranch. The weather was cooler now—he could head home anytime—but something compelled him to stay on in Shotgun; more specifically, to stay on with Griffin. He'd sent word to his oldest brother and folks about where he was, but right now he couldn't leave. Walking next door and going through the back, just like family, made him very glad he'd stayed.

Griffin led the way through the kitchen, through the dining area they'd eaten in last Sunday, and into the parlor. Zach was reading a book, Liberty had sewing in her lap, and Laura was swathed in quilts on the chair, bright-eyed with fever and remarkably wide awake.

"Hi, Griff." Zach was the first to spot him.

"Hey, Zach," Griffin said as he leaned down to hug the boy. "How was your day?"

"It was good. I lasted three rounds in the spelling bee."

"Good job. Do you remember Mr. Rawlings? He lives with me now."

"Hello," Zach said with a smile.

"Hi, Zach. You can call me Slater if you want to."

"All right. My sister's sick."

"I heard about that."

Griffin took a seat, so Slater did the same thing. From his place next to Zach, Griffin looked over at his younger sister.

"Are you going to come and see me, Laura?"

"Papa says I'm not supposed to run around."

Liberty's hand came to her mouth, and Griffin smiled.

"It won't be running around just to come over here to my lap."

Laura looked to Liberty, but that woman only smiled at her. Dragging along one small blanket and a stuffed bunny that had seen better days, Laura left the chair and went to Griffin's lap on the davenport.

"Where's Mam?" Griffin asked Liberty as soon as he hugged and kissed his very warm sister.

"She feels miserable, so Duff is putting her to bed."

Griffin looked down at the hot bundle in his lap. "Did you share your cold with Mam?"

"I think so, but her throat doesn't hurt."

"And yours does?"

"I'm not supposed to talk."

"Well, we both know how long that's going to last."

Laura only smiled and laid her head against him.

"How's the work on the porch going, Mr. Rawlings?" Liberty asked.

"I would say we're about half done. Mrs. Tobler doesn't want us there before 8:00, so by midafternoon the sun gets a little intense."

"It's anyone's guess why she doesn't want you there earlier," Griffin speculated.

"I think she said something about disturbing her breakfast."

"I'm amazed that Hank puts up with it. He's pretty much his own man," Liberty commented.

"He's not as eager to work as he once was," Griffin said. "Has he talked to you, Slater, about missing Price?"

"Not in so many words, but one day he expected me to lift the wagon for him and muttered something about Price never having any trouble. It made me wonder about the man I've replaced."

"Price is big," Laura suddenly put in, and Zach came alive.

"He lifted Miss Amy's horse right out of the creek. I saw it! He didn't even groan."

"I think they should have been married," Laura stated, and the occupants of the room stared at her.

"Who?" Griffin finally asked.

"Price and Miss Amy. He won't find a nice girl like her in Austin."

Zach looked at her as if she'd grown two heads, but the adults in the room were all working not to laugh. Griffin hugged her close so he could hide his face, and Slater dropped his head down to check for stains on the front of his shirt. Liberty became very involved with her sewing.

"That's just dumb, Laura," Zach told her mildly. "Why would Price want to get married?"

"Because it's fun," Laura told him. "Mam and Papa have fun, and when I marry Bobby Fossett, I'll have fun too."

"Bobby Fossett is a whole year older than me," Zach felt a need to remind her, his voice very logical.

"Well, Papa is older than Mam," Laura argued.

"I thought we decided that you weren't supposed to talk," Duffy said as he came into the room and stood looking down at his daughter.

"I had to set Zach straight."

Duffy looked at her sternly. "It's not your job to set anyone straight, and you need to be quiet when your throat is sore. Do you understand?"

Laura nodded, and Duffy turned away. Griffin was behind him, but Slater and Liberty could not miss the way his eyes lit with laughter and tenderness the moment Laura could not see him.

Five

"Do you have family, Slater?" Duffy asked after he'd taken a seat and they'd all talked a little more about the day.

"I do. I'm the youngest of three boys."

"Are you from Texas?"

"Not originally, and in fact, my parents moved back to St. Louis about five years ago. But my grandmother is still in Texas, and so are both my brothers."

"What do they do?" Liberty asked.

"One is a Texas Ranger, and the other runs the family ranch in Kinkade."

"So would you consider Kinkade home for you?"

"Yes. I was thinking about heading in that direction when I found myself detained in Shotgun."

Liberty and Griffin both smiled at his dry tone.

"Why have you stayed?" Duffy asked. This young man seemed very straightforward, but he was living with Kate's son, and it wasn't unusual to see his eyes stray in Liberty's direction. Duffy wanted to take him at face value, but he wasn't going to be heedless.

"Mostly the church. If I hadn't found work so easily, I probably wouldn't have had much choice but to move on. Griffin's hospitality was a draw too."

"Has he complained of your snoring yet, Griff?" Liberty asked.

"If I could get up, you'd be in trouble," Griffin told her. Laura had fallen asleep on him.

"I can hear it," Slater admitted, "but it doesn't keep me awake."

Liberty enjoyed sending a teasing look at her brother.

"What did you enjoy about the church?" Duffy asked.

"The way your pastor preached from the Word, and the way he didn't skip around the issues or make excuses. He's obviously studied, and I learned quite a bit. I've been reading in Nehemiah all week, and I'm looking forward to going back."

"There's a picnic," Zach told him, and Duffy looked surprised.

"You were so quiet, Zach, that I forgot you were there. I think you'd best head up to bed."

"All right. Are you coming?"

"Indeed, I am. Get changed and wash your face. I'll be right along."

"Mam told me about the picnic," Griffin explained to Duffy after Zach had kissed Liberty and Griffin and told Slater goodnight. "Do you think she'll feel up to going?"

"I don't know," Duffy admitted. "She tells me she's been tired lately. I think maybe she should stay home just so she can rest."

"It's not the picnic itself, Duff," Liberty put in. "It's all the work beforehand. I can take care of it, but she can't stand to lie around."

"I'll talk with her, Liberty," he said, sounding very much like a doctor. "But it wouldn't hurt for either of you to realize you don't need to bring enough food to feed the entire congregation. Everyone brings food to pass, and we always have an abundance."

Liberty nodded, knowing he was right. They always brought food home. Liberty was still thinking about it, even going so far as to figure out what she would make this time—two or three dishes to share instead of the usual four or five would be reasonable—when she realized she was alone with Slater. Duffy had gone up to tuck Zach into bed, and Griffin had carried Laura to her room. Slater was staring at her, his expression unreadable.

"That was rude of me," Liberty said. "I was thinking and didn't realize we were alone."

"I don't need to be entertained," Slater said politely.

The moment he said this, Liberty became thoughtful again. She looked at Slater and made no pretense that she was doing otherwise.

"It's terribly rude for a man to ask a lady what she's thinking, but I must tell you I'm very tempted."

"I'll tell you," Liberty said. "I'm trying to figure out which man is the real Slater Rawlings: the man who spent 48 hours in the jailhouse, or the man I see now."

Slater nodded, regret knifing through him once again. "I can't begin to tell you how sorry I am for the way I handled myself, Miss Drake. I was completely wrong. It's not surprising that you don't know what to think of me."

Liberty was impressed with his humility and said, "I'm glad you understand, but please don't think I'm looking for something. I'm not watching to see you slip up or make a wrong move, but it does take a little getting used to. Everyone calls me Libby, by the way."

"I hope you'll call me Slater."

"That's an unusual name."

"A family name from my mother's side. My oldest brother is named after my father but goes by a nickname. And my middle brother was named after the territory my father always wanted to visit. My mother finally got her way with me."

Liberty smiled at him and the story. Slater Rawlings was so straightforward and courteous. People had come and gone over the years, and Liberty's family had helped out whenever they could. Some made more of an impression than others. After she met Slater, he had glared at her; just days later he teased her. For some reason the contrast stayed in her mind. As Duffy and Griffin came back to the room and suggested a board game, Liberty knew that even if this man left town the next day, she would never completely forget him.

⚜ ⚜ ⚜

"It looks good, Hank," Griffin complimented the old man, who grunted but still managed to look pleased. He slapped the horse and set the wagon into motion.

Slater watched his boss for a moment, still amazed at how few words the man said. Some days he worked them both like there was no tomorrow, but not on Saturday. After a few hours of work, Hank wanted to start the weekend early. Griffin rode up just as they finished for the day.

"Don't tell me you'll actually be a man of leisure today," Griffin teased Slater as he stacked some large boards against the house, his final chore.

"Well, someone has to do it."

"What in the world?" Slater suddenly heard Griffin exclaim. He looked to find the lawman watching a man who was backing toward them. He had come around the corner of the house, clearly watchful, and it took him some moments to realize Griffin was approaching from the rear.

"What are you doing, Critter?"

"Nothing!" The younger man was instantly belligerent. "And you can stop tryin' ta pin things on me I didn't do. Just leave me be. I won fair and square!"

Griffin's gaze narrowed as he watched him stalk away. He hadn't gone 15 steps before he was back to looking over his shoulder and moving behind trees and houses.

"I think I'll check on Lib," Griffin said quietly.

"Mind if I come along?" Slater asked, his voice belying the way his heart slammed in his chest upon the mention of Griffin's sister.

"Not at all," was all Griffin said in return. A minute later they both rode for downtown.

⚜ ⚜ ⚜

"Can you come?" old Davis Marks panted as he hobbled into the jailhouse on Saturday afternoon. Liberty immediately stood.

"What's up?"

"Guy with a whip. He says young Potter cheated in cards, and he's mad. Potter made off, but this guy's still cracking that thing and..."

Liberty didn't wait to hear more. Checking her gun for bullets, she jumped into Morton's saddle and rode for the Crescent Moon Saloon at the far end of town. Slowing as she neared and eventually dropping off Morton's back, Liberty moved close to the window for a look. She was glad to see he was at the rear wall. No one else was in sight, but the man was talking wildly, which meant the others were probably all against the walls, a wise place to be if the whip was as long as it looked.

Seeming for all the world to be on an afternoon stroll, Liberty walked down the boardwalk and through the swinging doors of the saloon. She stopped inside, her eyes scanning the room and summing up the situation. The afternoon was growing long, and the saloon was already getting crowded. A good 25 customers were backed away from the angry man, who for a moment was in profile to her.

"I want him found," he said, his voice low as he lashed at a chair.

"Is he looking for Critter?" Liberty asked Smiley, who tended the bar.

"Yeah, but Stumpy was at the table, and he said nobody cheated."

The man turned suddenly, his eyes scanning the room. "Don't nobody move until I find him."

"We'll find him for you, but you have to put the whip down," Liberty told him, taking a few more steps inside. The man seemed to notice her for the first time. He wasn't a big man, but the bullwhip looked to be a dozen feet long, and even with his staggering gait, he looked like he could use it. Crescent Moon's bouncer was against one wall, a red slash on his face and one on his arm. The only disadvantage to Shotgun's laws concerning firearms in the saloons was the owner's inability to protect himself or his clientele.

"What did you say to me?"

"I said, put the whip down. No one wants to fight with you. Just put it away." Liberty's voice held authority, but it didn't carry like Griffin's. She wasn't sure she would get any response at all.

The whip suddenly cracked with terrific force, giving Liberty her answer. Nevertheless, she held her ground.

"Do you know what I can do to you?" he started to say, but Liberty drew and put a bullet past his ear.

"I want the whip put down," she said, her voice deadly calm. She also heard riders but couldn't be certain that help was on the way. She tried again. "Set it gently on the floor and take a seat at the table there."

The man watched her suspiciously. He noticed that she was holding a gun, but he still wasn't certain she had fired the shot. He shook his head a little and went to sit down, the whip still in his hand.

"What's his name?" Liberty asked of Smiley.

"I think Leonard something."

"Listen to me, Leonard," Liberty said as she approached. "You need to drop the whip and kick it toward me."

"You can't have my whip!" he stood with a roar as he shouted, the whip going into action again. Liberty had stayed well back, and from the corner of her eye she caught Griffin and Slater as they entered. Keeping her target in view, she shot the hat from Leonard's head. That man stopped in surprise, reeling a little in his boots. He turned in a deliberate fashion when he heard the cock of a shotgun from his other side.

"Put the whip down, or I'll take your arm off," Griffin said, his tone telling everyone in the room that he meant it. Slater had moved around and was coming at him from behind. When he drew close enough, he stepped on the whip and waited. He certainly hoped the man would do as he was told. It wasn't fun to shoot any man. It was extremely hard to shoot a drunk, when your heart told you he would act differently when sober.

"I want my whip," the man said pathetically, and Slater was close enough to see it go loose in his grasp. He removed the whip gently, the man having never seen him, and stepped back against the wall, where he began to wind it into a circle. Griffin moved toward him, and Liberty repositioned herself in case Leonard had more tricks up his sleeve. Griffin was cuffing him when Slater reached her side.

"Are you all right?" He dropped his head slightly to see her face beneath the brim of her hat.

Liberty blinked in surprise. "I'm fine."

Slater nodded, but his heart smarted a little in his chest. Did no one ever check with her? Was she ever frightened or rattled? He had all he could do not to shake his head. He would be treating this woman like a precious flower, not like a gunman. He stopped the judgment going on in his mind. It wasn't his place. He didn't have all the facts. He was also out of time. Griffin was taking the cuffed man away. After taking the whip from his hand and thanking him, Liberty followed in her brother's wake.

🦎 🦎 🦎

"And I hope ya'll can join us at the picnic," Pastor Caron said after the closing prayer. "If you've never joined us at one of our fellowships, just ask and someone will give you directions to the Millers'. We picnic on the creek at the back of their place. We'll gather for a blessing under the big oak tree in about 30 minutes. I hope you can all come."

Slater stood, his Bible going under his arm and his hat in his hand. He smiled at the two young ladies who kept looking back at him and then moved out the door, wishing

Griffin could have been there. Griffin said his mother usually made plenty, but not expecting to be on his own, Slater felt very awkward in just assuming he was welcome to their food.

"Slater," Zach piped up, suddenly speaking from his side.

"Hi, Zach."

"Papa asked me to tell you that you can come with us."

"Oh, thank you, Zach. I'll do that."

The little boy smiled up at him, and Slater saw Griffin's dark eyes.

"You can come with me, and I'll show you the wagon."

"All right."

Slater passed a group of young ladies—others had joined the two who had smiled at him after the service—and he would have been blind not to see their interest. Even if he had been blind, he would have still heard someone say his name as he walked away. They all looked sweet—nice girls—but his mind was elsewhere at the moment.

"Thank you, Zach," Duffy said as soon as he and Slater neared. "We weren't sure if you knew the way."

"Thank you, sir. I was hoping Griffin would get here, but I don't see him."

"Maybe he'll join us later."

"We need to go by the house, Duff," Liberty reminded him.

"All right. Laura, are you sitting down?"

The little girl's seat landed fast. "Yes."

"Is your mother still not well, Libby?" Slater asked from the seat beside her. The wagon had one wide seat. The younger two children were in the back.

"She is feeling better but still tired. She was ready to come, but Duffy put his foot down."

"You make me sound like an ogre," Duffy said, his hands controlling the reins.

"I think the word Mam used was beast, Duffy; never think of yourself as an ogre."

Duffy shook his head. For all Liberty's rather quiet ways, she could be quite a card.

She was also a good cook, and the food they brought from the kitchen not many minutes later smelled wonderful.

"Gingerbread?" Zach asked after peeking into the basket.

"Yes, just like you asked me."

"Thanks, Lib."

"You're welcome, Zach."

Brother and sister shared a smile, and watching them, Slater thought he might have missed something by not having a sister.

"The Millers have water in their backyard," Laura told Slater. "They can get wet anytime they want."

"That sounds fun," Slater responded as he turned to talk with her. "Will you get wet today?"

"If I'm lucky," Laura said in all seriousness and turned back around.

Slater faced forward again, his shoulders shaking a little. "Has she always been so profound?"

"No," Liberty told him. "She couldn't talk until she was two."

Smiling to himself, Slater suddenly knew just where she'd picked up her charming wit.

❧ ❧ ❧

"What a privilege this is, Father God," Bill Miller prayed from his place under the big oak tree after the group had quieted, "to gather in Your name for fellowship and food. We thank You for each person here, and pray that our time in You would be sweet. Bless this food as we partake. In Christ's name we pray. Amen."

Tables had been set up. Baskets, pots, bowls, and platters had been laid out. Towels were lifted and the contents displayed. Plates in hand, the congregation lined up to make their choices. A few mothers had to coax children from the water's edge, but most of the younger set were ready.

"It's time to eat," Liberty told Laura and Zach.

"Do you think they catch fish in here?" Zach asked, his eyes on the creek bed and the minnows that swam near the bank.

"I'll bet they do. You should ask Mr. Miller if you can fish here sometime."

"I could too," Laura put in. "I won't poke anyone with the hook."

"Papa won't let you fish yet, Laura," Zach said, his voice regretful. "You might get hurt."

Laura looked stubborn over this until she caught her brother's look. It was impossible to get mad at him when he *wanted* her to fish.

"We could ask," she said in a quiet voice, all stubbornness gone. "You could ask, Zach...you could."

Zach contemplated this. His father wouldn't get angry, but if he said no, Laura would be disappointed. Zach's soft heart could hardly handle the thought. He wished she hadn't even asked.

"Are you ready to eat?" Duffy called as he came toward them. Liberty had come off the quilt she had laid out and was holding the plates, but she didn't answer for the children. She was too busy trying not to watch Slater. He was surrounded by a group of women.

Zach stood staring up at his father until Duffy lowered his brow in puzzlement. Laura was pulling on her brother's sleeve.

"Papa," Zach began, "could Laura come fishing with us sometime?"

"Sure, Zach. I think that's a great idea. You were very kind to think of her."

There was no missing the little boy's sigh. He grinned at his sister, who grinned right back, and then smiled up at his father in a way that always melted the hearts of those who loved him.

"Let's eat," Duffy said softly, and the four proceeded across the grass. Liberty had a plate for Slater, but she suddenly felt awkward. She approached the food tables, fully expecting him to already have a plate in hand. She hadn't counted on Laura.

"Here," Laura said, as they neared the group that Slater was a part of and she took a dinner plate from her sister. Her family watched as she stepped right into the midst and handed it to Slater.

"Here's your plate, Slater. Are you going to come to our quilt?"

"I am. Thank you, Laura. I'll just come and stand in line with you right now. Excuse me, ladies."

Liberty could have sunk into the grass. She hadn't put Laura up to anything, but the looks on the female faces that watched Slater leave the circle were certainly speculative, or were they just fascinated with this new man?

"I hope I didn't hold you up," Slater said as they gathered at the rear of the line.

"Not at all," Duff put in before Liberty could speak. "We hope we didn't interrupt your conversation."

Slater didn't answer, but Liberty could have hugged her stepfather. He must have seen her strained, surprised look when Laura took things into her own hands. Indeed, her stepfather was bending over to speak to Laura right then. It wasn't hard to guess that she was being reprimanded over interrupting.

"Did Griffin happen to tell you how long he would be?" Slater asked Liberty.

"I didn't talk to him at all. Did he have to stay at the jail?"

"Yes. It was a busy night last night. He didn't get in until quite late."

Liberty nodded.

"Do you never work on Saturday nights?" Slater asked, no longer able to squelch his curiosity over the arrangement.

"Not usually, but that's why I go in on Monday and Tuesday mornings, so he can do a little catching up on his rest."

It was on the tip of Slater's tongue to ask how long she had been at this, along with a dozen other questions, but he felt he'd asked enough. Pastor Caron had taken most of the service that morning to tell them what a prayer warrior Nehemiah had been. Slater determined to emulate that Bible character and to start immediately.

Covertly watching Slater, Liberty tried to figure out what he might be thinking. Had he been very disappointed to be taken from the group? Had Laura rescued him, or was he being polite to a little girl? Liberty had no idea how she could find out and made herself rest in the matter. Easier said than done. She found herself glancing at him often to see where he was looking. She was quite fascinated to note that she never once saw him glancing back to the group of young women who had finally fallen into line.

"I don't like beets," Liberty heard Laura say. She watched as Duffy gave her something else. Zach's plate wobbled a little, but before Liberty could reach for it, Slater's hand was there. For the briefest of moments, Liberty had the unwanted feeling of not being needed but managed to push it away and concentrate on getting her food. While she did this, she had a stern talk with herself.

You enjoy Slater's company, and he's chosen to eat with your family. After all, Griffin invited him. Now, you can relax and take pleasure in this, or you can examine every move the man makes and be miserable. You're too old to be so distracted by a pair of warm blue eyes, a tall build, wavy blond hair, broad shoulders, a great smile... Stop it, Libby! Liberty shouted to herself just in time.

"Why don't I take our plates, Libby." Slater turned and offered, "and you can get our drinks?"

"Oh—all right," Liberty said but moved away from the crowd only a little and stood looking at him.

"I'm getting that look again," he said, his eyes smiling.

Liberty's eyes narrowed in an effort to hide her feelings. "I'm still figuring you out."

Slater smiled slowly. "Well, I hope you keep at it."

Liberty had no idea what he meant by this, so she simply said, "I think there's coffee, lemonade, and water. Which would you like?"

"Lemonade, please," Slater said, watching her closely and thinking he found her a little more fascinating every time they talked.

Liberty ended up with a tray holding five lemonades and then walked beside Slater back to the quilt. The Millers had a quilt next to theirs, and Laura joined their family to be with little Kathy Miller. Slater waited until Liberty had doled out the drinks and taken a seat on the quilt and then gave her her plate. Watching his solicitous manner, Duffy couldn't stop his smile.

"You're looking pleased with yourself, Duffy Peterson," Liberty said, knowing her stepfather well and reading his sparkling eyes.

"Am I?" he evaded.

Liberty only looked at him and smiled when he winked. She might have given him a hard time, but Zach suddenly said, "It's Griff and Tess! Over here, Griffin."

The couple made their way over to the quilt, Tess' mother coming with them. It was on Liberty's mind to find out what Duffy had been thinking, but the afternoon suddenly rushed on, and she never got back to it.

Six

"DID YOU POP THE QUESTION?" Liberty came right out and asked her brother.

"No," he told her honestly, his voice mild.

"Why not?"

They were still at the picnic, but Laura had wandered too close to the bank and fallen completely into the water. Slater had plucked her out, and Mrs. Miller had told Duffy to bring her to the house. Slater had gone with them. Zach had wandered off with a schoolmate, and Tess and Mrs. Locken had gone to see the Carons, who were sitting closer to the house.

"I have my reasons," Griffin said, effectively shutting the door in his sister's face. Griffin didn't realize this until he looked over at her. Liberty's eyes, large and somber as she looked at the children playing near the water, were hurt.

"I didn't mean it that way, Lib. I have some more thinking to do and someone I must talk to. I just know it's not time right now. It may never be time."

Liberty stared at him. "Then why do you spend so much time with her, Griff?"

Griffin sighed before admitting, "Because I'm selfish and unfeeling. I want to be with her—I want to see her—even if it hurts later."

Liberty nodded, glad that he had been so honest. Knowing she needed to be careful about what she said, she reminded herself that her brother was not answerable to her; she was not in charge.

"Griffin," Liberty said suddenly, "Slater is headed this way, and I want to ask him something. You may not like it, so I won't if you don't want me to."

"About what?"

"Marriage and law enforcement."

Griffin shrugged. "I don't care."

"Is this a bad time?" Slater asked as he neared—little wonder with the serious looks on Liberty's and Griffin's faces.

"No," Griffin told him. "Please join us."

"Does Duffy need me to do anything with Laura?" Liberty asked Slater.

"I don't think so. She had Mrs. Miller laughing when I left."

"What did she say this time?"

"She assumed the Millers had special get-wet clothes. When Kathy didn't know what she was talking about, Laura asked, 'So you just get wet in whatever you're wearing?'"

Griffin laughed, and Liberty shook her head.

"Her logic is always a challenge," Griffin said.

"I was looking at her as her head came out of the water. She was very shocked to have fallen in," Slater told them.

"Well," Liberty said, "Duff told her she couldn't wade in because it meant removing her stockings, but I know she still wanted to. I don't think getting completely wet was in her mind at all."

"Probably not. I think I heard a few tears when she thanked me."

"I'm glad she remembered to do that," Griffin said quietly.

"Slater," Liberty began, choosing that moment to plunge in, "may I ask you a question about your family?"

"Shoot."

"Did you say your brother is a Texas Ranger?"

"Yes."

"Is he married?"

"No."

Liberty nodded but didn't go on.

Slater watched her.

"Why did you ask, Libby?" Surprisingly enough, this came from Griffin, who felt she'd left Slater at sea.

"I just wondered if he had any views on the subject because of his job, or if he wasn't married because the right girl hadn't come along."

"His job requires him to move around a lot, and Dakota, that's my brother," Slater explained, "enjoys his work, even though it doesn't make marriage very practical."

"Do you think he worries about leaving a widow if he were to marry?"

"I would say he does. He's not at all easy on people who break the law, but he's usually very polite and caring of women. I think he would consider marriage a serious move for someone in his position."

Liberty nodded. She'd gotten her answer, but it wasn't one that would comfort Tess if she'd heard it. Liberty glanced at Griffin but only found him staring at Slater. He appeared to be waiting for something, and Liberty wondered if Griffin had wished she'd kept her mouth shut.

Slater, on the other hand, thought that Liberty's questions stemmed entirely from her own situation. Did she fear marrying someone because her job was so dangerous? Again, Slater was pained at the thought that she had to live like this. His own gaze swung to Griffin, whom Slater felt was very responsible for his sister. But that man was watching Tess and her mother return to the quilt. Asking God to help him be patient over matters that might never become clear, Slater shifted his mind away from the torturous thoughts.

❧ ❧ ❧

"How are you feeling?" Liberty asked Kate first thing Monday morning. Kate was still in bed; Duffy had gone downstairs to start breakfast.

"As well as can be expected," Kate said, her voice light.

Liberty stared at her mother, and Kate smiled at her.

"Duffy and I were talking last night and again this morning. Sometimes surprises are very nice things."

Liberty caught on swiftly, her eyes growing in size. "Oh, Mam, are you really?"

"Well, Duffy thinks so, but he's only a doctor."

Liberty rushed over and hugged her mother for a long time. Kate eventually pushed up against the headboard and the two sat talking.

"You didn't have Laura's cold at all."

"I don't think I did. I'm just tired."

"Not queasy?"

"Only around certain food."

"When do you think the baby is due?"

"Well, by my calculations, sometime in June—mid to late."

Liberty smiled. "Remember Zach's first day of school? You cried, not only because he was leaving, but because you knew that next year Laura would be gone too."

"I do remember that." Kate's voice was fond. "I asked the Lord to give me strength on that day and all the ones to come, but not to worry about tomorrow. It never occurred to me that we would have more children, but I can't tell you how pleased I am."

"When will you tell Zach and Laura?"

"Not until I'm ready for the whole world to know."

Liberty laughed. "But, Mam, Laura would tell the world in such a warmhearted manner. It might not be something we'd want to miss."

"This sounds like fun," Duffy offered as he came in the door with a steaming mug of coffee for his wife. Zach was close on his heels.

"Thank you, dear," Kate said as she took a sip and then set the drink aside so Zach could come close and cuddle with her. "Are you all ready for school?"

"Yes. We had oatmeal."

"Was it good?"

"Yes, but I think it's the only breakfast Papa can make." Zach looked over at his father. "What did you eat before you married Mam?"

"Oatmeal," Duffy told him, and Zach laughed at the way his eyes crossed.

Their voices woke Laura, who did not always rise with the rest of the family. Tousled and sleep-warm in a small flannel gown, she came in to snuggle next to her mother as well. Liberty had to be at the jailhouse soon, but she made time before she left to thank God for this new little person and to pray for his safe arrival. As she watched her family—Duffy was on the bed too—she didn't think that God could give another child to a more godly, loving couple. In her opinion, next June couldn't come soon enough.

೪ ೪ ೪

Did you pop the question? Why not? The questions Liberty had asked Griffin more than two weeks earlier were almost constantly on his mind. He had even double-checked with his sister to make sure she wasn't upset by his cold reply.

And why had he been so formal with her? He had thought it might help to speak with his mother, but Griffin used the excuse that she wasn't feeling well long after it was valid. No longer. Slater had left for work, Liberty was at the jailhouse, Zach was at school, and Duffy would also have gone to work. It was time to pay a visit to his mother. Griffin spent some time in prayer about their meeting and then went next door, hoping very much that she didn't have plans or company for the morning.

"Well, Griff," Kate greeted him warmly as they exchanged a hug, "I was just about to have some coffee and read my Bible. Would you like a cup?"

"I would if it wouldn't be interrupting."

"Not at all. You've been busy lately, and I don't want to miss a chance to talk with you."

Griffin realized that she always did that: made him feel special and wanted.

"Unless I miss my guess, you have something on your mind," Kate said as she put a steaming mug in front of him, not even giving him a chance to ask how she was feeling, especially with the baby coming.

"How did you know?"

"Because Libby told me she said something to you at the picnic and felt bad about it. She got the impression that you were upset by her probing. Did she not get back to you as she planned?"

"Well, I had to talk to her about the way I acted, and she tried to make sure I was all right with her, but now that you mention it, I think I was a little too busy making sure she wasn't upset with me to listen."

Kate nodded. "You're in terrible pain, Griff. I can see it."

Griffin dropped his head, his hand going to the back of his neck.

"All this time I should have been talking to you, but it never occurred to me. I think you could give me some answers—you have insight into being a lawman's wife— and it only just recently occurred to me to ask."

Kate smiled. "Sometimes we're like that, a little slow to start."

"Hi, Griff!" a cheery voice called just before Laura launched herself at her oldest brother. "I didn't know you were here."

Griffin gave her a hug and kissed her cheek. "How are you today?" he asked.

"I'm drawing a picture of our house. I did Mam and Papa's room and the kitchen."

"Well, you still have a lot of rooms to cover."

Laura agreed with a nod of her head but still plopped down in a kitchen chair as if she had all day.

"Laura," her mother said gently, "I need you to play on your own for a little longer."

Laura looked between the two adults.

"Are you talking to Griffin?"

"Yes."

"Is it because he loves Tess?" Laura asked, a little frown on her brow.

"That is none of your concern," her mother told her, and Laura tucked her lower lip under her teeth and gave Griffin an apologetic look. She left, looking back at them only once, and when she was gone, Griffin smiled.

"Just so long as she doesn't see you laughing," Kate told her son. "She's precocious enough as it is, and at times, nosey. Now! Let's get back to you. Ask me anything, Griff, and I'll try to answer."

Griffin sighed. "You married Thomas Drake before he was a sheriff, but did you know he wanted to be the sheriff?"

"Yes, I did. I can't say that I didn't worry, Griff, but I will admit that I didn't worry much. My father hadn't died from a bullet wound, so I didn't have that on my mind like you do. I knew the risks, but not until your father pushed to have the laws changed did I really start to see how dangerous his job would become."

"Tell me about the firearms law," Griffin requested. "I can't remember how long he waited to implement that."

"Less than a year after he took the job. And then he died not long after it went into effect. Because of that, there were some who said the law didn't do any good. All this clamping down on guns, only to have your father shot while enforcing the new statute. But he was the only one killed for a long time, and even though the job came with risks, we both believed in it. I still do. And thankfully, so did the town fathers. Innocent people still die, Griffin—they always will—but there's no comparison to what it used to be like."

"And you would have no trouble with my marrying a woman who could end up alone like you did?"

"It's crazy to say I don't have any trouble with it. I would be crushed if I lost you, but I remind myself of one thing: God is still in control. If it is God's will that you die, then you could go swimming with Tess on your honeymoon and drown. If it isn't God's will that you die, then a thousand bullets fired at you wouldn't make it happen."

In so many words, both Duffy and Pastor Caron had voiced the same thoughts to him. It was good to be reminded. Too often he wanted God to reveal His will before it was time. Griffin knew he was suffering from a lack of trust and that he needed to grow in this area.

"Thanks, Mam," Griffin said. "I'm still not certain what would be the wise course, but I needed that reminder."

"I'll keep praying for you, Griff, and if you need to talk again, come straight back. You know Duffy feels the same way."

"Can I come back in now?"

"*May* I come back in," Kate corrected, "and, yes, you may."

Laura flew through the doorway, kissed her mother, and scrambled into Griffin's lap. Watching her, Kate's prayers intensified for her son. It was so easy to skip through life without thought of the future. Griffin was wise to take it seriously. Looking at Laura, Kate was reminded that she might someday be forced to look at Griffin's children, just as she had her own, and wish that their father was still there to hold them.

❧ ❧ ❧

I don't know her well—at least not yet, Slater prayed a few weeks later. He was on his horse and headed to dinner at the Carons'. *But I like her...I like her so much. I've been here only six weeks, and already I feel at home and cared for. Can that be possible? I loved my job, Lord. I fought You tooth and nail about leaving it. But I don't miss the long rides, unpredictable hours, and meager pay. I've never known such a sense of completeness. I want to stay in Shotgun. I miss taking care of folks, and it's not always easy to work with Hank, but the thought of leaving Griffin and his family, especially Libby, really bothers me.*

I need to know Your will in this. The letters from the ranch have been encouraging. I'm glad they want me to stay here since I've found a good church, but I should probably visit them sometime soon. I'm still surprised that Dakota hasn't shown up. Please be with him, Father; touch his heart wherever he is.

Slater could have prayed on for the next hour, but the Carons' house was in sight. He had honestly appreciated being asked over, but he had been more thankful before Duffy extended an invitation for the same night. He'd had no choice but to go to the Carons'—he'd been asked there first—but it was hard to see Griffin head next door and know that he had to go elsewhere. With a prayer for a thankful heart, Slater tethered his horse and went to the door.

☙ ☙ ☙

"Do you think he's cute?" Mayann asked her mother while they were preparing the coffee tray.

"Mr. Rawlings? Yes, he's very nice-looking," Felicia said kindly, but she was not going to do too much encouraging. Mayann was growing up fast, but she was not ready to be in a relationship, especially one with a man Slater's age. Felicia wasn't certain, but she figured him somewhere in his midtwenties; not to mention the fact that they were still getting to know him. However, Betsy, their oldest daughter, suddenly sprang to mind. Felicia was not about to start pushing her daughter at anyone—she did not want to play God in the matter—but if Slater should show some interest in Betsy, Felicia didn't think she'd have any trouble with that at all. Felicia determined to discuss it with Ross later that evening.

"I think Betsy is in love," Mayann said, her voice a little too loud. Felicia came and put a hand on her daughter's shoulder.

"I don't want you to talk like that, Mayann. If Betsy has feelings for Mr. Rawlings, then we'll deal with that in its time, but don't you start planting ideas."

"All right. But do you think he likes her?"

Mayann had Felicia there. In truth, she had never seen Slater Rawlings give any of the young women preferential treatment. He was extremely polite, a real gentleman, but not at any time did she feel he was playing games with the young women of the church.

"Papa sent me out to help," Tanner, suddenly appearing in the doorway, said. "Do you want me to carry the tray?"

"Thank you, Tanner," Felicia responded, but his question brought her up short. How many minutes had she stood here daydreaming?

Lord, she prayed as she followed her children out of the kitchen and into the living room. *Mr. Rawlings needs my love and hospitality, not my matchmaking skills. Please help me to want his spiritual growth more than a husband for my daughter.*

"So where will we go after Nehemiah?" Felicia heard Slater ask her husband as she entered.

"I think the book of Mark. I try to alternate Old and New Testament books, but before we do that, I have some topics I feel we need to cover. Tell me, Slater, does sharing your faith come easily to you?"

"Not as a rule. I don't know how to open the subject with strangers."

"That's my point exactly. So often I think we try to press Jesus Christ onto someone who has given no sign of interest. What if we got to know our neighbors? What if we loved the people we worked with, without ever mentioning our faith, and then when they noticed the difference in us—*making sure they've seen one*—we lovingly explained why we're different and how they can be different too?"

Slater sat back and stared at him. "I almost want to laugh with the irony of your suggestion. I work with Hank Hathaway, and it's been on my mind to share with him, but he never wants to talk. He never lets me into his world, even a little, and for that reason I just haven't felt free to mention my decision for Christ. You've put it so well. He needs to see a difference in my life first."

Ross Caron nodded, thinking this young man was a balm for his heart. Unless he missed his guess, both his daughters thought he was nice to look at, but that wasn't Pastor Caron's main concern. He believed the church needed strong male leadership. If Slater Rawlings stayed around and continued to grow, he could be a help in leading this church to strength and maturity.

"When did you come to Christ, Mr. Rawlings?" Felicia now asked.

"Less than two years ago. A man I'd been working with talked to me. I had a tendency to search in all the wrong places. Some of my family had come to Christ, but I didn't think it was for me." Slater smiled. "I'll never forget that day. I told the Lord that I didn't think I would be any good as His child, that I could never love and serve Him like my brother was trying to do, but if He wanted a rotten sinner like me, I would do my best." Again Slater smiled. "I was in for quite a surprise. The Bible, a book I had always found dry as dust, became so exciting to me that I couldn't get enough of it."

Slater was on the verge of saying that that was just the beginning when he looked over to see the oldest Caron girl, he thought she had been introduced as Betty, staring at him with a dreamy look on her face. Slater smiled at her but stopped just short of pulling at his collar, which suddenly felt tight. Had he been invited over here as a prospective son-in-law? The thought chilled Slater to the bone, until a glance at his hosts put him at ease. They were looking at their daughter, neither one happy, and when the younger Caron girl saw it, she dropped her eyes and turned red. Slater busied himself with his coffee cup and was glad when Tanner changed the subject.

They fellowshipped for the next hour, and everyone, even Betsy after she realized what she'd been doing, joined in the conversation and had fun. Slater left, his heart at peace and very thankful as he rode through town toward Griffin's house. The church family was wonderful. All he'd wanted to do was escape to the cool of the mountains. Never in his wildest dreams did he think God would—

Slater's mind ceased its wandering. From the corner of his eye he'd caught movement on a downtown roof not far from the bank. He thought he heard a raised voice, but one of the saloons was nearby and he couldn't be sure of the direction. A second later he brought Arrow to a full halt. Another man was on the roof, and this one looked like Griffin. Slater was out of the saddle in a flash, tying Arrow's reins to a post and moving silently toward the alley between the buildings. Slater had gone only ten feet into the alley when someone moved ahead of him. Thinking that the bank was being robbed or cased, Slater touched the Bowie knife in his boot for reassurance and crept forward, not making a sound. A moment later he grabbed the guy in front of him with an arm around the neck, and Slater knew in an instant that this was not a man. With a swift hand to what was sure to be Liberty's mouth, he pulled her into the shadows.

"It's Slater," he whispered in her ear to stop her struggling and to also keep from being shot. The moment she calmed, he turned her to face him but did not let her out of his arms. He bent again to catch her ear. "What are you doing in this alley?"

"Leonard is drunk again," she spoke against his chest. "He's on the roof with his whip."

"Where's Griffin?"

"Up there with him. He wanted me here."

Slater sighed. Her voice was so pragmatic. Didn't anyone know this wasn't normal?

"What does he expect you to do?"

"Just to keep watch if something should happen, or if he calls."

Slater sighed again, this time over his emotions. Even in what was sure to be her deputy outfit, she smelled so nice, and holding her, even loosely in his arms, was nothing short of delightful.

"How do I let Griffin know that I'm here to help?" Slater, making himself concentrate, asked.

"I don't know. He wants me to stay quiet."

"Put it down!" The shout came from overhead, and Liberty scrambled loose and ran, Slater right behind her. They both heard Leonard's drunken wailing and the crack of the whip as they raced up the alley. Liberty, knowing the town well, ran for a ladder at the side of the bank building. She started to climb but found herself lifted by the waist and set back on her feet.

"Give me your gun!" Slater said in a voice that was not to be argued with. Liberty obeyed automatically. "Stay put!" was the next order before Slater started up the ladder. Liberty stood in shock. It took her a moment to realize she was not up there to take care of Griffin. Would Slater really know what to do? All cowboys carried guns, and she had originally found Slater with one, but did that mean he knew how to use it? In the next moment more shouting came to Liberty's ears, and without thought she climbed the ladder. She had just reached the top when she heard Griffin's voice.

"I've got him, Slater. Do you have the whip?"

"Yes. How do we get him down that ladder?"

"We don't. There's a stairway at the back here."

Liberty stepped across the roof then, and both men spotted her.

"We've got him, Lib," was all Griffin had to say.

"Good."

Slater, on the other hand, was speechless. He could not believe she'd come up that ladder. He opened his mouth to say something but closed it again. Now was not the time. They had a drunk to put in jail, but in his mind, the incident was not over.

❧ ❧ ❧

"I take it Leonard's moved into town, since he's still here?" Liberty asked Griffin.

"Smiley tells me that he lives out a ways, but when he gets lonely, he brings his whip to town for a drink."

"Smiley needs to get smart and have his bouncer take the whip away from Leonard while he's still in his right mind."

"I'll have to tell him," Griffin said. "In fact, I need to head over there right now and confirm what happened. Can you stay here for about 30 minutes?"

"Sure."

"All right. Thanks for your help, Slater. I'll be back long enough to check on him and then I'll come home."

"All right."

Both Liberty and Slater watched Griffin leave. Liberty walked to the cell and looked in to where Leonard was sleeping off his bottle before turning back to Slater. His look gave her pause. Indeed, after seeing the intensity of his gaze, she stopped a few paces short of the desk and stood very still.

Slater wasn't still at all. With the reach of one long arm, he hooked a finger in the bandana Liberty had knotted around her neck and pulled her toward him.

Seven

THE BANDANA AND HIS FINGER still holding Liberty captive, Slater spoke when their faces were scant inches apart.

"I thought I told you to stay put at the bottom of that ladder."

Liberty looked hesitant before her chin rose just a little. "Just because you have a gun doesn't mean you can handle it."

Slater's eyes narrowed, his finger still in place.

"All right," he began, his voice saying he would let it go this time. "But just for the record, Liberty Drake, I can handle a gun."

Liberty nodded, her eyes on the ones that watched her so sternly. She stood still while he removed his finger and even when he brushed that finger gently across her chin, but her heart was trying to beat a hole in her rib cage.

"How long did Griffin say he would be?" Slater asked.

"Thirty minutes."

"I'll stick around and walk you back."

"All right. Slater?"

"Yeah?"

"How did you happen to be in the alley?"

Slater explained where he'd been, and Liberty worked hard to quell an emotion she'd never before experienced: jealousy. For a moment, all she could see was Betsy Caron's face. Betsy was a good friend—a remarkably sweet woman—but Liberty had a hard time seeing her with Slater. Liberty almost shook her head. She had no right to picture Slater with *anyone*. His life was not her business.

"Did I hurt your neck just now?" Slater asked.

"No," Liberty said with some surprise. "Why did you ask that?"

"You got so quiet all of a sudden."

"I'm not hurt. I was just thinking, and before I forget to say it, thank you, Slater, for going up and helping Griff."

"You're welcome. I was glad to do it." *I would do it all the time if I could just figure out a way.*

"Where'smywhip?" was suddenly slurred from the cell, and both Liberty and Slater heard a thump. Investigating the noise confirmed to them that Leonard had rolled onto the floor. Liberty began to get the key, but Slater's voice stopped her.

"I would leave him there. He'll be stiff in the morning, but this way he won't fall off again and possibly hurt himself."

"All right," Liberty said, but she couldn't help but notice the way he spoke. He was so confident, more so than she would have thought he would be. Her mind recalled the way he had climbed that ladder going to Griffin's defense, seemingly without a qualm. Was there something they were all missing?

"Okay, Libby," Griffin called as he came back through the door. "Oh, Slater, you're still here."

"I told Libby I would walk her home."

"Well, be my guest. I'm going to make sure Leonard is settled and then head home myself."

"He fell off the bunk," Slater put in. "He's probably safer there."

Liberty nodded. She knew that if Leonard woke and caused a fuss, someone would just head to Griffin's house and shout him out of bed.

"Thanks again, Slater," Griffin said.

"You're welcome."

Slater and Liberty headed out the door then, both a little quiet. Slater was still thinking about the way Liberty seemed to withdraw from him just before Griffin returned, and Liberty was still speculating on the way Slater handled himself. Griffin, staying back at the jail for a few minutes longer, reminded himself not to start matchmaking when clearly he was no expert.

🌹 🌹 🌹

Slater woke early. It was still dark out, but his body told him he was done sleeping. Thankful for an untroubled night, he rolled to his side, lit the lantern, and reached for his Bible. He was still studying Nehemiah's life, wanting to keep up with Pastor Caron, but he was also spending time in 1 Corinthians. The early church was teaching him a great deal. Slater was now in the seventh chapter and began to read there. Reading verse one, he was ready to move on but got no further. Slater read it a second time.

Now concerning the things whereof ye wrote unto me: It is good for a man not to touch a woman.

Slater felt his breath leave him in a rush. The verses right before this had spoken of the sacredness of the body. Because a believer was bought with a great price—God's blood—his body was God's temple.

So what were you thinking in the alley last night, Rawlings? You knew immediately that it wasn't a man, and as soon as you figured out it was Liberty, you hugged her and held her as if you had the right. Slater rolled to his back and looked at the ceiling.

She was so soft and smelled so good, but she's not mine, Lord. I've got to apologize to her. I've got to put things right. I can't have intimate thoughts about her. It's wrong. You have better for me. As You do Liberty. She was so quiet as I walked her home. I can only imagine how offended she must have been.

Slater was sincere in his confession and planned to make amends, but his heart was still heavy. He had a feeling that it would be until he could go next door and ask to speak to the woman who occupied his thoughts so much of the time.

❧ ❧ ❧

"Here, let me try," Liberty said, as she worked on the button on Zach's pants. He had to leave for school soon. "The problem is, Zach," she continued, panting a little, "if it's this hard for me, how will you ever get them off to use the privy at school?"

"I don't know," the little boy worried. "Should I change? Do I have time?"

"Let me work the hole for a few more seconds," Liberty suggested. "Maybe that will loosen it."

"I even soaked those," Kate said as she put a platter of eggs and toasted bread on the table. "New denim pants should be outlawed."

"Now you try," Liberty encouraged Zach.

She was still watching him as he tried to unbutton and button his pants when his mother said he had to eat. Zach had just taken his place at the table when Liberty heard a knock at the door. Laura, fork in hand, began to rise.

"I'll get it," her older sister said. Liberty went through the house, opened the front door, and found Slater on the porch.

"May I see you a moment, Libby?" Slater said as soon as he saw her, relieved that she had answered the door.

"Certainly. Come in."

Slater cleared his throat. "I think out here might be better."

At a complete loss as to what could be going on, Liberty joined him on the porch and shut the door behind her. She watched Slater turn his hat in his hands and waited.

"I acted inappropriately last night, Libby, and I want to tell you I'm sorry."

Liberty's mind raced but she came up blank.

"I grabbed you in the alley and should have let go as soon as I knew it was you. I didn't, and that was wrong of me."

Liberty had forgotten all about it, but she was suddenly standing in his arms again. He was taller than she was, and his arms had been very gentle. The recollection was not unpleasant.

"I hope you can forgive me."

"Of course, Slater. Don't give it another thought."

Slater studied her eyes to see if she truly was all right and then nodded. It was so tempting to tell her how sweet she was and how lovely she'd been to hold, but that would have canceled everything he'd just said.

"I hope in the future you won't be afraid to be around me or untrusting of me because of the way I acted."

Liberty's mouth nearly fell open, but she saw the pain in his eyes and knew she had to make him understand.

"You don't feel threatening to me, Slater, not in the least. And as for the hug in the alley, I had forgotten about it, but I can honestly tell you that I wasn't offended." *Quite the opposite* were the words in her head, but she wisely held them, along with Slater's eyes, as she looked up at him.

Slater thought he could get lost in her gaze. She was so sweet, and unless he missed his guess, she had not objected to the hug. Slater was on the verge of asking when the verse came to mind. She was not his.

"I was reading in 1 Corinthians this morning about the fact that a man shouldn't touch a woman, and I realized what I'd done."

Liberty nodded. "I know the verses, the ones that go on to say that each man should have his own wife and such."

Slater nodded but realized he hadn't kept reading; he would have to do that.

"Thank you, Libby," Slater said.

"Thank you, Slater."

Slater put his hat on but still stood for a moment. He had to get to work—it wasn't wise to be late—but it was certainly hard not to stay and talk with this woman.

"Are you and Griffin still coming to dinner tonight?" Liberty asked, working not to read anything into the look he gave her.

"I wouldn't miss it," Slater told her before forcing his eyes away and admitting that he had to get to work.

"Take care," Liberty wished him and then watched as he left the porch, hoping he would turn so she could wave. He did that just before he disappeared around the corner. Liberty went back inside, a smile on her face as she thought about the evening to come.

❧ ❧ ❧

"I have something I need to thank you for," Liberty told Duffy over lunch that very day.

"What's that?"

"Do you remember when I told you I'd fallen into a slump in my Bible study and prayer time?"

"Yes, I do remember."

"Well, you told me that I had lost my wonder over the cross, and you know what? You were right."

Duffy smiled. They had been planning to go to lunch all week and were now at the hotel, just the two of them at a quiet corner table.

"So what did you do?"

"I began looking at those passages that cover Christ's death, and I realized I wasn't thankful, not deeply thankful, for the sacrifice God made on my behalf. I was saved when I was so young, Duffy, that it's too easy to take it for granted. I've been thankful and, I think, more obedient lately because my focus has changed."

"That's great news. I've been reading in the book of Revelation. There's so much to come, Lib, and we can't waste a moment in sin; it's just not worth it."

The waitress came with their lunch. They ate in silence for several minutes, but Liberty had something more on her mind and could wait no longer.

"Slater was over first thing this morning," Liberty told him. "Right after you left."

"Oh?" Duffy's coffee cup went to his mouth. "Something wrong?"

"He thought so," Liberty said, watching Duffy's brows shoot upward.

"But you didn't?"

Liberty gave a quick rundown on what had happened in the alley. She ended by saying, "I honestly didn't think anything of it, Duff. I didn't even remember it until he brought it up, but that's not my biggest problem."

Duffy waited, but she didn't tell him. Finally he asked. "What is, Libby?"

"I enjoyed it," she said so softly that he almost missed it.

Duffy's eyes lit with tenderness. "I'm going to say something that may surprise you, Libby girl. I'm glad."

"Why, Duffy?"

"Because it could have scared you, and I wouldn't want you to have that kind of memory. I don't know who the Lord has for you, and Slater was right, he had no business hugging you, but your response was normal. If it causes your thoughts to wander where they shouldn't, that will be very hard for you. But God made us to enjoy one another. I would not have chosen for it to happen, but now that it has, it's good to know that you'll enjoy your husband's embrace someday."

"I think about him a lot," Liberty admitted. "You're right, we don't know who the Lord has, but Slater is the first man I've even been able to imagine. Is that bad, Duffy?"

"Not if you handle it well. You can't be in a hurry, no matter what your emotions or body says. If God has a plan for the two of you, He will reveal it in His time. Neither you nor Slater should rush or push the point."

Liberty smiled at her stepfather. He was a gift to all of them. The subject shifted soon afterward to various topics—dinner that night, the barn raising on Saturday, and eventually the baby and how Liberty could help Kate take it easy from time to time. The tender light in Duffy's eyes caused Liberty to pray and ask God to let this child be healthy and live to fill their hearts for many years to come.

🌿 🌿 🌿

Nevertheless, to avoid fornication, let every man have his own wife, and let every woman have her own husband. Slater knew there was much more to chapter 7 than the verse he'd read that morning and the one now, but for the moment he stopped.

It was late at night, and he had just gotten home from next door and an evening full of good food, fellowship, and fun. Liberty Drake was one of the most special women he'd ever met. She was bright and talented. Slater smiled when he remembered her at the piano. She was compassionate and caring—he smiled again over the way she helped Duffy with the kids so Kate could put her feet up. And the whole family had made him feel welcome, even when Griffin had to leave right after dinner to go on duty.

At the moment, Slater was never more glad that he had saved himself for marriage. His parents, although not believers, were very moral people and had strong convictions on the subject. Respect for women and future mates was instilled from a young age. Slater had been unbelievably tempted over the years to throw it all away, but he had not. Even though his faith was new, he did not regret his actions in that area of his life.

Sometime after midnight, Slater woke to find the lantern still burning. He blew it out, realizing he must have fallen asleep while praying. It took a moment to remember what had been on his mind. Liberty floated back into his consciousness just before sleep, and right after he told the Lord he would talk to Him in the morning.

🌿 🌿 🌿

Liberty knew that being called to the saloon on a Saturday before noon was nothing to worry about. Saturdays didn't heat up until evening, and mornings were especially quiet, stemming from Friday late-nighters. For these reasons, Liberty walked into the Brass Spittoon with confidence, a confidence that died as soon as she spotted him. Like the last time, the room was sprinkled with regulars. The gun-toting stranger stood out like a sore thumb. And he was big—big and dark—making him look all the more menacing. Liberty approached, praying for calm and for her own safety, and stood next to the table until he looked up.

"Excuse me, sir," she began politely, "I'll need you to surrender your firearm to me. Shotgun has outlawed firearms in the saloons and after dark."

Liberty steeled herself when his hand instantly went down to his side. All he did, however, was set his side arm on the table and keep his hand on top of it. It seemed to be going fine until he didn't move his hand. Black eyes weighed Liberty, and with more calm than she felt, Liberty stared right back. This was the reason she knew the exact minute his gaze shifted behind her.

"You're going to get yourself shot," she said in a voice that was measured and in control, "as well as whoever you're looking at behind me, if you don't gently push the gun across the table."

The dark man did just that, his touch light, his eyes back on Liberty.

"Thank you," she said simply. "Do you have any more?"

"No, ma'am," he replied softly.

"You're welcome to pick this up at the jailhouse later today. It's a block and a half down, on this side."

The black-haired, black-eyed man nodded, and Liberty glanced at the man at the table with him, his crooked-tooth smile in place.

"Well, at least ya didn't haul this one away."

Liberty shook her head. "As always, you're a big help, Lance."

The man only cackled, and Liberty turned to go. She glanced around but didn't see anyone who appeared to know the stranger. Realizing there was still a chance that he could be ornery enough to pull a hidden gun or a knife and get her from the back, she made herself walk away. He had certainly looked big, without even standing up. She spoke with Gordie before going back to the jailhouse, all the time hoping Griffin would be back before the man at the table came looking for his gun.

※ ※ ※

"Did that really just happen," Dakota Rawlings asked his brother the moment he exited the saloon, "or did I imagine the whole thing?"

Slater smiled. "At least you didn't get thrown in jail."

Dakota's look was shrewd. "Meaning you did?"

Slater nodded, and Dakota's gaze narrowed a bit more. "Why didn't you come inside?"

Slater shrugged. "You didn't seem to need me."

Again, this response was carefully weighed as Dakota's eyes narrowed. "Where can we talk?" he asked bluntly.

"You mean, where can we go so you can give me the third degree and then lecture me?"

"That about sums it up," the older Rawlings said without apology.

Slater had all he could do not to laugh, but he didn't think Dakota, his senior by just one year, was in the mood for levity. Slater turned and started down the boardwalk. Dakota moved to untie a huge black horse at the hitching post and then followed slowly behind his brother.

Dakota missed little. His experience with the Texas Rangers had made his senses as honed as the knife in his boot. He noticed the way Slater walked with ease and even greeted by name some of the folks he passed, and how they passed the sheriff's office on the way out of the downtown and into a residential neighborhood. The last thing he noticed was the way Slater walked right in the back door of the house he approached.

Dakota saw the barn out back but opted to tie Eli's reins to a tree before following his brother inside. Slater was waiting in what Dakota found to be the kitchen, but the younger man turned and led the way the moment Dakota shut the door. When he walked into a nicely furnished living room and sat down like he owned the building, Dakota was more intrigued than ever.

"Start talking," Dakota, recovering swiftly, ordered, his seat having just hit the chair opposite Slater's.

"About what?"

"Don't play games with me, Slate. I've seen Brace, and I've been tracking you for days. Now I want to know why you left the Rangers."

"You won't like the answer."

Slater's voice and expression calmed Dakota immediately. He loved his brother; he was devoted to him. The last thing he wanted to do was make him feel attacked over his beliefs. He was, however, desperate to understand.

"Can you tell me this?" Dakota began again. "Why don't you think God wants us to keep law and order in Texas?"

"I do think that God wants that, Dak. I know He does. But I can't keep roaming around the country. I can't keep on the move like I have been. I want to be settled in one place and regularly attending church. I need consistent teaching and fellowship, not grabbing what I can, when I can."

"And Shotgun gives you that? How did you even hear of this place?"

"I didn't. I was just traveling at an easy pace and found myself in jail. When the sheriff asked me to church, I went. I haven't wanted to leave. It's not any more complicated than that."

Dakota didn't agree, but for the moment he kept silent. In his opinion, this whole thing was miserably complicated. He was still getting used to the first change in Slater; now he'd gone and made another one.

"Just so I have it straight," Dakota began. "You now believe the way Grandma and Cash do—that the only way to heaven and happiness on this earth is through the Christ?"

"Yes."

Dakota nodded before asking, "What was wrong with your life, Slate, that you needed that?"

Slater had to think about that one. The question didn't stump him, but wording the answer for his brother did.

"If you've never experienced a gnawing ache, Dak, then this won't make any sense," Slater began, his voice soft and serious as he remembered the pain. "But gnawing ache is the best way I can describe how I felt. Texas is a big land. It's easy to look at the sky and landscape and feel completely insignificant. I felt that way often. I found myself asking more and more what the point was. I believed in my work, and I was glad when I did a good job, but the fulfillment I once had was gone. I knew I had to find something that gave my life more meaning.

"That's why I talked with Desmond Curtis. I know there are men who can both walk the path God has laid out for His children and travel. Des is a good example of that. But I couldn't, Dakota. That's all the more I can tell you."

Dakota worked to calm the frustration rising inside of him. Slater was a good Ranger. He needed to be on the job. Dakota had just figured out what to say to him concerning that very subject when Slater stood.

"I've got to get cleaned up."

"We're not done talking." In the blink of an eye, Dakota became authoritative again.

"I'm afraid we are," Slater said calmly. "I'm going to a barn-raising party. Now, you're welcome to join me—in fact, I hope you do—but for right now the discussion is over."

"Slater," Dakota began, but the blond man was already headed toward the stairs. Dakota rose, went to the bottom step, and called his name again.

"We have to leave here in about 30 minutes, Dak," was all Slater would say. He didn't even turn around. "You won't want to smell like a horse."

For the first time in days, a smile threatened at Dakota's mouth. His brother knew just where to hit. With a shake of his head, he went for his saddlebags, seeing no help for it but to get cleaned up so he could accompany his little brother and keep an eye on the whole situation.

Eight

NO ONE KNEW EXACTLY HOW THE fire started, but the Coppersmiths' barn had burned down three weeks back. The stock was rescued, but the building was lost. The townsfolk, many of them from the church, now gathered on the third Saturday of November to build a new structure. A level wooden floor had been laid on a stone foundation, and the plan for the day was to raise the walls and the roof before dark—all of this after the square dance.

Wagons arrived bearing families, baskets of food, and tools for the workers. Stacks of lumber, boxes of nails, and work supplies were set in place for the main event. Quilts were laid out, but many tables were set up too. The children chased each other, the adults visited, and in one corner of the barn, a small trio was tuning up—two fiddles and a strum bucket. In no time at all, the floor was being used.

By the time Slater and Dakota arrived, the square dance was in full swing. From her place under a tree, Liberty happened to look up and see Slater joining a group of men as they were talking. She noticed the dark-haired man with him but didn't make the connection. She was telling herself not to stare when Tess joined her.

"Hi, Tess."

"Hi, Libby." Tess smiled in her direction, but Liberty could see that she was not her bubbly self.

"How are you?"

"I'm okay. How are you?"

"Fine," Liberty said honestly but kept an eye on Tess. "Are you sure you're all right?"

"How's your mom, Libby?" Tess asked, ignoring the question.

"She's feeling pretty good. Duffy had to work until 2:00, so she'll come with him then."

The women were silent for a moment. The floor was quite full now, and the music was wonderful. Both women enjoyed a good square dance, but each wanted to be asked only by certain men. Liberty suddenly caught sight of Slater again. This time many women had joined the group, and as Liberty watched, one put her hand on his arm. Liberty glanced at Tess in an effort to shift her gaze and knew she had to forget herself and ask the question again.

"Tess?" Liberty's voice was soft. "Are you sure you're all right?"

Tess sighed and admitted, "I will be, but Papa said he would come today, and then he backed out. Mama didn't want to come either, so I rode with the Millers. I was okay until I got here and saw all the families grouped off. It makes me feel a little lonely."

Liberty's heart ached for her, and wishing to be a comfort, she said, "Maybe you'll have a family of your own one day, Tess."

"I suppose it could happen," Tess said. "I guess I have to keep trusting."

"Is that your way of saying that you haven't been?"

Tess' blue eyes met Liberty's gaze. "I will admit to you, Lib, that it's been pretty hard lately." Tess gave a little shake of her head. "It's so awful, Libby—all this hurt. I really am glad for your family that Griffin is still alive, but it occurred to me just as I was turning in last night, that for me, he might as well be dead."

Liberty's breath caught in her throat. The pain on Tess' face was unlike any she'd ever seen. Her words only confirmed the fact that this was miserable for her.

"I'm wicked, aren't I?" Tess whispered, tears coming to her eyes.

"No, Tess," Liberty whispered right back, a hand going to the other woman's arm. "I would never think that. And do you know what? You're right. I wish it wasn't so, but you're completely right about Griff. There's nothing anyone can do. There's certainly nothing I can say. I wish there were."

Tess nodded, her eyes going to her hands, which were fiddling with the pleats in her dress. Liberty dropped her own hand, thinking she would have both of them sobbing if she didn't let the subject go. For a time the women sat in silence. Liberty was slowly growing more stunned over what Tess had revealed, and Tess felt guilty for having the thought and admitting it.

"Hello, ladies." Slater was suddenly in front of them, his eyes smiling and kind. Liberty thought him adorable in a crisp plaid shirt and dark denim pants. His light-colored hat was in place, and Liberty thought as she had before that the hat always worked to accentuate his eyes.

"How are you, Mr. Rawlings?" Tess asked.

"I'm fine. Are you enjoying yourself?"

Tess smiled, not wanting to lie, and said, "It's certainly a nice day for a barn raising."

"Indeed. Is your family around?" Slater asked now, this time of Liberty.

"They're coming in a little while," she explained. For a moment she had been rather lost in the sight of him, but her gaze had drifted as she wondered whether Griffin knew of Tess' thoughts.

"Would you care to join me in the next set?"

Probably not. Tess said that it had just occurred to her last night.

"Would you like to dance, Libby?"

Then again, they may have seen each other earlier today. I'd like to think that this news would affect Griffin like it has me, so maybe he doesn't know after...

"Libby!" Tess' voice came through to the daydreaming deputy at the same time she shook her arm. "Mr. Rawlings is trying to ask you something."

"Oh, I'm sorry." Liberty looked to Slater to find him smiling in great amusement.

"Would you care to dance?"

Liberty blinked. "You want me to dance?"

Slater's smile grew. "Well, we could start to work with the hammer and nails, but I thought dancing might be a bit more fun."

Liberty laughed and stood. Slater offered her his arm, and just a minute later they had joined a group. There was no time for talking, something that suited Liberty fine. She smiled and laughed as they spun around, changed partners, stood opposite each other, and promenaded from one end of the floor to another. They were breathless when the set was through and only too glad to turn the floor over to the next group.

"Thank you," Slater said as they stepped off the floor. "How about some water?"

"That sounds good, thank you."

They stood in line with the other couples for a chance at the dipper, and it was there that Slater caught Liberty looking back at Tess. He looked as well and saw that Griffin had joined her. Liberty's eyes took on a look he hadn't seen before.

"Here you go, Libby," Slater said as he offered her the ladle. Liberty drank and handed it back. She watched Slater drink, realizing only then that she'd been distracted. Even so, she took one more peek at Tess and her brother.

"Why don't we come over here out of the way," Slater was saying, her hand captured in his as he urged her along. "You might even feel like telling me what's bothering you."

It was said so smoothly that for a moment Liberty missed it. When they stopped and she looked up at him, his raised brows told her she had heard him right.

"I'm sorry I was so distracted, Slater. Did it ruin the dance for you?"

"Not at all, but you could have told me no; I would have understood that Tess needed you."

Liberty was horrified to feel tears fill her eyes.

"Did you see the size of this gopher mound?" Slater quickly asked, his hand to Liberty's arm now as he moved her a few feet away. "They sure make a mess of things."

Liberty worked to catch her breath as he turned her away from the gathering and chattered inanely.

"Thank you, Slater," Liberty said when she had herself under control.

"My pleasure."

Liberty smiled a little. "Do you have a sister, Slater?"

"No, why?"

Liberty shrugged, almost sorry she'd said anything. "You just seem to know what to say. It makes me think some older sister influenced you."

Slater laughed. "My mother would be pleased to know that all of her work paid off."

"Did she keep on you?"

"On all three of us, yes. She had very definite ideas, and woe to the son who forgot to hold the door or let a lady go first."

"What would she do if you forgot?"

Slater shuddered a little. "She'd give us the eye."

Liberty found this highly amusing.

"You wouldn't laugh if you could see it," her told her, his eyes filled with dramatic fear. "She was tough."

"You poor baby." Liberty was teasing him when she saw that Tess and Griffin were approaching. She was relieved to see that Tess was looking more like herself, but her heart still speculated on what the other woman had said to her. The four of them talked for a few minutes, but the two walls that were built were ready to go into place, and the walls remaining to be built needed crews of men. Hank Hathaway was giving orders as though the barn were his, and Slater and Griffin went over to put their hands to the task. Some of the women started to lay out the tablecloths and set out the food, plates, and flatware. Tess and Liberty joined them.

"Is it my imagination, or is Mr. Rawlings rather interested in you, Libby?"

"I don't know," Liberty told her honestly, although she wished it was true. "Have you seen something that makes you think that?"

Tess smiled. "You mean, other than the way he stares at you and then asks you to dance?"

"Oh," Liberty said quietly, suddenly at a loss.

Tess put a hand on her arm. "Oh, Lib, sometimes I think you don't have a clue."

Liberty laughed a little. "Why is that?"

"You're so busy looking for lawbreakers, you never notice how cute any of them are or how much they watch you."

"Tess Locken!" Liberty had a good laugh over this. "Where do you come up with this stuff?"

Tess' jaw dropped. "Libby, it's true. I swear to you."

"Swearing, Tess? I'm ashamed of you."

Both women turned to see a smiling Dr. Duffy Peterson behind them.

"She's been coming up with all sorts of wild notions, Duff," Liberty told him. "You might hear anything out of her."

"Yes, Dr. Peterson," Tess chimed right in, hands on her hips, a smile in her voice and eyes. "I was telling Libby how men notice her, and she thinks I don't know what I'm talking about."

Duffy turned such a surprised face to Liberty that that woman shook her head.

"No, Duff," she began. "Don't join Tess and tease me about this."

Duffy looked a little more stunned, his brows rising slightly, as he saw that his stepdaughter was quite serious.

"Duffy?" Liberty began, her face now showing that she was very confused. Duffy put a hand on her arm.

"We'll have to get back to this, Lib. All right? Don't give it any more thought right now."

Liberty's eyes went back and forth between the two of them, their faces reminding her how much they cared. This was a subject she would need to know more about, but Duffy was right. This was not the time or place.

"Hi, Tess. Hi, Libby," Laura greeted them as she arrived. "Did you dance yet?"

"I did," Liberty said, glad to have the subject changed. Her mother was coming, Zach in tow, and all hands fell to food preparation as Duffy went to help the men. In no time at all dozens of people would be gathering to eat. Time for small talk had ended.

☙ ☙ ☙

"My brother is in town," Slater told Griffin when he had the chance.

"He is? That's great."

Slater nodded, his face thoughtful.

"Is it great, Slater?" the lawman asked sensitively.

"It is," Slater agreed, "but he came looking for some answers, and I know he won't like everything he hears."

"Well, let me know if I can help."

"Thanks, Griffin."

"Oh, and don't hesitate to have him stay at the house for as long as he needs."

"Okay."

"Where is he, by the way?"

Slater nodded his head toward a large, dark man some 30 feet away who was driving nails into the wood with one blow. Griffin, surprised that he was even there, stared at Dakota for a moment and then turned his attention back to Slater.

"Was your brother in the saloon earlier today?"

Slater smiled. "Yep. Libby was ready to put him away, but he gave up the gun."

"She said it was some big guy with dark hair. Does she know he's your brother?"

"No. I'm not sure how long he'll stick around or how much he'll want to become known. He moved away from me the moment we arrived. Actually, I was surprised that he even came here today. I'm going to invite him to every-thing but let him make the choice," Slater chuckled, "not that I could do much else."

"Is he older than you?" Griffin thought Slater might have said but couldn't remember.

"Yes, but not by as much as it looks. Do you want to meet him now or later?"

"Later is fine. Be sure and tell him that Mam and Duffy are expecting us after church tomorrow."

"I'll do that. I'll be very satisfied if he joins me for either one." This said, Slater went back to work, his heart asking God to let Dakota stay long enough to have contact with folks who could make such a difference in his life.

☙ ☙ ☙

"When did you meet her?" Dakota asked the minute they were in the door that evening.

"Who?"

"The woman you're going to marry."

Slater blinked. "You spent too much time bending over a hammer today, Dak. Get some rest."

"Not until you tell me."

"How can I tell you when I don't know what you're talking about?"

"I'll tell you what I'm talking about. You arrive and every female under 25 comes crowding around. They look at you as if you've just dropped from heaven, but do you ask one of them to dance? No. You leave them all for the small, dark-haired beauty who wanted to put me in jail this morning."

Slater was speechless. Dakota had perfectly described the scene. So why had the younger Rawlings thought that no one would notice his special interest in Liberty Drake?

"I haven't asked Libby to marry me, not even close," was all Slater could think to say.

"What's her name?" Dakota pressed him.

Slater closed his mouth. If Dakota wasn't going to stay in town long, he wasn't sure how much he wanted to share with him.

"You can meet her tomorrow," Slater finally said, "if you're sticking around that long."

Dakota's eyes narrowed. Slater had always held Dakota in high regard, and Dakota respected Slater in return, but if Dakota ever wanted the upper hand, he knew just how to get it. Having his younger brother refuse him anything or not answer a question took some getting used to.

"I take it she goes to your church."

"Yes, she does, but that's not where you would meet her. Griffin and I go to lunch at her parents' home on Sundays."

"And Griffin is the one who owns this house?" Dakota asked as he gestured to the room in general.

"Yes."

"How is he tied into this Libby woman?"

Slater opened his mouth but shut it again. Finally he said, "Why don't you come tomorrow and find out?"

Those dark eyes narrowed in his direction again but nothing more was said. Griffin came in a short time later, met Dakota Rawlings, and then took himself downtown to check on the Saturday night activity. Both Slater and Dakota turned in without another word on the subject.

❧ ❧ ❧

Slater didn't know when he'd been so distracted. Never in his wildest dreams did he think that Dakota would be sitting next to him in church. His presence caused Slater to listen with new ears. Things that made complete sense to him caused him to wonder if Dakota had a clue. His brother had not seemed overly intrigued or even resigned, but fairly early that morning he had come to Slater's room and asked when he needed to be ready for church. Slater was glad that he had some time alone after telling him. He spent that time praying, thanking God for His work, and asking Him to soften Dakota's heart.

"I want you to pay close attention to Nehemiah's prayer life," Pastor Caron instructed now. "Almost a dozen times the verses tell us that Nehemiah engaged in prayer. I'm just going to point out a few. He goes to God in prayer starting in chapter 1:4, and then while he's talking to the king in 2:4. Chapter 4 has several verses on the subject; 6:9 is a prayer, and the book ends with a plea to God from Nehemiah." Pastor Caron went back and read those verses before pausing and meeting the eyes of his congregation.

"As I've been saying for weeks now, this man teaches me so much. Is he teaching you? Are you trying to serve God without talking to Him? Are you forgetting that after we believe, He is with us always? How many of you can spend hours in someone's presence and not utter a word to him?"

Slater had to stop himself from smiling. Thinking that if Hank Hathaway were present he could raise his hand, he forced himself to concentrate on the sermon.

"If your goal is to grow and to serve the Lord, you've got to be praying. I don't know that any of us will be called to do something as huge as Nehemiah did, but no matter what your task, God is standing by to help you. He doesn't want to just observe; He delights in the prayers of His children and wants to give you the power and strength to succeed."

Slater felt Dakota shift beside him, and for a moment he thought he might rise and leave. In an effort to accept God's will in his brother's life, no matter what it was, Slater prayed and steeled himself for the worst, but nothing came of it. The service ended and Dakota headed right for the door, but not a mention was made of the service. Slater found him by the horses, asked him if he wanted to go to the Petersons', and took his quiet nod as a yes. Tempted as he was to question the older man's look, Slater held his tongue, praying all the way down the street.

🌿 🌿 🌿

"Zach can read," Laura told Dakota, leaning from her chair to make sure he could hear. "He goes to school."

"Does he?" Dakota's words were soft, his tone warm. The change had come over him as soon as he met Laura Peterson. "Do you go to school?"

"Next year. I'll be big then."

Dakota smiled, learning swiftly what many already knew: Laura was a heartwarmer.

"Is your horse the big black one?"

"Yes, it is."

"He looks like you," she announced.

"Laura!" Zach's shocked voice could be heard as he entered the room.

"Oh," Laura's eyes widened. "I'm sorry," she apologized. She had learned what Zach's looks meant. She wasn't sure what she had said, but her brother was looking horrified.

"That's all right," Dakota reassured her. "I guess Eli and I do look alike."

"His name is Eli?" Her face showed her disillusionment. "I was hoping it was a girl."

Dakota smiled before exchanging looks with Slater, who was glad to sit back and take this all in.

"I'm glad you don't have handcuffs on," Laura proclaimed.

Dakota blinked at her. "What?"

"Slater did when he first came."

This got another shocked tone out of Zach, even as Dakota turned compelling eyes onto his brother. Laura simply sat back and shut her mouth. The last time she had said too much she experienced a visit to the pantry with the wooden spoon. Laura had only just made her wise decision when Liberty came through the door.

"I think we're ready to eat," she announced.

The children scooted from the parlor on this note, but both men stood on her entrance, Slater ready to do the honors.

"Libby, this is my brother, Dakota. Dakota, this is Liberty Drake."

Liberty's eyes told the men that she was thinking fast, even while she heard Dakota say, "I've been wondering what you would look like for a long time."

"Dakota," his brother warned, but Liberty only looked confused. A moment later, still not having heard what Dakota said, she made the connection she'd been working through her mind.

"Oh, my," she said softly. "I didn't know." Indeed, Liberty was shocked. With his hat off, a freshly shaved face, and warm eyes, Dakota took some moments to place.

"It's all right." Dakota came to her rescue. "You were just doing your job."

Liberty suddenly bit her lip. "I did the same thing to Slater," she admitted on a laugh, relieved when the men joined her.

"Did Slater say the name was Liberty?" Dakota asked after she invited them to follow her to the dining room.

"Yes."

"Born on the Fourth of July?" Dakota asked, his eyes not missing a thing.

Liberty laughed again. "As a matter of fact, I was," she told him, all the time causing Slater to wonder why he had never asked.

"Here you are," Duffy said as they entered. "I'm sorry we didn't get to do more than meet you, Dakota. Did Laura do a good job as hostess?"

"Yes." Dakota told the truth, but Laura's eyes darted to their guest and swiftly away.

"Do we need to talk, Laura?" her father asked quietly.

"I shocked Zach two times," she admitted.

Duffy's hand came to his mouth, but he managed, "Well, did you say you were sorry?"

"I think so." She looked on the verge of tears, and Slater, feeling free to do so, stepped in.

"She handled it very well, as did Zach."

"Thank you, Slater," Duffy said with a nod. "Good job, children." He smiled at both of them before bowing his head. "What a privilege it is, Father, to gather around this table to eat, and also to have Slater's brother join us this day. We thank You for all Your blessings, from the food to the warm shelter You have lovingly placed over us. In Your will and timing, we ask that Griffin's business downtown will go smoothly, so that he may join us for dinner. In Your Son's holy name I pray. Amen."

The bowls were passed, and in an instant, Dakota was experiencing what Slater had experienced the first time he sat at this table. He hadn't heard anything too disagreeable from the preacher that morning, but he didn't think he wanted to go to church all the time. He was, however, gaining a glimpse of why Slater wanted to stay in this town. Dakota thought he might stick around himself.

"Hello," Griffin suddenly called as he came through from the kitchen. "Any food left?"

"Oh, Griff." Kate shook her head at him. "As if I would let you starve on the one day you let me feed you."

Griffin smiled before kissing his mother's cheek, taking a seat, and serving himself. He was in the midst of telling them what had happened downtown when someone else came in the back door.

"Doc! Doc!" the man cried frantically.

"In here," Duffy said calmly but started to rise.

Pat Brewster came panting to the doorway, his face a mask of fear. "Meg's pains have started. Doc, can you come?"

"I'm on my way," Duffy told him.

"I'd better get back," Pat panted, suddenly whipping the hat off his head. "I'm sorry, Mrs. Peterson," he said to Kate.

"It's all right, Pat. Tell Meg I'm thinking of her."

"Thank you, ma'am."

In the next few seconds Pat left and Duffy grabbed his bag, kissed Kate, took a hug from Laura, and made his way from the room. The diners had all fallen silent.

"My Papa's going to make a baby be born," Laura said after a moment. The pride in her voice made the rest of the room smile.

Nine

"Was Laura serious about your handcuffs?" Dakota asked much later that day as both men rode on horseback along the creek line. The men had spent most of the afternoon with the Petersons. They were still there when Duffy returned to announce that he had delivered a healthy baby girl.

"I'm afraid so," Slater replied, shaking his head with regret. "I told you I went to jail."

"True, but why would the sheriff take you to his mother's house?"

Slater gave him a rundown and watched Dakota's brows lift. He didn't have to say it. It was written all over his face: Were these people real? Since Slater believed their actions were all spiritually based, he was glad when Dakota didn't press him over answers he wouldn't believe.

"Do you think Libby will like being a Ranger's wife?" Dakota asked.

"You'll have to ask her when you propose," Slater replied calmly, not rising to the bait.

"That's not what I meant, and you know it."

"Well, then she knows some other Ranger, because I turned in my badge."

The look Dakota sent him was dark, and not just from the color of his eyes. He looked ready to begin a lecture but turned away, his eyes on the water.

"How long do you plan to keep this up?" Dakota asked, his voice soft.

Slater sighed. "I'm not on vacation, Dak."

"Then what would you call it?"

Slater weighed his words and spoke, a slight edge to his voice. "I don't know where all of this is going to lead, but rare are the times in my life when I've felt such a peace. I felt a peace when I told Brace, and I felt a peace the first Sunday I sat in that church and was taught from the Word. I don't think I can tell you how much I needed that. If you have peace right now, I'm glad for you, and I will welcome your questions, but badgering me will stop, Dakota. I'm staying here right now, and that's the end of it. If you stay around, you'd better know one thing: I'm not going to have you constantly on my back."

Dakota nodded but kept silent. Lately Slater had become very even-natured. He hadn't been as a child, so there was no missing the change. It wasn't often in the last two years that he grew angry or overly passionate on an issue, so when he did, his family had learned to listen. It was on Dakota's mind to tell Slater that he would go along but that his eyes would be open. He changed his mind. Why would he want to threaten his brother? Much as he disagreed with his decision, the idea was ludicrous. They eventually turned and rode silently back toward town. No tension lingered between them—they cared for each other too much for that—but each brother wondered what the future would bring.

❧ ❧ ❧

"Hey, Griff," Liberty said softly as she followed Griffin out the door.

"Yeah?" He turned while still on the porch. The sun was falling fast, but they could still see each other well. The already visible moon was full.

"Did you see Tess today?"

"Not to talk to. Why?"

Liberty opened her mouth but hesitated.

"What's the matter?" Griffin asked, his voice telling her he wanted an answer.

"She was having a pretty hard time at the barn raising yesterday. I just wondered how she was today."

"Was it something to do with me or her family?"

"Some of both. She didn't talk to you?"

"Not a word."

Liberty nodded, saddened by the fact. She wanted to help her friend—she wanted to help Griffin—but the situation seemed impossible.

"What did her family do?"

Liberty explained the way they had backed out of coming and how lonely she felt.

"How did my name come up?" Griffin asked, no censure in his voice.

"Oh, Griff." Liberty sounded annoyed. "Sometimes I'm such a dolt. I told Tess that maybe someday she'd have a family of her own. She was already upset. I don't know what I was thinking." Liberty stopped and then admitted, "Then she told me some of her most recent thoughts. I wanted to sob for her."

Griffin could see that she didn't want to go on, but he had to know. "Tell me, Libby," Griffin said, his voice indicating he was at a loss in the whole situation.

"You won't thank me, Griff—not if it hits you as hard as it did me."

Griffin gave a mirthless laugh. "Sometimes I think a hit is just what I need. Please tell me."

Liberty looked up at him. "She said she was glad for your family's sake that you were alive, but where she's concerned, you might as well be dead."

Griffin could barely find air to fill his lungs. He put his hands on his sister's upper arms, harder than he intended, and brought her up close.

"Did she really, Libby—did she actually say that?"

A small cry broke Liberty's voice. "I'm sorry, Griff. I'm so sorry."

Griffin slowly let go of his sister, his arms dropping to his side. What a fool he'd been. All this fear of leaving her when he'd already abandoned her. He looked over to see Liberty staring at him, tears caught on her lower lids.

"Did I hurt you?"

"No," she replied, shaking her head. "Not at all. I just feel so bad."

"I've got to go see her," Griffin said, his voice still stunned. "I'll talk to you later."

"Okay."

Griffin was ten steps off the porch when he turned and ran back. He hauled Liberty into his arms and hugged her tightly.

"Thanks, Lib," he whispered.

Liberty stood still long after her brother moved out of sight. Her heart in her throat, she prayed that God would give Griffin wisdom and that Tess would just keep trusting.

🌿 🌿 🌿

"Well, Griffin," Mrs. Locken said with a smile, "come in."

"Thank you, Mrs. Locken," Griffin said as he removed his hat, "but could I possibly see Tess here on the porch?"

Mrs. Locken smiled. This man had never done anything to make her worry, but it was a cold evening.

"Tess is in the kitchen, Griffin; you won't be disturbed in there."

"Thank you," he said softly as he crossed the threshold. The house was warm, and with his heart trying to jump into his mouth, he began to perspire.

"Just go on through, Griffin," the lady of the house invited. "Tess is working on a pie."

Griffin greeted Mr. Locken as he passed through the living room, but he only waved his hand and kept the newspaper to his face. His legs feeling weighted, Griffin made his way to the kitchen at the back of the house. Whoever had built this home had not spared in space. It was roomy and comfortable. The dining room was dim, but more light peeked from under the closed door to the kitchen. Griffin pushed open the door without knocking, standing just inside until Tess looked up from her work.

"Well, Griffin," she said in surprised delight.

In just a few strides, Shotgun's sheriff covered the distance between them and took Tess' flour-covered hand in his.

"Marry me, Tess," he barely managed through suddenly dry lips.

Tess closed her eyes for a moment and sighed. She then smiled into his worried gaze and said, "Just name the date, Griffin, and I'll be there."

"Oh, my wonderful Tess," the sheriff breathed as he drew her gently into his arms. "I love you so."

"Oh, Griffin." Tears were coming now, and Tess could not stop them. "I never thought..." she began.

"I know," he said as he moved back and smoothed the hair from her brow. "I just didn't understand until Lib told me what you said."

Tess wasn't long in catching on. "It was horrible of me."

"It wasn't," Griffin said emphatically. "It was horrible of me, but to be honest, I really thought I was doing the right thing. Now I see that you're right: I might as well be dead for you if I'm going to keep us apart."

Tess couldn't take it. She sobbed into his shirt front and couldn't stop, even when she heard the door open again.

"I'm sorry," Griffin said, turning to see Mrs. Locken. "I didn't know she would cry."

"What is it, Griffin? Has something happened?"

"I asked her to marry me."

As though he was watching the scene all over again, Mrs. Locken began to cry too. She and Tess came together in a hug and then laughed at each other's teary faces.

"I'm sorry," Mrs. Locken told Griffin. "You can't have bargained on both of us sobbing all over the place."

"Well, I left my sister in tears when I came over here, and something tells me my mother will do the same."

"So Libby knew?" Tess asked. "What did she think?"

"No, she didn't know, but she told me what you'd said and that was upsetting."

Tess briefly explained the conversation from the day before, and Mrs. Locken hugged her again.

Ready for a lighter subject, the older woman said, "Tell me, Tess, a big wedding or a small affair?"

Tess looked at Griffin. "I don't care, just as long as I become Mrs. Drake."

"Oh my, Tess," her mother complained. "You'll have me going again. Come. Let's go tell your father."

The next few minutes went much better than Griffin could have anticipated. Mr. Locken actually put his reading material down long enough to smile at his daughter, congratulate the both of them, and ask about the date, something that would have to be considered. One of Tess' brothers even came home from downtown and heard the news as well before going off to his room. When Griffin was finally ready to leave, Tess walked him onto the porch.

"I won't sleep tonight," Tess said, "and that means I'll have bags under my eyes. If I see you tomorrow, you'll change your mind."

Griffin laughed. "That's not going to happen."

Tess could only stare at him. "I love you, Griffin."

"I love you, Tess, so very much. Thank you for helping me see what I'm missing."

Tess nodded. "We have to trust. For all we know, something could happen to me."

"I hope not," Griffin said softly. "I hope we're still gazing into each other's eyes 30 years down the road."

All Tess could do was smile. It was the last thing Griffin saw before he turned and headed for home—not home exactly but more like the house next door, where just as he suspected, his mother, joined by his sister, cried when they heard the news.

🌷 🌷 🌷

The man working with Hank Hathaway when Slater landed on the job the next morning was one of the biggest men Slater had ever seen. A vague remembrance of someone lifting a horse from the creek passed through his mind even as he went forward to see if he still had a job.

"I'm Slater Rawlings," he said as he put out his hand to the stranger.

"Price Hathaway," the huge man said in return, just before he engulfed Slater's hand in a gentle grip. "I hear you've been fillin' in."

"Yes," Slater said congenially, even as his heart sank. It sounded as though he was no longer needed.

"I've been in Austin," Price informed him.

"I'd heard that. How was it?"

An odd light flickered in the larger man's eyes. "Not like I thought."

"Did you make friends there?"

"I thought I would, but I didn't."

Slater ached a little for this gigantic young man. He had the face and eyes of a boy, and maybe the heart of one too.

"What do you want Slater to do, Pa?" Price turned and asked.

"Same as always," the older Hathaway grunted, not bothering to look up.

Price turned back to Slater with a huge grin. "Pa's as informative as ever."

Slater smiled before he went for a hammer. He came back and began to stack and organize the lumber. Right now they were building a house. It wasn't long before Price was working beside him.

"You ever been to Austin?" the young Hathaway asked.

"I have, yes."

"It's big," he said with awe. "I had heard that, but I wanted to see for myself."

"Did you get work there?"

"I tried, but nothing panned out."

"What did you want to do?"

"I wanted to build houses—big, fancy ones—but everyone I met told me I should be in the saloons. I finally ran out of money and had no choice. I was hired right away."

Slater took in the pained look on his face. Yes, he was the perfect size for a bouncer but clearly not a rough individual. The combination would not have worked.

"How'd you get home?" Slater asked as he began to place a board against the studs and nail it into place. Price worked on a plank of his own.

"I finally saved enough to go. They actually owed me a little more pay, but I wanted out."

Slater wanted to ask if it was nice to be home, but the pain on Price's face was too raw.

"Where is that saw I asked for?" Hank called.

Unlike Price's last communication with his father, this time he didn't smile. His look was clearly longsuffering as he turned to help his parent. Slater watched the two of them for just a moment, wondering what the week would bring.

☙ ☙ ☙

"I'm here for my gun," Dakota told Liberty as soon as he opened the office door.

Liberty laughed as she stood and took the weapon from the wall cabinet.

"I really am sorry," she said as she handed it over, eyes brimming with pleasure.

"You look sorry," he teased back and then shook his head. "It wasn't a very nice welcome to your fine town."

"That's true," Liberty had to admit.

"Think of my feelings. You've got some patching to do."

Liberty laughed again. "All right, I'm *very, very* sorry."

Dakota shook his head. "That won't do. Nothing short of lunch with me will help."

Liberty's mouth opened in surprise, and she gave an incredulous laugh. He was certainly smooth, but she was not going to agree. When her features were composed once again, she told him plainly, "I'm going home to have lunch with my mother and sister. You're free to join us, but that's my final offer."

Dakota smiled. He liked a lady who would not let anyone push her around. Not getting her alone would make it harder to find out her feelings for Slater, but maybe he'd learn something after all.

"Your mother won't mind?" Bold as he'd been, he felt a need to check.

"No." Liberty shook her head. "I've brought stray pups home before; Mam will understand."

Dakota fought hard not to smile, but it wasn't working. He had seen how fun she was on Sunday but not had it directed at him. He'd just found a comeback when a woman's stringent voice cut through the air.

"I tell you I want something done!"

Both Liberty and Dakota turned as Griffin came through the door, closely followed by Maddie Flowers.

"I swear those Potters were up all night! Now, are you the law in this town or not?"

"Have a seat, Mrs. Flowers," Griffin returned calmly as he took the desk chair and pulled out his report folder. He began to write, his head bent, while the lady in front of the desk went puce with outrage.

"My dog's hair is falling out! If they shot those guns once, they shot them a hundred times, and I want to know what you're going to do!"

Griffin took a few notes and then looked up.

"I'll come out and check on things, probably later today or this week for sure."

"Why not now?"

"Because if they roughhoused until that late, they'll all be dead asleep for most of the day."

"Well, you wake 'em up! That's your job."

Griffin let her rail for a time but eventually turned a deaf ear.

"How'd it go?" he asked Liberty.

"Fine. I never left the office. Duffy stopped by with the mail. I left it there for you."

"All right. Thanks, Lib. What are you up to, Dakota?"

"I just talked my way into lunch at your mother's," he answered, but went on to say what he was thinking. "Has Slate ever mentioned what I do?"

"Yes, he has," Griffin remembered even as he said it.

Dakota nodded. "If I can be of help while I'm in town, please say the word."

"Thank you."

Maddie's voice had quieted, but she was still sitting there seething and muttering to herself. Knowing that Griffin would best know how to deal with her, Liberty moved to the door, Dakota on her heels.

"Tell me, Libby," Dakota asked almost as soon as they were outside, "how did you become the deputy?"

"My father taught me to shoot, and I've filled in as Griffin's deputy ever since he's had the office. I think most of Griff's deputies have come into the job with stars in their eyes. They think it's going to be exciting and action-packed, but Shotgun's a very peaceful town. Deputies hear of something bigger or better and move on."

"But not you."

"No, not me. I grew up here, and I love it. My father was the sheriff for years. He died in the line of duty."

"And what compelled him to teach you to fast-draw?"

Liberty shrugged. "He worked with Griff, and I was interested. He let me try." Liberty shrugged again, and

Dakota, even though he'd never seen her draw, sensed that there was more to it than that. He might have tried to find out, but the house was in sight. Much as he wanted to know more about Liberty's work with a gun, Dakota actually hoped that her heart would be revealed at lunch.

🌸 🌸 🌸

"My brother is getting married," Laura told Dakota, her eyes shining with the news. They had just sat down to eat.

"He is?" Dakota asked; the Ranger had not heard this.

Laura nodded. "He loves Tess."

Dakota smiled. He had certainly seen Shotgun's sheriff with a lovely blonde on Saturday but not made any suppositions.

"I get to watch," Laura went on. "Mam and Papa said. I just have to stay quiet."

Dakota smiled again and looked up to see Kate watching her daughter, her eyes alight with love.

"Well," Dakota put in, "let me offer my congratulations on your getting a new sister-in-law."

Laura's eyes widened, and she told her mother. "Another sister! And she's going to help Libby when she helps Griffin with the law."

"No, dear," Kate said gently and explained Tess' title to Laura. The little girl did a lot of nodding but waited only until Kate turned away before whispering to Dakota, "Did Tess break the law?"

Dakota could not stop laughing. He had never encountered a child quite like her. She was so full of wonder and news. He was still trying to compose himself when Liberty tried to explain. More nodding followed, but no one was very certain if Laura understood.

"Dakota," Kate began kindly, thinking they all needed a change, "did Slater say you are older than he is?"

"Yes, ma'am, by just a year."

"And I can't remember if you have other siblings."

"I'm the middle of three brothers. Cash runs the family ranch in Kinkade."

"Well, if you don't think you can make it home for Thanksgiving, the church always has a dinner. We attend, and we'd be happy to have you join us."

"Thank you, Mrs. Peterson, I think Slater talked about doing that, so I'll probably tag along."

"What will your family do?" Liberty asked.

"My parents, who moved back to St. Louis about five years ago, will dine with friends, but my brother will do as you're doing, meet with families from the church he attends. My grandmother, who lives in Hilldale but visits the ranch each winter, will probably do the same thing."

Dakota said all this very politely and had no qualms about sharing, but he did have a motive. He wanted to know more about *this* family—more specifically, Liberty. He spent the next hour hoping some tidbit would be revealed, but it was not to happen. Much as he enjoyed the meal and company, he left the house feeling as though he hadn't accomplished a thing.

❄ ❄ ❄

Liberty suddenly made the connection from the comment in the sheriff's office. Dakota was the brother who was a Texas Ranger. Liberty had already changed into her dress, but she felt a need to check on Griffin. Heading from the house with a brief word to her mother, she moved swiftly back downtown.

"What's up?" Griffin asked when she came in panting just a little.

"I just realized I heard you say you might go to the Potters'. I wondered if you needed me."

"Thanks, Lib, but Dakota's going with me. He was just in to check about it and went back to get his horse. I figure now is as good a time to go as any. They might be a little more docile if they're still feeling the effects."

Liberty nodded, working successfully to hide the confusion and hurt inside of her. Never before in her life could she remember Griffin not needing her. It was one of the most awful sensations she'd ever experienced.

"Well," she said to hide the hurt, "let me know how you fare, and be careful."

"I'll do that," Griffin said sincerely, but he wasn't looking directly at her. He might have seen her confusion if he had been.

Liberty took that moment to make her exit, hoping against all hope that Dakota would not be coming down the street. She slipped away, going a strange, indirect route in an effort not to see him. She slowed her pace when she thought it was safe and tried to pray and think clearly. She knew she could talk to her mother, but what would she say exactly? *Griff didn't need me, and I've never been so crushed and rejected.* Even to her own ears, she sounded like a five-year-old. It was, however, exactly how she felt.

"Hey, Lib," a male voice suddenly said.

Liberty looked up to see Price Hathaway next to a half-built home, a hammer in one hand, a board in the other.

"Well, Price, when did you get back into town?"

Price gave his boyish smile. "When in actual time, or how I feel?"

Liberty laughed as she moved toward him. It had been a long time since they'd talked; the two of them had been in school together, and she had always cared for this gentle giant. And right now she welcomed the chance to get Griffin and Dakota off her mind.

Ten

"You still totin' a gun?" Price teased Liberty as soon as she was near.

"Yes, I am, so you'd better not have brought any bad habits back from Austin. They could land you in trouble."

"If you'd stay at the jailhouse and talk to me, I wouldn't mind," he returned, flirting with her a little.

"What would Miss Amy say?"

A sad light filled Price's eyes. "She wasn't too happy when I left."

"Does she know you're back?"

"I haven't talked to her, so I don't know."

Liberty nodded but didn't press him. She glanced around and heard pounding but couldn't see who it was.

"Did you meet Slater Rawlings?"

"Sure," Price said easily enough.

"Did your father keep him on or is he out looking for work?"

"He's around the corner, trying to please Pa."

As if Slater had heard the calling of his name, he suddenly appeared from around the other side of the building. He paused when he saw Liberty, but only because he was a sweaty mess. He thought as he always did that she looked wonderful.

"Hi, Slater," Liberty greeted him, giving no thought to the signs of hard work on his shirt or face.

"Hi, Libby. What are you up to?"

"I'm headed home," she said, trying not to think of her conversation with Griffin.

"Price!" Hank suddenly bellowed from around the corner, and that man withdrew from Slater and Liberty.

"I'll talk to you later, Price," Liberty called to him.

"All right, Lib. Take care."

Liberty watched him move away and then noticed Slater's eyes on her. She smiled in genuine pleasure.

"I'm glad you didn't lose your job, Slater."

Slater's brows rose a little. "It's been an interesting day."

Liberty nodded, not needing much more of an explanation. Hank Hathaway's reputation preceded him. Price's desire to leave had been no mystery.

"Price and I were in school together," Liberty put in. "I've always liked him."

"There isn't much not to like."

"That's true. I've always hoped he would marry a certain woman here in town, but I don't know."

"Miss Amy?"

Liberty looked hopeful. "Did he talk of her?"

Slater shook his head no. "Some of the neighbors around here are a might busy. One came by and asked him questions for far longer than I would have allowed."

"He's so kindhearted. I don't suppose he wanted to wound Mrs. Hurst."

Slater smiled at the way she knew exactly who it was.

They talked for a few minutes more, but Slater knew he had to get back to work. Liberty went on her way, and Slater returned to help Hank and Price. The temptation to simply follow Liberty and talk to her for the remainder of the day was powerful indeed, but he resisted. Instead, he prayed for her almost the entire afternoon.

❧ ❧ ❧

"And how long have they been giving the town trouble?" Dakota asked as they rode away from the Potters' house.

"For as long as anyone can remember. Maddie Flowers didn't mind for a long time, and they're far enough out that not much was said by anyone else, but Maddie's getting older and more intolerant of the noise."

"And you say she has her own still."

"Yes. If rumor can be trusted, Rush and Possum Potter built it for her. Maybe that's why she stayed quiet for so long."

"What will you do next?" Dakota asked as they arrived in Shotgun's downtown area.

"I'll lie low. Critter is as mean as a rattlesnake, and Ned can be. If I rush things, someone will die. I want to avoid that, but my eventual goal is to shut them down. If I succeed at that, they'll probably move on. I wouldn't wish that on any other town, but I've got to think of how fast our city is growing."

Dakota was impressed. He'd been impressed for a long time, but his respect was steadily growing. His first meeting of the town sheriff had not given him much to hope for, but behind that smooth, young face was an intelligent, clear-thinking sheriff—one who cared about the people as much as he did his job.

They parted company after they reached the jailhouse, Dakota heading to Griffin's house and Griffin into his office. Dakota had not thought of Slater and Liberty since earlier that day, but now they came to mind; more specifically, Liberty did. He wished that she had gone to the Potters' with them so he could see her in action.

🍃 🍃 🍃

"Thanks for putting the kids down, Lib," her mother said that evening. "I swear, some days I don't think I'll even get up the stairs to put myself to bed."

Liberty came over and kissed her mother's cheek.

"What was that for?"

"That was from Laura. She said you needed another one."

Kate chuckled and began to loosen the pins in her hair. If they had unexpected company, she'd have to put it back up in a hurry, but right now it felt too good to massage her scalp.

"Why don't you head up?" Duffy asked as he watched her.

"Because I'm not sleepy, just weary. And when I go to bed too early, I wake so early that I have to just lie quiet or wake Zach." Zach was the light sleeper in the family. He was very good about staying in bed, but his mother knew how much he needed his rest in this first year of school.

"Duffy?" Liberty had sat down, but she was not relaxed. Duffy looked over to see her perched on the edge of the davenport.

"Yes?"

"I need to ask you about something. Are you too tired?"

"Not at all," the doctor said sincerely. "What's up?"

Liberty took a moment to start, and Kate looked to Duffy for answers. His raised brows told her he was in the dark, so they both waited.

"Do you remember talking to Tess and me as soon as you got to the barn raising on Saturday?"

Now knowing exactly what was on her mind, Duffy nodded.

"Duffy, do you really agree with Tess that I don't see when men are interested in me?"

Duffy did not immediately answer. He weighed his words and then started. "I don't want you to misunderstand me, Lib, and you might because the single women in our church so dreadfully outnumber the single men. I do agree with Tess that you don't seem aware of the looks that come your way, but most of the time I'm glad you don't see the attention of those men, since they're probably not the ones for you. Does that make sense?"

"Yes, but I still don't see it," she told him, frustration punctuating every word. "I think you and Tess are doing more hopeful thinking than witnessing any great male interest in Liberty Drake."

"That's easy to understand," Kate suddenly inserted. Both Duffy and Liberty stared at her.

"How do you figure?" Duffy asked.

"Well, she's a deputy. She has to keep her eyes open. She hasn't had time to relax like a lot of her friends have." Kate suddenly looked sad. "I wish she had."

Liberty sat back. For the first time in her life she asked herself if she might be too involved in her work. She suddenly found her eyes on her mother and had to ask her a question.

"Do you wish I wasn't helping Griff, Mam?"

Kate smiled. "Now that's a hard one, Lib. Do I want both my children in danger or do I want one of them in extreme danger because he has no one to back him up?"

Liberty nodded. That made very clear sense, but there was more. As seemingly slow as she was about men, Liberty now asked herself what godly mother didn't want her daughter to meet and marry a wonderful man?

"I keep praying that God will send the right man to help Griff, but so far that hasn't happened," Kate continued.

"I pray for the same thing," Duffy added. "Every day."

Liberty felt as if she'd been hit. She had never once asked God to send someone to replace her. Why was that? The question gave Liberty pause. She suddenly wasn't sure that she wanted to know.

A moment later Duffy asked Liberty if she was all right. Admitting that she didn't know, she was ready to change the subject. She double-checked with her mother about Thursday's preparations. They talked of Thanksgiving for the next hour. When she finally went to bed, her mind immediately moved to Slater, Griffin, and her job. She pushed them all away and repositioned her mind to the baking she wanted to get done for Thanksgiving, telling herself she didn't want to rush this holiday time away with all sorts of other thoughts. It was not a solid reason and Liberty knew that, but she just kept justifying it by reminding herself that all too soon it would be December, with Christmas rushing up on the calendar.

❧ ❧ ❧

"Do you know what happened to me on Sunday?" Tess whispered to Griffin in the general store. She had been shopping and turned to find him next to her, something that never failed to delight her.

"What?"

"A very wonderful man asked me to marry him."

"No kidding?" Griffin's eyes were impressively large.

"No kidding," Tess answered, her own eyes alight with pleasure as she looked up at him. "I said yes."

"Did you?" Griffin smiled down at her. "When is the big event?"

"Well," her brow dropped in the way he loved, "I'm free tomorrow."

"Tomorrow is Thanksgiving," he reminded her, feeling intoxicated by her nearness.

"Friday then?" Tess asked hopefully, and Griffin had to laugh.

Tess smiled complacently and then noticed the eyes that watched them, mostly older women who should have known better.

"I can tell this is going to be interesting," Tess said as she turned to examine a row of shoes and belts.

"Why is that?" Griffin asked, studying her profile with pleasure.

"You might be the most well-known person in town. It's like courting in a house made of glass."

Griffin had noticed the attention as well, but there was little he could do or say. He opted for a lighter note.

"You sound as though you're changing your mind."

No longer caring who might be watching, Tess' eyes met his.

"Not even close," she said softly.

Griffin reached for her hand, their fingers entwining for several seconds.

Not long afterward, Griffin went back to work, comforted by the fact that in two days he could see her almost all day. Nevertheless, he asked God to help him concentrate on the job. Remembering Tess' sweet smile and love for him, he thought he might endanger someone if he even touched his gun.

❧ ❧ ❧

The second week in December was cold. Slater had not paid much attention to the weather so far, working with Price and Hank no matter what. But today his head felt full, and every time he bent over the hammer, his forehead and cheeks pounded. He told himself he could make it all day, but by midafternoon, he knew he had to get inside.

"I don't feel well," Slater wasted no words in telling his boss. "I'm going to head home. I'll try to work tomorrow."

Hank looked up, a frown on his face, but Slater's glassy eyes and red face softened him a little.

"Just take off till it's gone, or you'll have us all sick."

Slater did little more than wave as he turned away.

"Hey, Slater," Price stepped in, "Miss Amy carries some medicine for colds. Stop by for some on your way home. Doc Bergram's or something like that."

"Thanks, Price."

Slater hadn't really decided to stop, but since he hadn't ridden Arrow to the job that day, he felt nearly frozen by the time he reached downtown. He stepped into the general store just to get his lungs out of the cold. Miss Amy happened to be standing right inside.

"May I help you?"

"Oh." Slater tried to smile and be polite, his mind fuzzy with the headache. "I'm looking for something for colds. I think Price said it was Doc Berg's or some name like that."

"Doc Bergrin's?"

"Yeah, that must be it."

"Right this way."

Slater followed her in something of a daze. She had a large selection of tonics and such. He watched as she plucked one off the shelf and handed it to him.

"That one will take all pain away—it's pretty potent. This one," she said, handing him another bottle, "doesn't have any alcohol in it at all, but it's still good stuff. Typically, husbands buy the first one and wives buy the second one."

No contest in Slater's mind. He took the second bottle and turned toward the counter, wanting nothing more than to get home and climb into bed.

"Price sent you, didn't he?" Miss Amy asked quietly as Slater was fishing for coins.

"Yes. He said you might have something."

"He hasn't been in since he got back," she murmured. A note in her voice got through to Slater. Working to ignore his own discomfort, he looked at the tall, well-built woman behind the cash register. She didn't appear to be quite as young as Price, but there was no mistaking the interest in her eyes.

"Maybe he doesn't know you'd like him to come in," Slater offered.

"Well," Miss Amy's gaze dropped, "I hope someone tells him." With that, she slid Slater's change across the counter, shut the drawer, and turned away. Slater watched her take a feather duster to shelves that looked immaculate, his heart turning over in compassion. He felt simply awful, but that did not stop him from praying for Price and Miss Amy and asking God to open the door if he should tell his coworker what this woman had said.

ॐ ॐ ॐ

"Oh! Dakota!" Liberty said when the door was opened, "I didn't know you were back."

Dakota had been called to work just after Thanksgiving and hadn't been in town since.

"I'm just in," he explained. "Come on in."

"Well, I don't want to be in the way, but Mam thought she saw Slater come in and wanted to send this soup for him. Is he here?"

"I don't think so, but maybe he is. Come on through and I'll check."

Dakota held the door wide, and Liberty took the pot of warm soup straight through to the kitchen. Since her brother had gained a housemate, she did not come and go as she pleased through his back door.

"Let me see if he's here now," Dakota said.

Liberty put the pot on the stove top and went ahead and added a little wood to the fire in the oven. The house felt chilly to her.

"He's sound asleep," Dakota announced when he returned from upstairs.

Liberty nodded. "He mentioned on the weekend that he thought he'd caught something. Well, tell him to rest, and hopefully the soup will help."

"All right. Thanks."

Liberty started back toward the front door, Dakota on her heels.

"Should I take this as a good sign?" Dakota suddenly asked, causing Liberty to turn before she reached the doorknob.

"For what?"

"Well," Dakota smiled charmingly. "When a lady brings a gentleman hot soup, I would say that means she cares."

Liberty's eyes lit with amusement. "My mother sent the soup, and to answer your question, yes, she cares very much."

"Come on, Libby," he coaxed now, "give a guy a break."

"Dakota," Liberty replied, trying not to laugh at his pleading look, "I don't know what you want."

His black eyes narrowed as they always did when he was in thought.

"All right," he finally said, "I'll play my hand. How do you feel about Slater?"

Liberty's look was remarkably calm. "That, Mr. Rawlings, is a question the gentleman himself will have to ask me."

"But you could give me a hint."

"No, I couldn't," Liberty said on a laugh. She thought he was so funny. "And while we're on the subject, what is it to you?"

"I'll tell you what. He's going to let you get away if he isn't careful."

Liberty shook her head. "I don't think I've ever seen the like."

"What's that?"

"A Texas Ranger with nothing better to do than play matchmaker."

Dakota was opening his mouth in outrage when Liberty slipped out the door. She didn't look back or even wave, but she smiled to herself all the way back to her own front door.

❧ ❧ ❧

"Did I hear Liberty's voice?" Slater asked when Dakota checked on him about 20 minutes later.

"Yes. Are you going to marry that lady or not?"

"This afternoon," Slater said as he rolled over to go back to sleep. "Didn't I tell you?"

Dakota took compassion when he heard Slater's rough voice. Thinking his throat had to be sore, he took himself from the room. It didn't look as though anything he could say or do would induce Slater back to the Rangers, but where Liberty Drake was concerned, he wasn't going to leave things so up in the air. He decided that before he left town he was going to wring a few promises out of his little brother.

🌿 🌿 🌿

A high-noon bank robbery the day after Christmas was not what Griffin and Liberty had been expecting, but that was exactly what they got.

It was a Monday, and Liberty was due to go off duty when a terrified Miss Amy came running to tell her what she'd witnessed across the street. Liberty knew better than to go alone. Thankfully, Griffin was in the mayor's office, and within minutes the two of them were making their way to the bank building. The only way in was through the front door, so they started to inch their way down the boardwalk. They had just gained positions at the window when a shot was fired and at least two women screamed. Wasting no more time, the Drakes rushed in.

"Don't do it!" a wild-eyed man screamed, his gun pointed right at them. "Get your hands up. I swear I'll shoot again."

Liberty and Griffin did exactly as they were told, coming in and leaving the door wide open. The man kept turning, moving around so fast that he gave them no time to reach for their weapons. At the same time, he didn't seem to notice their gun belts. Standing with her hands in the air, helpless for the moment, Liberty took in the scene and felt very sick.

Seven people stood against the tellers' windows. One of them was three-year-old Josie Frank, who stood frozen as she stared at her mother's body. What had compelled this man to shoot Desna Frank was unclear, but the pool of blood underneath her and her motionless form did not look good.

Liberty forced her mind back onto the robber just in time to see him spot Griffin. It seemed as though he had forgotten him.

"You there!" he screamed. "Get that gun off and shove it away from you."

The robber was so wild-eyed that it was terrifying to watch him, but Griffin slowly removed his weapon and quietly placed it on the floor. He pushed it away with the flick of his boot, his calm face seeming to irritate the man even more.

"Now come here! Help him," he ordered, gesturing wildly with the gun. "Help him put money in the bag."

Griffin went slowly forward. Liberty didn't dare move. She was small enough not to be seen behind Griffin's back if she wanted to pull her gun, but if the robber caught any movement, Griffin would be right in the line of fire.

"What bag do you want me to use?" Griffin asked calmly. The man looked panicky until he remembered and pulled a sack from his waistband.

Griffin had deliberately moved between the gunman and the innocent folks against the counter, but now the head teller had no choice but to move out of their ranks and join Griffin. The gunman started to follow but pulled back. Suddenly grabbing Bill Miller, who had come in to withdraw some funds, he pulled him close and held the gun to his head.

"Make it fast!" he yelled.

Griffin and the teller did just that, taking money from the drawers and shoving the bills into the bag. They were finished in less than two minutes, but the man was so agitated it looked as though he would shoot anyway. He had to let go of Bill to grab the money, and when he did, Griffin stepped in such a way as to put himself between them. The gunman was instantly irate.

"What are you doing?"

"Just waiting on you," Griffin said. He was close enough to see that the man was out of his head.

"I'll shoot him if I want to," he said suddenly and gestured with his gun. "Move!"

"I can't let you shoot him," Griffin said calmly, and the man lost control. He brought the gun directly in front of him and aimed at Griffin, giving Liberty no choice. The look of surprise on the man's face as the bullet entered his body was pathetic. He froze, dropped everything from both hands, and crumpled to the floor.

In the next instant, Liberty was across the room taking Josie in her arms. She scooped the child up—she was stiff with shock—and cradled her close. Looking to Griffin, who motioned her out with his head, she turned for the door. She didn't expect to see Slater and Dakota, who had just slipped in the door, both with guns pulled. The look on Slater's face shocked Liberty. She had never seen such a look of revulsion, and it was directed at her. In an instant she was angry.

"This baby's mother is gone, and Griffin was next," she said quietly. "I suppose you wanted me to slap his hand for that."

This said, Liberty pushed past both men and the crowd that had started to gather outside. Questions about what happened flew at her, but she ignored them. She had to get to the Franks'. She had to find this little girl's father. She only hoped that in time the memory would fade. There was no chance that Liberty would ever forget, but she prayed that Josie would never remember a thing about this day.

Eleven

"HOW ARE YOU?" Duffy asked Liberty as he joined her in the living room several hours later. Kate had called Duffy home as soon as she'd heard. She had given Zach and Laura a snack at the table, but Liberty had wanted to be alone. She'd opted to grab her Bible and sit in the living room where she could hear their voices, but she had yet to open the book.

"I feel bruised all over," she said as she looked at him. "I never get used to it, Duffy. Today's not the first time, but it might as well be. The shock and hurt are just the same."

"If you did get used to it, I'd be worried about you."

Liberty nodded.

"Thank you, Libby," he said now.

"What for?"

"For saving our Griffin."

Liberty cried then. "I had to, Duff, I had to do it. He was going to kill Griff!"

Duffy moved to put an arm around her. She hadn't cried yet, and this was what she needed. Not even her mother's arms had provided the needed cathartic, but having Duffy, who loved them as though they were his own, thank her for her brother's life had been enough.

Duffy had yet to go to the Franks', but he was headed there next. He left as soon as Liberty fell asleep on the sofa and he'd covered her with a quilt. He held Kate for the longest time and then his children. The Frank family went to church with them, but it was more than that: As a doctor, Duffy had to check on that little girl.

❦ ❦ ❦

"Why have you never asked me to be your deputy?" Slater asked later that afternoon. It had been an emotional day for all of them, but Slater could not keep his thoughts to himself any longer. He had even asked Dakota to take off for a while to give him and Griffin privacy.

Griffin, who was headed to Tess' for dinner, looked at him from across the room and was suddenly all ears. He took in Slater's intense eyes and had sudden hope.

"Tell me something, Slate," Griffin requested right back. "Why have you never told me why you left the Rangers?"

Slater looked confused. "I thought I did."

This was not what Griffin expected at all. "Tell me again" was all the sheriff said.

"I couldn't keep on the trail for the Rangers, constantly moving around and never having a home church. It was wreaking havoc with my walk with Christ. I knew I had to settle somewhere; most Rangers can't do that. I don't understand why knowing that is so important."

"I wasn't sure it would be, but for all I knew, you'd accidentally killed an innocent man or a child and never wanted to be in law enforcement again. You had opportunity at one point to tell Liberty you were a Ranger, but you didn't do it. Other than me, I've never heard you tell anyone what you were. I didn't know what to think about that. Much as I need a new deputy, I have to be pretty selective about who I have at my back. I think you can probably understand."

Slater nodded. He had no idea Griffin's thoughts had run along that line. No wonder he'd not said a word. But there was more, and Slater thought it was time to come out with it.

"I would like to serve as your deputy, Griffin; I think I would do well. But there's more to it than that. I don't want

Libby working as your deputy. I've had a hard time with that from day one. I don't think she should be in such a dangerous position."

"Liberty takes care of herself very well." Griffin defended his sister with calm self-assurance. "And she has a natural ability. Not to mention I use her only when I have to."

Slater still shook his head. "I can't tell you what to do, Griffin, and I won't leave in a huff, but I don't like it. No, that's not true, I hate it. I want to marry your sister, Griffin. It's not fair of me to tell you before I've spoken to her, but that's the fact. I don't want her packing a gun and putting her life in danger, no matter how good she is. I'm glad she saved your life today and possibly the lives of others, but I don't like Libby being an option when you don't have help."

Griffin nodded very slowly. Liberty had never let him down—he would be the first to say that—but had he done the right thing by her? Sheriff Drake questioned this for the first time. He knew this was going to take some thinking.

"Can you use me?" Slater asked, naturally wanting an answer.

Griffin looked him in the eye. "Yes, and with you on as deputy, Liberty can go back to her own life."

Slater nodded but didn't let his satisfaction go too far. That Griffin would use Liberty at all told him his bias was altogether different. But he would have to be content with that for now. Thanking him, Slater stood.

"Are you headed out too?" Griffin asked. "I could give you a rundown on a few things before I have to go."

"Is there any way it can wait for morning, or even later this evening?"

"That's fine."

Slater put his hat on his head. "I've got to find Hank Hathaway and tell him I've got another job. I'll ask him if he needs me to put some time in until he finds someone else. Then I need to see your sister."

Griffin looked at the grim line around the other man's mouth and said, "Something tells me you're not going to propose."

"You're right. I'm not even sure she'll speak to me, but I've got some explaining to do."

"I'll give you one word of advice," Griffin offered.

"What's that?"

"They don't think like we do." Griffin's voice was dry. "Don't expect Liberty to be the exception."

Serious as Slater's business was, he found himself laughing on the way to the door.

☙ ☙ ☙

"Mrs. Peterson," Slater began as he stood at her door some time later, hat in hand. "May I see Libby?"

Kate hesitated. Liberty had said something about seeing Slater and Dakota at the bank, and even though she had not explained, her mother could see that it had upset her even more.

"Please," Slater tried again.

"She's sleeping, Slater," Kate said honestly. "I'm not sure what Libby would want, but I can't ask you to wait because she's asleep in the living room."

Slater was nodding and trying to fight his discouragement when a disheveled Liberty appeared behind her mother.

"Did I hear the door, Mam?" she asked in a small, croaky voice. A moment later, she spotted Slater, stiffened, and turned away.

"You misunderstood my look," Slater promptly said, looking past Kate to see her. "I'd like to explain."

When Liberty stopped and looked back at him, Kate slipped away. Slater took this as consent, stepped inside, and shut the door. Dim as the light was, Slater could see Liberty's eyes as he walked forward and stopped in front of her. His hand came up, and with just the tips of his fingers, he touched the hair at her temple.

"How are you doing?"

"I just woke up."

"You might feel drained for a few days," he offered.

Liberty nodded. "I always have in the past."

Slater had all he could do not to close his eyes and sigh with pain. How could she do this? How could this be so normal for all of them? He had to force his mind back to why he was here.

"I'm sorry you misunderstood my look," he repeated, his eyes looking directly into hers. "I was sick inside that you had to go through that. I was sick inside over that poor woman lying in her own blood. And all I was thinking was that I wish I'd been there to spare you. I would have done exactly as you did," he told her softly, "but I'm sorry *you* had to do it."

Liberty bit her lip and admitted, "I thought you despised me."

"Not even close. I just wish I had been on the scene faster."

Liberty shook her head. "I think I should tell you, Slater, that that's not really anything I've ever expected."

"I can understand how you would feel that way, and it's time I told you that I was a Texas Ranger, Libby. I gave up that job right before I came here."

Liberty blinked, taking a moment to let it sink in. Finally, "Why, Slater? Why did you give it up?"

"I want to tell you—it's not even that complicated—but right now I need to let you know that I asked Griffin whether he could use me as deputy, and he hired me. I hope you're pleased. If not, I hope you'll talk to me. It may not have been my place to tell you, but I wanted you to know."

"Oh, Slater, that's wonderful. I'm very pleased," Liberty said sincerely even as she took in the full import of his news. She didn't have to back up her brother or stay on edge any longer. She didn't have to worry about someone being there to protect her brother's back. A former Texas Ranger would be on the job to do it. Liberty was slightly amazed, so much so that it took a moment for her to hear her mother calling.

"Yes?" she answered after the second call.

"Can you come here a moment, Lib?"

"Excuse me," Liberty said to Slater and slipped around into the dining room where she followed her mother into the kitchen.

"Are you all right? Did you need me to rescue you?"

"No, thank you, Mam. He was just explaining what his expression meant earlier. I had completely misunderstood."

Kate smiled at the daughter she adored. "Would you like to invite Slater for dinner? We have plenty."

"I'll ask him."

Intent on doing that, Liberty went back to the hallway but found Slater leaning against the wall, his eyes closed. She hesitated, and almost instantly he opened his eyes.

"Are you all right?" she asked.

"Yes," he answered right away. "I was just praying. I—"

Liberty waited, but it took a moment for him to continue. Slater had just told Griffin that he wanted to marry Liberty, but he suddenly realized that he wasn't ready to ask her on the spot. He suspected that she might need some time as well.

"There's so much in my heart, Libby. Sometimes I think I could burst with all the things I'm keeping inside. Does that make sense?"

Liberty nodded.

"I guess I just wanted you to know that. I want to have a chance to figure out what I'm feeling toward you. I don't want us to rush, but I want you to know I'm feeling things and to ask if you might be feeling some things too."

"I am, Slater. I have been for a time now," Liberty said, not able to keep the breathlessness and fear from her voice. "It's all so new."

Slater nodded. The light caught her face for a moment, and he thought she looked so pale. He chastised himself for his timing.

"I should have waited to talk to you, Libby. It's been a rough day. I am glad to learn, however, that I'm not in this alone."

Liberty felt a wonderful warm feeling spiral through her. He was so honest and open. Her mother had told her that women seemed to deal better with their thoughts and feelings than men did, but she wondered if Slater might be an exception.

"My mother said you could stay for dinner," Liberty suddenly said, wishing she'd come up with something a little more profound.

"I'd like that," Slater replied, not wishing for any other words from her. For right now it was enough just to stand with her, knowing she was not upset with him anymore and that the subject of the future—their future—was an open one.

🌿 🌿 🌿

"How are you?" Tess asked Griffin the moment she saw him. For more than two weeks they had been planning to celebrate their Christmas the day after, but neither one had expected the evening to follow a bank robbery and shooting.

"I'm all right."

"How about Libby?"

"I stopped for a moment before I came over here. She's pale, but they were just sitting down to dinner, and she seemed to be doing fairly well."

"Who was the man, Griff? Was he from around here?"

"Not that I'm aware of. I did find a poster that looked like him, but I'll have to write some letters and check it out." Griffin shook his head. "He didn't seem to be in his right mind."

They fell silent for a moment. They were the only ones in the living room—Tess' mother had said she would finish preparing dinner, and her father and brothers were not yet home. They never waited dinner for the men—they would starve if they tried—so Tess wondered what the evening would be like.

"I'm sorry I couldn't get over here sooner," Griffin said. "Slater needed to talk with me."

"Was he upset?"

"Yes, but mostly because of Libby," Griffin told her before explaining Slater's past work experience, their conversation, and Slater's new position as deputy.

"I hope Lib will be pleased."

Griffin gave her a shrewd look. "Do you have some doubt about that?"

Tess looked surprised. "Don't you, Griff?"

"I didn't, no."

Tess bit her lip.

"Talk to me, Tess," he said in that tone she could never argue with.

Tess hesitated but still said, "I don't want to be too harsh on Libby, but I wouldn't have said she could give it up that easily. But then you know her better than I do, Griff. If you say she'll be fine, I'm sure you're right."

Griffin felt the air leave his lungs. What was Tess saying that made him feel so breathless? He wasn't exactly sure, but doubts about Liberty handling this change began to assail him. She had honestly looked very calm that night at the dinner table, but would that be the end of it?

"Have I upset you?" Tess asked after studying his thoughtful face.

"Yes, but that's good. I'm going to have to keep my eyes open."

Not really knowing what he was referring to, Tess innocently said, "Maybe Slater isn't the man for Libby after all."

"Why do you say that?"

"Well, you've told me when you were explaining about the change that Slater didn't want Libby in that job and was glad to become your deputy." She suddenly smiled. "Maybe I've misunderstood all these years, but I've always thought that when a woman loved a man enough to marry him, she would be willing to do anything he wants."

Griffin smiled a little but couldn't speak. Was Tess right? Would Liberty still want to work for him even if it mean losing Slater?

Tess missed all of this turmoil. She heard a bang in the kitchen and told Griffin she was headed to check on her mother. By the time she returned, Griffin calmed his thoughts. He knew that time and prayer were needed here, but right now it was more important that he celebrate Christmas with the family he would be joining.

"Dinner's not ready yet," Tess said as she returned to her place across from Griffin. "Did I tell you that my father came home and told me you were all right?"

"No, you didn't. How did he know?" Griffin asked, working hard to get back into Tess' life.

"He saw you downtown and came home and told me." Tess gave a small, incredulous laugh. "You could have pushed me over with a small breeze. My father left the office and came all the way home to tell me you were all right. He went back as soon as he'd let me know. My mother and I could only stare at each other after he left."

"Maybe with your getting married and leaving, he has realized how much he's missed."

Tess smiled hugely. "I love it when you talk about our getting married."

Griffin smiled back at her. "Then you should get downtown more—that's all I hear from people. And they all want a date set right now."

"Well, maybe we'd better do that," Tess said softly.

"We don't have to..." Griffin's tone was just as hushed.

It was not logical to people who knew of their plans, but Tess Locken did not want to set a wedding date too soon. She hadn't thought she would ever be engaged to the man of her dreams, and she wasn't about to rush things. It wasn't that she didn't look forward to being married—she looked forward to it all the time—but this was special. This was a once-in-a-lifetime experience for her, and she wanted to savor it.

"Maybe we could at least pick a season," Tess capitulated. "Would people be pleased about that?"

Griffin shook his head. "We don't have to do anything. I was just teasing."

"I suppose everyone would be crushed if we just up and married one of these days."

Griffin could only stare at her. A moment later Tess caught his expression.

"What is it, Griff?"

"You're so easy to love, Tess."

"Why is that?"

"You're never the same, but everything I discover is wonderful."

"Oh, Griffin," was all Tess could say; she was so much in love with this man. She couldn't be having intimate thoughts about him, not yet anyway, but the desire to crawl into his lap was so very strong.

"Dinner," Mrs. Locken called from the other room.

Griffin stood immediately, took Tess' hand, and pulled her from the chair. With his hand under her chin, he bent and kissed her mouth.

"Merry Christmas, Tess."

"Merry Christmas, Griffin."

They walked hand-in-hand to the dining room where Mrs. Locken was waiting. It seemed that some weeks her husband and sons never ceased to cause her pain with the way they overlooked her and took her efforts for granted, but this couple who loved the Lord and each other was like a gift from God and the best Christmas gift she could possibly imagine.

❧ ❧ ❧

Dakota could not dispel Liberty's image from his mind. He had tried closing his eyes, which only made it worse. He had tried concentrating on the creek line, dark as it was, but he could still see her in the bank building. He shook his head a little at how fast she had been. He'd seen many a quick draw in his business, and he thought she might rank among the smoothest. And her aim! If it hadn't been so sad, he would have called it beautiful. That thought today, however, only made him ache.

"I wanted to see her in action," he said quietly, causing Eli's ears to twitch, "but not like this."

Slater had asked him to head out for a time. Dakota had been only too glad to oblige him. He needed to be alone. He needed to think. For a moment his mind lingered on some of the things he'd seen and heard from the pastor and the church family, but it didn't take long for him to feel uncomfortable with his thoughts. He pushed them away to concentrate on his brother. As though he'd never had a problem with Slater giving up his job, Dakota was now resolute.

Slate should stay here, he decided. *Slate needs to step in as deputy. I don't know why I didn't see it before. I'm still not certain what to do with the change in him, but he's made a life here. A man with his skill and level head shouldn't be building houses. He should be helping Griffin with the law, not Libby. And I'm going to tell him as soon as I get back.*

❧ ❧ ❧

"This is my room," Laura told Slater after dinner, her drawing of the house in her lap. The whole family was gathered in the living room. "It used to be Griffin's room, but he moved next door, and Mam gave it to me. It's my very own."

"What's this?" Slater pointed to a circle on the floor.

"My rug. It's all red and blue and green colors."

"It sounds nice."

"Libby's is almost the same, only hers has some yellow."

Slater nodded and smiled down at her.

"If you marry Libby, then you can come upstairs and see all the rugs."

"Laura May Peterson!" Duffy wasted no time in exclaiming.

The little girl looked across at him, clearly upset and uncertain, but her silence didn't last for more than a few seconds. Tears already filling her eyes and her chin tilted upward, she said, "Well, he should marry Libby and make her smile all the time!"

The room was silent with shock—not just over her talking back—but at the words as well.

"Libby's sad because she had to shoot that man, and when Slater comes she always smiles." With that Laura put her face in her hands and sobbed. Kate was sitting closer than Duffy, so she was the one to move and put her arms around the little girl. It took some time for her to calm, the others quietly waiting.

Laura would not look at anyone, but they all had eyes on her. Duffy waited but could see that she was going to keep her face buried against her mother's side. He went to her, hunkered down in front of both his wife and daughter, and spoke quietly.

"Laura, you need to look at me."

Laura obeyed at once, her little face blotchy and tearstained.

"I know you meant well, but Slater and Libby's relationship is not your business. If you have questions, you may ask Mam or me, but you can't just sit and give your opinion whenever you feel like it. Understood?"

Laura nodded, and her father gave her knee a little squeeze.

"You need to apologize." This said, Duffy returned to his seat, fully expecting to be obeyed.

"I'm sorry, Libby," Laura said to the big sister who sat across the room.

"I forgive you, Laura."

"I'm sorry, Slater."

"Thank you, Laura, and I want you to know that I do appreciate the nice words you said."

"I can be nice sometimes," Laura told him, "but not always."

Slater had to smile over this. He looked over at Liberty to find her smiling at Laura too. He was still watching her when she noticed him. Duffy asked Zach a question just then, and the little boy began to answer, but it took several minutes for Slater and Liberty to hear.

Twelve

"I WANT TO TALK TO YOU," Dakota greeted Slater the moment he walked in the door.

"All right. Let me get my coat off."

Dakota waited with ill-concealed impatience, and Slater wanted to laugh. It was always clear to him when Dakota had a mission.

"When are you headed back to work, Dak?" Slater asked as he sauntered his way toward the living room and took a seat on the davenport.

"Not until I'm through with you, at the very least. Now, I've been doing some thinking."

"About my life or yours?"

"My life is fine," Dakota clarified for him. "Yours could use a little work."

Slater laughed, which only got him glared at.

"Are you going to listen?"

"Yes." Slater schooled his features and worked not to smile.

"Now, I think the most logical thing for you to do is apply as deputy of Shotgun. You're good enough to be the sheriff, but Griffin already has the job, and he's doing fine. However, a man with your talents has no business pounding nails for a living, and I don't want to hear any arguments.

"My first choice would be to have you come back to the Rangers, but since you're being mule stubborn about that, this is the next best thing. I'll also concede," Dakota went on even as both men heard the back door open and close, "that there's a very sweet lady in town who makes staying a very palatable option. *But*, if I find out that you've let her get away, you'll have some fast explaining to do."

"Hello," Griffin greeted the men as he walked in and took a chair. He saw that Slater was on the sofa, relaxed as a cat, but Dakota was standing as though giving a lecture. Griffin, not worrying about offending anyone, spoke to Slater.

"Did you tell Dakota about the job as deputy?"

"Not yet," Slater replied and let his gaze swing back to his older sibling.

Not surprisingly, Dakota was looking right back at Slater.

"You could have stopped me," the older man said.

"That wouldn't have been half as much fun."

Dakota dropped into a chair and shook his head.

"Someone should fill me in," Griffin suggested.

Slater did the honors, and both men had a laugh on Dakota.

"How's Tess?" Slater asked when the laughter died down.

"She's fine."

"Price asked me this morning if the two of you had a date."

"That seems to be the common question. Tonight Tess suggested that we just up and marry."

"That would be fun," Dakota agreed.

"Spoken like a man," Griffin stated. "I know I would like it, but somehow I think the women in my life, namely Kate Peterson, Liberty Drake, and Rebecca Locken, would not find it so amusing."

"You never know," Slater put in. "Our mother wanted to elope, but our father wouldn't hear of it."

"Did she really?"

"That's what they've always told us," Slater confirmed. "Our father hailed from modest means, and our mother had been reared in the lap of luxury. *Her* mother desperately wanted a large wedding, the kind befitting a young socialite, but our mother had had that her whole life. I guess Grandma Slater, who had a terrible time accepting our father, was won over in an instant when he took his future mother-in-law's side and opted for a grand wedding."

"What did your mother say?"

"She was ready to call the whole thing off," Dakota continued. "She can be rather stubborn, but our father talked her around."

Griffin looked between the two of them, so mismatched in appearance.

"By the way, where do you two get your coloring?"

Both Rawlings laughed.

"He should see Cash," Dakota said to Slater.

"What does Cash look like?" Griffin took the bait.

"Dark red hair, brown eyes."

Griffin's brows rose. The two men before him were so different. One was blond with blue eyes, and the other had black hair with eyes so black you couldn't even see the pupils.

"And you all have the same mother and father?" Griffin clarified.

Both brothers nodded, smiles on their faces.

"No sisters?"

"Nope," Dakota supplied, "but if you're giving up Laura, I'll take her."

"She's a card, all right," Griffin agreed with a small sigh. "She's another reason not to just up and marry."

"She gets to watch it happen," Slater supplied the words, "if she's quiet."

"I'm not sure that's possible." Griffin's tone was dry. "Actually, I shouldn't be surprised at how different you two look, considering Zach and Laura are like day and night in personality."

"Zach's a nice little guy," Dakota said, and with that the men fell quiet. It had been a long day, emotionally and physically. And speaking of the children reminded them of a little girl who no longer had a mother. It wasn't long before all three men opted to turn in, knowing that the next few days promised to be just as draining. On Wednesday they would all be attending the funeral of Desna Frank.

�» �» �»

"Are you up to this?" Duffy asked Kate Wednesday morning. She had been crying since she rose and hadn't wanted anything for breakfast. She now washed the dishes with slow, distracted movements.

Kate shrugged. "Even if I'm not, I can't stay away. Desna was my friend, and I need to see Lloyd and Josie."

Duffy eyed her face. Her color wasn't good, and he naturally thought of her condition.

"Stop looking at me, Duffy," she told him as she handed him a plate to dry.

"That's like telling me not to be a doctor, Kathleen," he replied firmly. "Now, you're not going if there's more than grief going on here. Do you hear me?"

"Yes, but it is grief, Duffy; I know it is. That can bring about problems of its own, but I'm not feeling *that* feeling or anything like that."

To just about anyone else, those words would have been cryptic, but to Kate, who had been expecting so many times, and for the doctor she was married to, it made perfect sense that she was in tune with her pregnancy. Duffy continued to watch her for a moment, and finally Kate came to him. Duffy slipped his arms around her and held her close.

"I don't want to lose you, Duff," she admitted. "I want you here with me. When I think of Lloyd I can hardly stand it."

Duffy pressed a kiss to her temple; he'd had the same thoughts about her. He held her a little closer, already feeling the baby between them. He never tired of touching or holding her. He wasn't a lot taller than she was, but the difference in their heights gave him wonderful access to her soft hair and brow, where he kissed her again.

"We should always have the attitude that we're not staying here permanently, but there's nothing like a death to remind us of how frail we are."

"I'm glad school was canceled. I want the children with me."

"I'd have kept them home anyway," Duffy told her. "Laura told me she wants to talk to Josie, but I told her I'd have to think about it."

"She means so well, but I'm a little afraid of what she'll come up with."

They heard noises behind them then and weren't surprised when Zach came forward and hugged his father from the side. Duffy slipped an arm down to hold him.

"Where are Libby and Laura?"

"Both crying in Libby's room."

"Maybe I should go up," Kate said and moved a little, but steps could be heard on the stairs. Sure enough, the teary-eyed sisters joined the family in the kitchen, and 15 minutes later, they headed for the cemetery.

᪥ ᪥ ᪥

"Second Corinthians 5 says, 'Therefore, we are always confident, knowing that, while we are at home in the body, we are absent from the Lord. For we walk by faith, not by sight. We are confident, I say, and willing rather to be absent from the body, and to be present with the Lord,'" Pastor Caron read these words to the crowd as they huddled close against the cold wind. Rain was threatening.

"Can there ever be good news at a funeral?" the pastor asked. "I just read verses to you that would give a resounding yes!" Pastor Caron went on to say, "Desna Frank was 24 years old. She was born in Dallas on May 1, 1857, to the late Henry and Lottie Jeffers. She lived most of her life in Dallas and moved to Shotgun after she married Lloyd Frank in 1876. Her daughter Josie was born to her in 1878. Desna is also survived by two sisters and a brother, all of whom live in the Dallas area.

"Desna wanted to be a schoolteacher but met Lloyd before she completed her training. She was actively involved in the church where she attended and was a regular at the women's Bible study. Desna also enjoyed attending the quilting bees that the Ladies' Legion holds each month. She was quoted just a few weeks back as saying, 'I love Shotgun. I hope we can raise all of our children here.' "

Pastor Caron took a moment to compose himself. He had just recently learned that Desna had been expecting. For an instant he wanted to sob with the loss of both lives. Almost a minute later he took a breath and continued.

"I had a long talk with Lloyd yesterday. He talked to me about Desna, a woman he'd known and loved for more than six years. Lloyd is confident, as am I, that Desna is indeed present with the Lord. Lloyd was with Desna the day they both realized they needed a Savior. He told me all about the camp meeting where they both sat, hungry for the truth about eternity, and how they needed to fill the ache inside, an ache that was spiritually based. Both Lloyd and Desna were saved that day.

"I didn't know Desna before she and Frank moved to Shotgun and began attending the church where I pastor, but we spoke many times, and on several occasions she told me about her life. Frank wanted me to talk about Desna today, but also to let you know that you can have the same hope in Christ that she had.

"I don't say that Desna is in heaven because she was a good person. Those of you who know me know that I would make no such claim. She's in heaven today because she repented of her sin and accepted God's Son as her Savior."

Taking in the words as best she could, Liberty stood very still at the graveside. She felt like her insides were crumbling, but she didn't want to break down. She was thankful beyond what she could express that her friend was in heaven, but Lloyd's pale face and Josie's confused eyes were almost too much to bear. When the service ended, many people went forward to have a word with Lloyd, but Liberty hung back until they were almost all gone. Griffin was close by, Dakota and Slater behind him.

"I'm sorry I didn't get there in time, Lloyd," Liberty said, tears coming without invitation. "I can't tell you how sorry."

"It's not your fault, Libby. I'm just glad no one else was hurt."

Tears fell as she nodded and shifted her gaze to Josie, who was standing next to some of Lloyd and Desna's family. As she watched, Laura came up to the other little girl.

"Hi, Josie. Mam said you can come and play with me. Do you want to come and play sometime?"

Josie nodded and Laura gave her a hug, one that the younger girl returned.

"We'll plan on that," the woman next to Lloyd now said. She was Desna's sister.

"Call on us," Griffin told him, his hand extended in friendship. "We'll do whatever we can, Lloyd."

"Thanks, Griff."

It was time to move on, but Liberty didn't want to. She stood in momentary indecision. Since she was ready to leave, Laura made it a little easier. She took Liberty's hand and even turned away. They hadn't gone ten feet when the five-year-old stumbled over the uneven ground and nearly fell. Slater was suddenly there, scooping her up to sit on his arm and taking Liberty's hand in his own.

"If I had just been a little faster," Liberty said quietly.

"Don't do this to yourself." Slater's voice came softly to her. "It won't help to go over it again and again."

Liberty turned her head to look up at him. It was too easy to forget that he would know that. The news about his past job was still so foreign. Dakota seemed like a Texas Ranger, but for some reason Slater did not. A moment of disquiet filled her. Was he capable of being Griffin's deputy? Had Griffin known what he was doing, or was the decision made in the heat of emotion? On top of these upsetting thoughts, Liberty abruptly realized how warm and solid his hand was and how confidently he'd taken over with Laura. Even amid her doubts about his serving as deputy, Liberty still thought him the most wonderful man she'd ever met.

"Here you go," he said gently, helping her into Duffy and Kate's wagon.

"Come and have some lunch," Kate invited Slater, her eyes taking in Griffin and Dakota as well.

"You're welcome to come by the house for lunch," Duffy cut in, his voice mild, "but your hostess will be lying down."

Kate's hand went to her mouth, and she looked away. She was just holding on, and her husband knew it.

"Do you want company, Lib?" her brother asked.

She nodded yes. It wasn't hard to guess that she found that easier than being on her own. The wagon pulled away then, and the men moved to their horses. Once at the house, her husband seeing to the task of settling Kate upstairs, all hands joined in to help with the meal. It was light fare, and because her mother was not with them, Liberty was committed to acting as normally for Zach and Laura as she could. Neither one of them had eaten a good breakfast, and she determined to see food into them now. Slater was feeling the same way about Liberty, and Dakota watched it all in silence. Not until the meal was over and he was in the living room with Zach and Griffin did he start to relax. It didn't last long, however, as the little boy began to talk with his brother.

"I don't like cemeteries, Griff."

"Why not, Zach?"

The little boy shrugged. "They scare me a little."

Griffin nodded.

"I'm not scared now, but I'm afraid I'll think of it tonight when I go to bed."

"Come here, Zach," Griffin invited, putting an arm around him when he joined him in the large chair. "Do you know one of the things I love about God, Zach? It's the way He's everywhere all the time. Do you know what that's called?"

Zach shook his head no.

"Omnipresent. That's a long, funny word, but it simply means that God is everywhere 100 percent of the time. I love that. When I have to ride into a dangerous situation, I know that He's with me, but that He's also where I'm headed. When I lie down at night He's with me, but He's also with Tess. I take great comfort in that.

"And now tonight, I'll be thinking of you especially. I'll be so glad that when God is with me, He's also with you in your bed, and with Josie Frank where she's sleeping, and even at the cemetery. There's no reason to fear if God is with us, Zach, and He always is."

"Papa has told me that, but I think I forgot."

"Well, I'll pray that you'll remember it the next time you're scared. You can pray that Josie will understand and remember too."

Without warning or word to anyone, Dakota suddenly stood and left the room. Zach looked to his brother, his eyes questioning. Griffin's eyes met the younger ones.

"I think maybe Dakota could use the same prayers too, Zach."

The six-year-old was still nodding when Griffin tightened his arm around him and bent to give him a kiss.

🌿 🌿 🌿

"How are you?" Slater asked Liberty as he took the wet bowl from her hand.

"I'm all right. I'm always surprised at how much it affects me physically. I still feel bruised all over."

"You might be in a way," Slater surmised.

Liberty looked up at him in question.

"You move very fast when you draw, Libby. That's bound to affect your muscles."

"I've never thought of that," Liberty said slowly. She had just handed another bowl to Slater when Dakota burst through the door.

"Oh," he seemed momentarily stopped. "I, um, I mean, thanks for lunch, Libby."

"Are you all right?" Slater asked before Liberty could reply.

"Yeah," Dakota answered, but he was clearly agitated. "I've got to go."

Both Slater and Liberty watched in surprise as he moved for the back door and left in a hurry.

"I need to see what's wrong," Slater said, even as he was setting the towel down and moving out the door.

Liberty didn't try to comment; she didn't want to distract him, but she stepped away from the washtub to see Slater catch up with Dakota halfway between the houses.

"Are you all right?" Slater asked again, this time taking his brother's arm.

"No, I'm not all right," he gritted. "But it's nothing you could possibly understand."

"Try me."

Dakota speared him with angry eyes. "I suppose you thought the service was great. I suppose you agreed with every word."

"I did, yes."

Dakota shook his head in disgust. "What's the matter with all of you, Slater? A woman is dead. Her husband and baby stood there in terrible grief, and who do we hear about? Jesus Christ! Unbelievable."

It was cold out, but neither man seemed to notice. Slater's mind scrambled fast for a reply, his mind praying for wisdom.

"What did you want Pastor Caron to say, Dak? What would you have deemed appropriate?"

"A little more about the woman herself, for starters. He turned it into a sermon!"

"What if the woman was who she was because of Jesus Christ, Dak?"

"What do you mean?"

"Well, you heard what he said. She was a changed person because of her faith."

Dakota's eyes narrowed. Slater knew he was not happy with that answer, but he went on anyway.

"If I'm a different person because of my beliefs, Dakota, and I were to die, I would want other people to know they could have the same hope. Lloyd Frank clearly feels the same way." Slater took a breath and said, "Maybe you should be listening instead of criticizing."

"My life is *fine*," Dakota did not hesitate to clarify.

"If that's true, then why does this have you so upset? If everything is fine, you should be able to shrug this off and go on with your life."

Dakota's eyes became dangerously black, but Slater held his ground.

"I'm leaving," he finally gritted out.

Slater stood still as Dakota stormed away and slammed into the house. Not until he reappeared with his saddle-bags and gear did Slater see how serious he was and follow him to the barn to try again.

"Please don't leave like this, Dak. Don't leave in a rage."

"I'm not angry at you, Slate," Dakota said tightly, throwing tack onto Eli in a hurry. "You're just a little confused right now, and I know how that can be. I just need to get away for a time. Maybe when I return you'll have come down off this cloud that says your way is the only way."

Slater had no idea how to reply. He believed with all of his heart that God's Son *was* the only way, but clearly that was the last thing he could say right now. Dakota mounted Eli and said goodbye, leaving Slater standing by the small barn. As he watched him ride away, Slater thought it most fitting that it had finally begun to rain.

🌿 🌿 🌿

"I brought you some soup," Liberty said as she entered her mother's room.

"Thank you, dear." Kate sat up and reached for her robe; the room was chilly.

"Did Zach and Laura eat lunch?"

"Yes. I think I got quite a bit into them."

"And what about you?"

Liberty chuckled. "Slater kept pushing food my way. He must have had the same plan I had for the kids."

Kate took a sip from the mug of soup and watched her daughter. A blush had stolen over her cheeks, and her eyes, which had a dreamy light in them, had gone toward the window.

"You're falling for this man, Libby," her mother said.

"I think you're right." Liberty bit her lip and met her mother's eyes. "I didn't know I could feel this way about anyone, Mam. I think he's wonderful."

"Are you going to be able to move slowly?"

Liberty nodded. "I do have feelings, though, ones I've never experienced before. I also have a lot of questions. We haven't talked about when he came to Christ, and he said he'd get back to me about why he left the Rangers."

"Cover all of it, Lib. I can't give you better advice than that."

"When did you and Duffy find time to talk?"

Kate smiled. "It wasn't easy. I had two children and he had a busy practice, but we made it work. I also listened to the people who were close to me. If someone I loved and trusted had felt any doubts, I would have slowed down or stopped."

"Do you and Duffy have doubts about Slater?"

"Not doubts, but we do want you to go slowly. We think Slater is wonderful. We're delighted that he's taking the deputy's position, but that doesn't mean he's the man God has for you."

Liberty nodded. "I think about what Tess said too— you know, about my never noticing male attention before. Maybe all I'm feeling is a first-time infatuation."

"That's what time will determine, dear. Give yourself lots of it."

Liberty stood and kissed her mother's cheek.

"Send the kids up, will you, Lib? I want to see how they're doing."

"Will do. Are you up to coming to the table for dinner?"

"I feel up to it, yes, but Duffy may come home and order me back to bed. I'll be down in about an hour."

"All right."

Zach and Laura were already in the hallway when she left the room, their little faces anxious.

"Can we see Mam, Libby?" Zach asked.

"Yes, Zach. She was just asking for you."

Liberty smiled as they raced down the hall and heard her mother's cry of delight. Again she prayed that God would allow this fifth child to come safely into their world.

Thirteen

"SO HE JUST STORMED OFF?" Griffin asked.

"Yep. He's fighting what he's hearing, I'm sure. That's not like Dakota, but then I guess I did a good deal of fighting myself."

"What do you suppose brought it on?" Tess asked; the three of them were at the sheriff's office the next day.

"The funeral," Slater said, filled her in, and went on. "He's not a man who cares how other people live as long as they obey the law, so this is a surprise. I haven't had hope until now."

"Zach and I were talking in Mam's living room yesterday when he left so suddenly."

"What were you discussing?"

"God's omnipresence."

Slater nodded.

"I find it so interesting that he wanted Pastor Caron to talk more about Desna," Tess said. "Do you remember what you pointed out to me, Griff, about the way the disciples wanted to talk about themselves when Jesus mentioned His death?"

Griffin nodded. "It's the same today. You talk about Christ's work on the cross, and most people start telling you how good they've been. They want to talk about themselves, not about Christ's death for their sins."

Slater's brows rose. That was exactly what he did for a time, but he eventually got so miserable that all the fight went out of him.

"Do you think he'll come back?" Griffin now asked.

"Yes, but probably not for a time. I know he thinks I need to get my head on straight. I'm not real anxious to have him return, knowing there will probably be another confrontation."

"Maybe not," Tess put in. "Maybe he'll run into the man who led you to Christ, and he'll have an impact."

"I only hope and pray that it happens," Slater said sincerely.

"Oh, there's Libby," Tess exclaimed, spotting her across the street. "Maybe she'll come over."

Slater's head whipped around at the sound of that name, and he was out the door so fast the other two almost didn't see him move. Griffin and Tess' eyes met, both people smiling in delight.

❧ ❧ ❧

"I think the pink calico," Liberty said to Miss Amy. "The one with the small flowers."

"Six cents a yard," Miss Amy quoted as she laid it on the counter. "I just got this in."

"And the navy flannel?"

"Eleven cents a yard" was the price as this bolt came down from the shelf.

"Thank you. I need to see a little of the blue-striped ticking too."

"That goes for twelve cents a yard."

"Okay. Thanks, Miss Amy. I'll look these over and do some figuring."

"Okay. I've got a special on buttons. There're some red ones that would be nice if you want that navy flannel for a shirt."

"Okay."

Liberty was fingering fabric and working sums on her paper when Slater approached. He said nothing but stood at her shoulder and watched her work. Without warning

Liberty's head came up, and she swung around to look at the buttons. What she encountered was Slater's chest.

"Hello," he said quietly, a smile in his eyes.

"I'm sorry. I didn't see you."

"I saw you," he told her warmly, and watched as she smiled, bit her lip, and dropped her eyes.

"How did you know I was in here?"

"Tess is across the street talking to Griffin. She spotted you."

Liberty nodded.

"What are you shopping for?"

"Mam gave me a list of things. Zach needs a shirt, and two of Laura's dresses are rather short."

"Nothing for yourself?" Slater asked, wishing he could purchase something for her, something as lovely and feminine as she looked right now.

"Not today."

"How are you doing, Libby?" he suddenly asked so seriously that Liberty wanted to lay her head against his shoulder and cry.

"Why did you ask me that?"

"Because with a list like that, it sounds as though your mother knew you needed to get out."

Liberty nodded. "She probably did."

"Is your mother feeling better?"

"Yes. She's up and around, and Duffy has stopped watching her like a hawk."

It was in that instant that Slater realized there was more to Duffy's actions the day before than his concern about his wife's grief. He felt a jolt of concern shoot through him. Griffin had once mentioned all the babies his mother had been forced to bid goodbye, and he found himself hoping and praying that this one would not be added to the list.

"Tell her I'm praying for her, will you, Libby?"

"I'll do that."

Liberty felt it again—that warm feeling spiraling through her over this man. He was so gentle and kind. Griffin and Duffy were that way as well, but this was different. Slater looked at her as if he couldn't pull his eyes away. Knowing that did strange things to Liberty's heart.

"Are you shopping for something?" Liberty asked, also happening to notice several pairs of eyes on them. She dropped her own and added, "I'm afraid we're drawing a crowd."

Slater glanced around, causing eyes to look away, but he still didn't move.

"I have a little time off after lunch," he said quietly. "Would you be free to go for a walk?"

Liberty nodded.

"I'll see you then," he assured her, his eyes warm and direct until he was forced to turn away.

Liberty watched him leave and then made herself go back to her list. She was still looking at the buttons when she felt a large presence beside her. Certain that Slater had returned, she looked up with a smile. Price Hathaway stood beside her, his brow showing determination.

"There are some goods in the back you need to see, Libby," he said. "Come this way."

Liberty was given no chance to argue. Her upper arm was taken in his huge fist, and she was urged along toward the rear of the store, and not just out of sight: Price walked her until they were at the far corner of the storeroom—cans of lima beans to Liberty's back and sacks of flour at her heels.

"Are you going to marry Slater?" Price wasted no time in asking.

"Of all things!" Liberty exclaimed. "Price Hathaway, what's come over you?"

Price bent until his face was close. "Slater Rawlings is the reason Amy and I are together again. He told me she still cared. Now if he's in love with you and wants to marry you, I want that for him."

Liberty blinked. There were so many things she could say to that, but all she could manage was "You want that for him? What about me?"

"He's a good man, Lib. I've never known a man like him. He works hard, and he's fair. You can't believe what he put up with with Pa and never said a word. He even invited me to church. Not since I've been grown has anyone ever done that."

"Are you going to go?"

"I don't know yet. Amy and I are still talking about it. Marry him, Libby. If he asks you, marry him."

Liberty saw the earnestness in his eyes.

"For the record, and just between the two of us, he hasn't asked me, but we are going for a walk today. And I do care, Price; I care very much."

Price stood to full height and smiled. "I knew he was the one for you. I just knew it. He believes like you do, and he's a lawman. He probably can't outshoot you, but you can still make it work."

Liberty had a good laugh over that, and Price continued to smile as though he'd won a ticket to the fair.

"I think I'd better get back to my list."

"Did you talk?" Miss Amy's anxious voice came toward them as she nearly ran into the storeroom.

"Yes," Price told her.

Miss Amy came right up to Liberty. "He told Price I still wanted to see him, Libby. I was never so glad in all my life."

Liberty smiled up at her. She was the perfect size for a huge man like Price, but Liberty had always found her so reserved. Not now, however. Her eyes were lit up with pleasure and love for Price, and all because Slater had gone between them.

"So when is *your* date?" Liberty felt free to demand of the two before her.

They both smiled, and Liberty's eyes grew.

"You didn't!"

"We did. Just before Christmas."

"When are you going to announce it?"

"Mama's planning a big party on January 14. You'll be invited."

Liberty hugged Price, who squeezed her in return. Miss Amy surprised Liberty by hugging her next, but Liberty returned the embrace just the same.

"Congratulations!" Liberty told them warmly, but then her eyes grew serious. "I hope you do come to church. I play the piano, so I sit down on the left-hand side. Just look for me and sit with me. You don't know how welcome you would be." This said, Liberty smiled and turned away. She gave a wave but didn't turn back when Miss Amy thanked her.

Not since I've been grown has anyone ever done that.

Liberty could not get the words from her mind. *How many people do I see every day? I've been keeping my eye on the behavior in this town and missing the lost souls.* Liberty finished her list—fabric, buttons, and all—but the subject stayed at the front of her mind for the next several hours. Indeed, she and Kate were still speaking of it when Slater arrived for their walk.

🌿 🌿 🌿

"His name is Desmond Curtis. He's been a Ranger forever. I was working with him, and he noticed how unsettled I was. I'm not an angry person, but I tend to get antsy and have to move around all the time. I just thought that was the way I was, but he asked me what I was running from. I didn't like that, just like Dakota didn't like it when I challenged him, but it got me to thinking."

"So you did know about Christ?" Liberty asked. They had planned to take a walk, but rain had threatened so they sat alone in the Petersons' living room.

"Yes. Both my grandmother and my oldest brother had come to Christ and had talked with me on several occasions, but I was convinced there was nothing wrong with my life." Slater shook his head. "I was blind for a long time."

"What was the turning point?"

"I think God used the solitude of my job to make me see. I was alone so much of the time and becoming lonely in the bargain. I would be on the trail and thinking about how insignificant I was. I found myself wanting to cry all the time. I would look at the magnificent world around me and think, 'If all this just happened, then what's the point? Why go on? Why try at all?' One day when I was in the midst of feeling that way, I realized someone was riding toward me. It was Des. Here I'm sitting in the saddle, tears pouring down my face, and Desmond Curtis rides slowly up.

"I'll never forget it. He stopped his horse right next to mine, looked me in the eye, and said, 'Would you like to talk about it, Slate?' All I could do was nod. We never moved or even got off our horses. He told me that Christ's love was so huge that it had sent Him to the cross for my sins. I was so hungry for that love. Des listened to me while I prayed."

"Oh, Slater," Liberty said, breathless with emotion.

Slater smiled. "I wasn't saved a year when I knew God wanted me to settle down someplace. I fought that one like a madman, but in the end, I gave up the Rangers and ended up here. I didn't know Shotgun existed, and I don't believe that a man should just wander around looking for signs from God, but I ended up here and felt I should stay."

Liberty couldn't take her eyes from him. "I'm so glad you did."

"Are you, Libby? It means a lot to hear you say that."

Liberty's head tipped and she admitted, "You came so suddenly. Sometimes I'm sure I'm going to wake up and find you've gone."

"I wouldn't do that, not to you or Griffin."

Liberty nodded, her heart very full. She wanted to tell this man she was falling for him but opted for a change in subject.

"How will you like the job?"

"I like it already. Griffin is great to work for."

Liberty nodded; she knew that very well. She was genuinely glad that Slater had the job, but on occasion she felt a twinge of regret. This worried her since it had been only a few days.

Someone knocked on the front door right then, and Laura, having been told to play in the kitchen, came running, glad for an excuse to escape.

"Hi, Tess!" they heard her say. "Come on in."

"Thank you, Laura. Are your mother and Libby home?"

"Yes. Mam is in the kitchen, and Libby is visiting with Slater. I'm not allowed in there."

Tess laughed.

"Hi, Tess." Kate had come around the corner. The two women hugged.

"I have news," Tess told her future mother-in-law. "I'd like to tell you all at the same time."

"Of course. Slater and Lib are right in here."

"We have a date!" Tess announced to the occupants of the living room just moments later.

"When?"

"January 21. Three weeks from this Saturday. We know it's short notice, but we didn't want anything too fancy."

"Will you be able to find a dress?" Liberty asked.

"I'm going to wear Mama's. She's so excited."

"When did you decide?"

"Just today."

"And I get to watch?"

"Yes, Laura, you do."

"Oh, I can't wait to tell Zach."

Kate happened to look over just then toward Slater. That man was just starting to get glassy-eyed.

"Did you want to ask what the dress looks like, Slater?" Kate teased.

He gave a small laugh. "That was on my mind," he told her and then shook his head and stood. "I hope I won't offend anyone, but I think this might be a good time for me to get back to work."

The women all laughed at his expense, but Liberty took pity on him and walked him to the door.

"Thanks for the walk," she said.

Slater smiled. "We'll do it again very soon, Miss Drake, and you can tell me your story."

Liberty nodded. Slater slipped out the door, and she peeked out to watch him walk away. Her brother was getting married in three weeks. For the first time in Liberty's life, she wished the wedding was hers.

☙ ☙ ☙

Price and Amy Hathaway's party did not turn out to be overly crowded, but a good time was had by all, including the smiling newlyweds, whose eyes were constantly turned to each other in love. That they had managed to keep their marriage a secret so long was nothing short of amazing. It was also amazing when Hank Hathaway approached Slater and offered him a room.

"In your house?" Slater had to clarify.

"Well, Price won't be needin' it! And the sheriff is gettin' himself hitched too."

Slater nodded slowly. "How about I come back on Monday?"

"Suit yourself," the crotchety old man said as he turned away. Slater looked to Liberty with raised brows.

"He's always a surprise, isn't he?"

"Yes, but Mrs. Hathaway is one of the best cooks in town, so you might want to consider it."

"Did he talk to you?" Korina Hathaway came up as if she'd heard her name.

"He did, Mrs. Hathaway. Did you know he was going to ask me?"

"It was my idea," she beamed at them. "Hank has talked about what a good worker you are, and I thought it sounded just right. Hank always tries to please me."

Both Slater and Liberty managed to smile, but they were stunned. It wouldn't seem that Hank tried to please anyone. Clearly he was not the same man at home that he was in public.

"Everyone seems to be settled in with their cake and coffee. Why don't I show the room to you right now?"

"All right," Slater agreed. He would not have suggested it, but he saw no harm in agreeing.

"Would you like to come too, Libby?" their hostess asked.

"Thank you," Liberty smiled and followed Korina up the stairs, Slater bringing up the rear.

"Price is so big that we've always given him the large room. We talked about switching, but we like where we are."

This didn't really make sense until they were upstairs, but in truth, both rooms were spacious and separated by a large closet that Mrs. Hathaway proudly showed them. Nevertheless, Slater questioned Mrs. Hathaway about disturbing them.

Brushing it off, she responded, "We both sleep like the dead. Price has always come and gone, and we never hear a thing. Lucky for us he's such a good boy because we would never have stayed awake to catch him in his mischief."

The room was lovely—spacious and beautifully furnished. The curtains even matched the bedspread. Slater found himself agreeing to the rent they wanted—a buy because it included meals—and asking when he could move in. Griffin and Tess were to be married in one week's time, and he thought the sooner he vacated, the better.

"Anytime," he was told, and looking at the immaculate room, Slater could see that it was in fact ready for occupation.

"That was a nice surprise," Liberty said when they finally joined the party back downstairs, and their hostess hurried away to see to the refreshments.

"Wasn't it? I would never have guessed."

"Do you have some reservations?"

"A few, but I'd already checked into the boarding house. If this doesn't work out, I can still try there."

Liberty made a face.

"You're spoiled," Slater told her, watching that adorable nose wrinkle.

"I'm sure you're right."

As had become normal for her in the last few weeks, Liberty looked around the Hathaways' home and tried to picture herself as wife and homemaker in a home of her own. It wasn't hard to do with a certain tall blond standing next to her.

Slater suddenly turned and looked at her, his eyes searching her face. The act made her wonder if her thoughts had shown, and she blushed at the very idea.

"I don't suppose you want to tell me why you're blushing," Slater asked, his voice low as he bent toward her.

Liberty refused to look at him.

"I'll find out," he teased, but Liberty only smiled.

The temptation to ask him how he would learn her thoughts was strong, but that might be stepping onto intimate ground, something Liberty was struggling with anyway. She made herself shift her thoughts and gladly took the cake and fresh coffee she was offered. Slater did the same, causing Liberty to wonder if he wasn't struggling with the same thing. With a heart asking for an extra measure of patience, Liberty asked the Lord to strengthen them both.

❧ ❧ ❧

Griffin and Slater had not been back from the Hathaways' party an hour when Maddie Flowers came in. She was obnoxious and shrill, but since Griffin's plan was to keep a close eye on the Potters' dealings, the men mounted up and rode out.

Griffin filled Slater in as they rode, and by the time they arrived, the new man felt prepared. He wasn't prepared, however, to have shots fly at them when they were still a ways off. Griffin wasn't either.

"That's enough, Ned!" Griffin bellowed at him from behind an outcropping of rocks.

"I didn't know it was you," the man called back. "I thought it was that Flowers woman."

"You and the boys come on out to the porch, Ned. Just leave your guns inside."

The front door opened soon after, and all four men trooped out.

"We weren't going to shoot the old bat, only shut her up a bit."

Griffin shook his head. "I oughta run you all in."

Ned was a mean one, but even the threat of jail time made his face pale. He'd been locked up twice in his life. Jail was a dry place.

"We won't shoot anymore," he told them in a petulant voice; he sounded like a spoiled child.

"Who's that?"

"Shut your mouth, Critter," his father turned on him, but Griffin answered.

"That's my deputy, Critter." The sheriff's voice was cold. "You take a good look at him. You too, Rush and Possum. We are not going to put up with this any longer. You'd best keep that in mind."

While Griffin held his shotgun on all of them, he ordered Slater to collect the guns.

"You can come for them in two weeks. Not a day before. Now keep it clean, boys, or I'll run the lot of you in and raid the house and barn."

The lawmen did not stick around much longer, but both were aware of the dark, angry eyes that followed them.

"It's going to come to a head one of these days, and someone is going to get hurt," Griffin predicted.

"I'm sure you're right. Some things you can avoid, and some you have to deal with when they come. Unless they up and move, it's probably going to get worse before it gets better."

Griffin couldn't have agreed with him more, but right now he had no solution. Ideas and plans shifted through his mind all the way back into town. They did battle with thoughts of his wedding in a week's time. Not for the first time, he asked God to let him be there for Tess.

Fourteen

"WHAT DO YOU MEAN, NO?"

"Just that, Libby. The answer is no."

Liberty stared at the man she thought she might be in love with and wondered if she knew him at all. The wedding had been wonderful. Tess had been stunningly beautiful, and Griffin's eyes had been full of love as they joined hands and vowed their lives to one another. Now it was Monday morning, and all that had faded. Liberty had gotten up, climbed into her work clothes, and headed to the jail, only to have Slater tell her to go home.

"Slater," she tried a new tact. "Griff and Tess don't come back until Wednesday."

"Be that as it may, you can't fill in."

"What if something dangerous comes up?"

"I'll call Price."

Liberty was instantly angry. "Price is no lawman!"

"But he does know how to use a gun, and he told me to call me if I needed him." Slater spoke with more calm than he felt. Liberty's coming to work was the last thing he'd expected. They had never talked about this, and now he wished they had. It was past time for her to know how he felt on this issue.

"You're going to get your fool head shot off," Liberty retorted, her anger still evident.

"At least it won't be yours" was all the deputy said, sending Liberty storming from the office.

Liberty was some ways up the street before she realized she'd left without Morton. She stormed back up the walk, swung into the saddle, and heeled him too hard for the short ride home. The poor horse had never been treated so roughly. By the time she stabled the beast and hit the kitchen door, she was in the finest rage she'd ever known.

"Liberty!" her mother exclaimed, naturally surprised. "What in the world?"

Liberty was ready to explode, but reason took over. Laura had come off the floor where she was playing, and a sudden view of her mother's expanding waistline caused Liberty to remember that she was not the only person in the world. Willing herself to calm down, she took a seat at the table and accepted the mug of coffee her mother set before her.

"Laura..." Kate began.

"You want me to play somewhere else, don't you?"

"Well," Kate hesitated, hoping she didn't do this too often, "only if you want to."

"I don't. I want to know why Libby's face is all red."

The room was silent for several seconds. Kate had no idea what to do, and Liberty was still working on calming down. She finally looked at her small sister's concerned face.

"It's nice of you to care so much, Laura," Liberty said. "I would like to talk with Mam. Do you think you could give us a few minutes alone?"

"Are you mad at me?"

"Not at all, and I'm very sorry that I acted that way when I came in."

Laura nodded. Liberty's voice had returned to normal. All was right in the world. Both older women watched the little girl skip from the room, and when she left, Kate sat opposite the small table in the kitchen.

"What's up?" She didn't hesitate; Laura would not want to stay gone all morning.

"I just had an argument with Slater."

"About?"

"My working. He told me that I couldn't fill in and to go home."

"I would think you would be glad of that, Lib. I thought you'd been rather relieved."

Liberty knew it was time for the truth. "I haven't been near so relieved as I've let on."

"Meaning?"

"I just don't feel needed by Griffin any longer," she said, finally telling the truth. "Slater has fit in so well. I thought Griff would need me from time to time. I know it hasn't been that long, but I feel so left out."

"So Griffin didn't ask you to go down there this morning and help?"

"He shouldn't have to ask me. He knows I'll just naturally fill in."

"But he didn't ask you, did he, Libby?" her mother asked again.

"No."

"So Slater's telling you to leave did not sit well."

Liberty shook her head in confusion. "I know he needs me, Mam. Why can't he see that?"

For the first time ever Kate saw how unhealthy her daughter's situation might be. It never occurred to her that Liberty wouldn't be able to give up the job. She'd always been too busy being thankful that her daughter could be there for her son. Clearly, Slater had other ideas. Kate was in a sudden quandary. Her natural bent was toward her child, but she certainly admired Slater's desire to keep Liberty safe.

"What was his reason?" Kate asked.

"I don't think he wants me hurt," Liberty said, some disgust coming back into her voice. "I can take care of myself, Mam. I think I've more than proved that."

Kate's brow lowered. "What's really going on here, Liberty? It doesn't sound to me as though you want to help so much as you want to prove that you can."

Liberty looked so crushed that Kate almost retracted the words, but she took long enough to decide that Liberty's face changed again.

"I don't know," Liberty admitted. "I want to say that's not true, but you might be right. Clearly my pride is involved, or I wouldn't have gotten so angry."

Kate only nodded.

"I think I'll head up to my room now. Tell Laura I'll play with her in a little while."

"All right. What are you going to do?"

"Spend some time reading my Bible and praying. I've got a lot of thinking to do."

Kate stayed where she was as Liberty left the room. She had work to do—lots of it—but right now her daughter needed prayer. She was still praying for her when Laura returned. Kate carried on, seeming as normal as ever to Laura, but her heart was full of doubts and questions, all of which she had to leave with the Lord. No easy task. It was close to lunchtime before she surrendered and knew God's peace.

�»🌿🌿

He divided the sea, and caused them to pass through; and he made the waters to stand up as a heap. In the daytime also he led them with a cloud, and all the night with a light of fire. He cleaved the rocks in the wilderness, and gave them drink as out of the great depths. He brought streams also out of the rock, and caused waters to run down like rivers. And they sinned yet more against him by provoking the most High in the wilderness. And they tempted God in their heart by asking for meat for their lust.

Liberty read these verses in Psalm 78 several times. The children of Israel had been brought from slavery and bondage, but all they did was complain about what they'd been forced to leave behind. God had given them an abundance. Every need was met. He showed His love for them over and over, but they still complained and wanted more.

I'm just like they are, Liberty now told the Lord, tears clogging her throat. *You've given me so much to thank You for, but I want something different. You allowed me to help Griffin, but when Slater doesn't want me, I grow angry. I'm sorry, Lord. I'm so willful and full of pride. I think Mam is right. I want to prove that I can do this. I've never seen it that way before.*

Liberty suddenly rolled onto her back. "I'm terrified," she whispered, her eyes on the wood molding at the edge of the ceiling. Liberty said the words, but not even that made it clear to her. She knew she was frightened, but she wasn't sure of what. Not being wanted? Not being good enough? The answer wasn't obvious to her, but one thing was: She had to go back to the jailhouse and apologize to Slater. She had behaved terribly. Griffin had put him in charge, and she'd treated him with contempt because she didn't get her way.

Liberty did take time to put a puzzle together with Laura, but when she left the house an hour later, she was in one of her best dresses, her hair brushed away from her face and falling long down her back. There hadn't been much color in her face when she left, but just the thought of facing Slater made her blush, and she knew there would be more than enough color when she saw him.

It was something of a letdown to find the office empty, but she was not put off. She paced around the small confines and hoped he wouldn't be hours. She was determined to see him before she left. She turned when she heard boot steps on the boardwalk, and sure enough, he opened the door a moment later. Liberty watched him freeze and then come in slowly. She spoke the moment the door was shut.

"I'm sorry."

Slater covered the distance between them in an instant, coming to stand close in front of her.

"Thank you," he said softly, his eyes taking in every detail of the face he loved.

"It was presumptuous of me and disrespectful. I am very sorry, Slater."

Slater's hand came up, and with the backs of his fingers he stroked her baby-soft cheek, wishing with all his might that it could be his lips instead.

"I was going to talk with you," he finally said. "I'm so glad you came to me. The time was dragging because I wanted to see you so much."

"Oh, Slater. Have you always been so understanding?"

He smiled. "Did you think I would order you into the street?"

Liberty chuckled. "No, but I wouldn't have been too surprised if you didn't want to speak to me for a while."

"That's never going to happen. Do you hear me?"

Liberty nodded. She desperately wanted to tell him what was in her heart—the fears, the love—all of it, but it had to come from him first. She thought he might be ready for that, but until it happened, she couldn't be sure. The silence was making her tense, so she invited him to dinner.

"I'd like to come, but I'm not sure I can spare the time."

Liberty understood. She had watched her brother as sheriff for a long time.

"Can you tell me something, Slater?" Liberty asked, wondering why she hadn't asked him before.

"Sure."

"Why didn't you want my help? Have I done something that makes you think you can't trust me?"

"Not at all. I know how good you are, but my answer may not be the one you want to hear."

Liberty frowned. He could very well be right, but she still wanted to know.

"Will you tell me anyway?"

"If you want me to, yes." Wondering if she could handle his feelings on the matter, Slater looked at her for a moment and then plunged in. "I haven't liked this arrangement from the beginning. I don't think Griffin should be using you as a backup. I think it's too dangerous."

Libby blinked in surprise but still said, "Slater, what does Griffin do when there's no one else?"

Slater tenderly put his hands on Liberty's shoulders, his touch light. "Don't misunderstand me right now, Libby. I'm glad that Griff is still here because you have a clear head and good aim, but I don't think Griff should even use you as an option. I can't help but wonder if he might not have looked a little harder for a deputy if you hadn't been so available."

Liberty's head was spinning. This was so new to her. They had always done it this way. Her father had taught her, and she had carried on to do what was needed, always feeling that even though he was gone, she had his blessing. She shook her head a little. She wanted to be available for Griffin, and right now she wasn't convinced that she couldn't do that.

"Are you all right?" Slater asked.

"I am, Slater, but I can't tell you that I agree. I don't know what I'm feeling right now. I've got to think."

Slater could only nod. He expected no less, but that didn't change his disappointment. This was a major issue in his mind. The pain in his heart forced him to go to the Lord, the only good thing he could see in this situation. Liberty didn't stick around much longer, but that wasn't all bad. He found he needed time to think as badly as she did.

❧ ❧ ❧

"A baby?" Laura's little face showed her shock and delight.

"That's right," Duffy told her. "This summer he or she will be here."

"Can he sleep with me?" Zach wished to know.

"Well," Kate told him gently, "the baby will have his own bed, but maybe when he's a little older."

"Does Libby know?" Laura asked.

"Yes."

"And Griffin and Tess?"

"Yes."

"Does Slater?" she tried again, and her parents laughed; she simply had to share this news.

"I don't think he does," Duffy said. "Did you need to tell someone?"

Laura nodded and looked down at her mother's stomach.

"You're going to get fat, aren't you, Mam?"

Kate smiled. "I suppose I am."

"Laura!" Zach looked shocked. "Mam will never be fat. It's not the same when you have a baby."

Laura nodded—she was always amazingly contrite when Zach rebuked her—but her eyes still strayed to her mother's waistline. Kate was increasing rapidly now, being over the halfway point. It was one of those things a child wouldn't notice unless told, and Laura was now noticing plenty.

"Does the baby make you tired, Mam?" Zach asked sweetly, and Kate leaned to kiss him.

"At times, yes. Have I been crabby with you?"

"No, but you fell asleep in the kitchen that one day, and I wondered."

"That was very observant of you, Zach," his father praised. "A woman does tire easily when she's expecting."

"Will there be more?" the six-year-old asked.

"We don't know. We didn't know that God would send us this baby, but we know that God knows what's best for us."

Zach sighed. "A baby. I've always wanted a baby."

Duffy and Kate shared a warm smile. God had surely given them the most precious children in the world. They were still thinking on this when Laura scrambled from her mother's lap.

"Where are you going?" Duffy wished to know.

"To the front porch in case someone walks by," she answered as she went.

"Why?" Zach asked first.

"So I can tell him Mam is having a baby."

"Laura." Duffy called her back even as Kate and Zach dissolved into laughter. Kate didn't know what God had planned for them, but if it was another Laura, it was sure to be fun.

🌿 🌿 🌿

"How is it?" Tess look anxiously across the table at her mate.

"Very good," Griffin told her after he swallowed. "Were you worried?"

Tess nodded a hesitant yes.

"Why?"

"Oh, well, I'm still getting used to a different stove, and this is a new recipe. I wanted everything to be just right."

Griffin sat back a little. "I was crazy not to marry you the first time I laid eyes on you."

Tess smiled. "Well, *I* think so, but sometimes it takes you a little longer."

Griffin reached over and took her hand. "I love you, Tess."

The bride sighed. "It's funny, but I can't hear that too much."

"I'll have to remember that," Griffin responded.

They continued to eat, but as Tess watched her husband, she could tell something was on his mind.

"Did anything happen today, Griff?"

Griffin looked at her. "Slater told me that he and Libby had it out while we were away."

Tess put her fork aside. "Why did he wait almost a week to tell you?"

"I don't know. Maybe he was still trying to gauge whether he should."

"Can you tell me what happened?"

"He didn't go into great detail, but he wanted to know if I had asked her to come and fill in while I was gone. She evidently arrived all ready for work, and he told her she couldn't stay."

"And she was unhappy about that," Tess stated.

"I think you were right, Tess. She is more attached to the job than I thought. I don't know how I feel about that."

"Do you think it would help to talk with her?"

"I would say yes, but I don't want her to feel that Slater snuck around her and reported. He said it ended well; she even came and apologized. I guess I'm hoping she'll mention it to me."

"And if she doesn't?"

"I don't know," he said honestly.

"Will you continue to ask her to work?"

Griffin stared at his wife. That really was the sticking point in all of this. When he needed help, his sister came to mind so easily. But Slater was so against it, and Griffin had such a high regard for his new deputy...

"I don't know," he said one more time and went back to his food. Both husband and wife were thoughtful for the next several minutes.

☙ ☙ ☙

"This fabric is nice," Mrs. Tobler told Liberty the second week of February. "I think this color would be good on you too."

"I've never had a purple dress." Liberty forced herself to be honest, even amid the generosity. "I guess I had blue or green in mind."

"Well, I've got those too. Just give me a minute!"

Mrs. Tobler was in the mood to sew. Liberty had never known her to be in any other mood, but this was the plan in her mind when she stopped by the day before and vowed to start with Liberty, move to Laura, and then make a dress for Kate, and even one for the baby if it was a girl. The ladies were all naturally pleased, and because Liberty felt at loose ends lately, she was glad that Mrs. Tobler wanted to start the next day.

"How's this blue?"

"Oh, this is beautiful."

"I like it too, but let's not be too hasty!"

Liberty smiled. Mrs. Tobler was always the same.

"What is that noise?" she exclaimed in irritation. "I just keep hearing it!"

Liberty thought she heard something too, but her host had gone back to excavating in the closet and grumbling again, so she wasn't sure.

Bolts of fabric and an hour later, they agreed on one. It was a deep green piece with a tiny yellow flower all over it. The yellow flower seemed to make Liberty's eyes come alive. Once Mrs. Tobler saw it draped over her, she would not look at anything else. In just a matter of minutes, Liberty was being fitted with a pattern.

🌹 🌹 🌹

"I think there's been a murder," Keaton Saint said almost as soon as he walked in the door.

"Why do you think that, Mr. Saint?" Griffin asked. He and Slater had come to full attention.

"Because my neighbor, Mrs. Mills, is missing, and I've been hearing strange noises."

"What kind of noises?"

"Digging."

Griffin took a moment to compute this.

"Her nephew was visiting, wasn't he?"

"He's still there."

"We'll check it out for you, all right?"

The tall man solemnly thanked him, turned, and went on his way.

"How reliable is he?" Slater asked as soon as the door closed.

"Very. He's lived here for years. He's retired now, but he used to run the library and teach part-time."

"Where does he live?"

"Two doors down from Mrs. Tobler. The house he's talking about would be next to hers as well."

"A small, two-story white house?"

"That's the one."

The men had exchanged all of this as they moved to their horses. They rode without haste toward the Mills place, both hoping Mr. Saint was wrong but knowing that such an announcement could not be ignored. Griffin led the way up to the front door, and it took several knocks for someone to answer.

"Yes?" an impeccably dressed man answered as he stood looking out at them. He had an eastern air about him, and his voice was clipped and precise.

"I'm Sheriff Drake," Griffin said congenially. "Could I please talk to Mrs. Mills?"

"My aunt is out of town right now," the man said.

"I see. And you would be?"

"Her nephew, Davis Mills."

"Well, Mr. Mills, when do you expect her back?"

"She didn't say," he said very swiftly and then seemed to reconsider. "Actually, I just remembered a letter she sent. Maybe she mentions her return date. I'll check."

Griffin and Slater exchanged a glance, both men wishing Griffin hadn't given him such an easy way out and also wishing that Davis had left the door open.

"Not a word, I'm afraid," the nephew told them the moment he reopened the portal.

"Where has she gone?" Slater asked.

"Dallas," he said very smoothly.

"And you have no idea when she plans to return?"

"I'm afraid not." His smile was almost angelic.

"Well, please do us a favor, Mr. Mills, and ask her to come by the office when she returns," Griffin said. "I'd like to speak with her."

"I'll do that."

The door was shut again, and the men had no choice but to move away, but neither one was buying the story. Plans bounced around in both men's minds, and they waited only until they were back at the office to discuss them.

Fifteen

"SINCE MR. SAINT CAME TO US," Slater began, "I wonder if he would be open to our using his home for surveillance."

"I was thinking the same thing. I would guess that he wouldn't care to be disturbed, but the very fact that he came to the office might indicate some willingness."

"How long do we want to wait?"

Griffin's look was grim. "If Mrs. Mills is dead, then there's no hurry to help her, but if Davis is planning to escape or do something with the body, then we need to keep tabs on him."

The door opened suddenly, and both men were surprised to see Mr. Saint enter.

"Did you speak to Mrs. Mills?" he wasted no time in asking; he wasn't nearly so composed as earlier. "Did you see her?"

"I'm afraid not, Mr. Saint. Her nephew says she's out of town."

The man dropped into a chair.

"She does like to travel, but she always tells me when she goes. This nephew has visited before, and she did go away the last time he was here, but not for this long. She seems very tense when he comes, and his manner is so stiff and formal. I suppose it's terrible to accuse him of anything, but something is not right in that house. I just know it."

"When was the last day you saw her?"

"Thursday. She was in her front yard and waved to me as I came down the street."

"This is Tuesday," Griffin murmured out loud, taking a minute to gather his thoughts. "I think I need to know more, Mr. Saint. Tell me everything you've heard and seen in the last five days."

Mr. Saint recounted things as best he could. There were times when he heard short bouts of the digging noise during the day, but it was especially loud and continuous at night. He talked to the men for the better part of an hour, and when he was done, Griffin knew what he wanted to do. Mr. Saint was very cooperative, and Griffin sent Slater home before lunch to get some rest. They would start their work right after sundown.

☙ ☙ ☙

"All right, Libby. I'm going to sew for a while. You come back in the morning for a fitting."

"Okay. Thank you, Mrs. Tobler."

The woman didn't even answer. She was already bent over her machine. Liberty let herself out the back door. She had walked instead of ridden and was all set to head for home when she heard the sound. It was coming from Mrs. Mills' and sounded like digging. Liberty had been wandering in and out of these homes since she was a child. For this reason she approached the back porch, opened the door, and called inside.

"Mrs. Mills? Are you here?"

Liberty heard nothing, which only caused her to move more fully inside.

"Mrs. Mills, it's Libby. I was just next door at Mrs. Tobler's and thought I would stop to say hi." Liberty didn't add that she wanted to know if she was all right. Some of the older ladies in town took offense to that idea.

"Mrs. Mills?" she tried again, this time moving through the kitchen toward the living room. What she saw caused her to blink. The rug was rolled back and there was a huge hole in the living room floor. The boards had been brought up, and even from several feet away, she could see a mound of dirt so high that it was above the line of the floor.

"What in the world are you up to?" Liberty said softly as she approached. She stared down at the bags still in the hole, her eyes huge. They looked like money sacks.

"Mrs.—" she looked up to try again but stopped. A man calmly stood to one side of the room. He held a derringer. It was pointed right at her.

"You shouldn't have come in here," he said congenially. "I wish you hadn't."

"Well, I can leave again," Liberty said, trying to be calm.

"I'm afraid that won't do at all. I've seen you around. You know too many people in town."

Liberty swallowed. "I just wanted to check on Mrs. Mills."

"Why is everyone so interested in Mrs. Mills today?" The man sounded testy. With that he motioned with the gun, and Liberty backed herself into the kitchen. She thought she might be able to bolt for the door but took too long to decide. The man came forward, shut it, and ordered her to sit at the table.

"Where is Mrs. Mills?" Liberty asked quietly, her eyes straying back to the hole in the floor. To her surprise the man smiled.

"You think I've murdered my aunt? How barbaric."

"Where is she?"

"Out of town. Just like I told the sheriff. I don't know why people can't leave well enough alone."

Liberty waited for him to take his eyes from her so she could make some kind of move, but he never did.

"I guess it will have to be the closet. The one by the front door locks."

"When will Mrs. Mills be back?" Liberty asked in an attempt to stay calm.

"I'm not entirely sure," he replied absently as he tried to think.

"Are you really her nephew?"

"On her late husband's side, yes."

"Does she know what you're up to?"

"Come along," he commanded, ignoring the question this time. "Back through the living room, and watch the hole."

Liberty moved as slowly as she could get away with. It wasn't much floor space to cross, but she moved at a snail's pace. The front door was almost in reach, but Davis took that moment to put the gun right against her back.

"All right now," he said as he opened the closet. It was full of coats, but there was plenty of room to stand. "In you go."

Liberty stepped inside and turned to look at him. She tried for her sternest deputy look.

"What's your name?"

"Davis. And yours?"

"Liberty."

His brows rose and he chuckled. "Rather ironic, isn't it? I'm locking freedom in the closet."

The door shut in her face, and she heard the key turn before she listened to the hollow sound of his shoes as he walked away. For several seconds she felt as though she were dreaming. Not in all of her years of law enforcement had she been held captive. Now here she was—no gun—and locked in a closet.

"Are you going to put up with this?" Liberty said to the darkness around her. With that she began to pound and yell. She kicked on the door, throwing herself against it with such force that she fell out when it opened. She would have continued to yell, but there was a derringer in her face.

"You can't do this," Davis said softly. His voice was still congenial, but his eyes were hard. "I have to leave town soon, and I can't have you disturbing me. Now you need to stay in here and be quiet. Have I made myself clear?"

Liberty nodded, very real fear covering her features. Davis turned her with a hand to her arm and closed the door while her back was still to him.

"That was stupid, Libby," she breathed. "He could have shot you."

She groped for the wall and slid down to a sitting position, her legs drawn up and her arms around her knees.

Show me what to do, Lord. Show me a way out of this. I don't know if Mrs. Mills is all right or not, but I could get myself shot. He's obviously stolen that money. He needs to go to jail for that.

Liberty stopped when she realized he had said he was leaving town soon. She let her head fall back against the wall and prayed again, wishing there was some way to go for help.

🌹 🌹 🌹

"This is for Libby when she comes home," Laura told Kate as they sat down to lunch.

"What is it?"

"A picture of our family with the new baby."

"Let me see."

"This is Papa and this is Zach. Libby is by me, and I'm holding the baby."

"Where am I?"

"You're still in bed."

Kate laughed. "I don't know whether to thank you or to be insulted."

Laura frowned at her, since the word "insulted" was new, but Kate only blew a kiss in her direction. Weary from a morning of work, Kate sat back a little in the chair, a sigh escaping her as she took a bite of sandwich.

At times like this, Lord, I feel as though I'm going to be tired for the rest of my life. My attitude has been anxious, and I feel achy and grumpy all the time. That's not fair to You or any of my family. Please help me to...

Laura was going to ask her mother for more milk but saw that her eyes were closed. Her mother's limp hand and sandwich lay in her lap, and for a moment Laura just stared at her. When she didn't open her eyes, Laura, carrying her own sandwich, moved to the chair right next to her mother and simply sat still until she awakened.

⁂

Liberty had moved as quietly as she knew how, but in the still confines of the closet it sounded so loud. She only hoped that all the digging and movement from the living room was muffling the sound.

Liberty had pushed the hem of her dress under the door as far as she could get it. She then proceeded to use first a hairpin, then the slim heel of a shoe she encountered, and finally what she thought might be a knitting needle, to try to push the key from the lock. She knew the sound of the key dropping might give her away, but she was determined to get out of this closet. She had sat quietly for the longest time before realizing that Mr. Mills was working. Feeling that she had little to lose, she decided to try. She thought she might have just gotten it when the door opened.

Without a word from her captor the sewing implement was plucked from her hand, and she looked up into enraged features.

"The thought of trussing you up is abhorrent to me, but if that's what it takes to keep you quiet, I'll do it. You must understand that I won't let anything stop me from leaving here. Now this is my last warning."

The door closing once again, Liberty let her shoulders slump. This was such a mess. How long would it be before she was missed at home? Quite possibly hours. Her mother knew what Mrs. Tobler was like and would assume that she'd wanted her to stay all day. Liberty worked to keep her head clear, but it was getting hard. For the first time since she could remember, she wanted to panic.

Stretching out on her side, she prayed and tried to calm her heart. She thought of every verse that would come to mind, going slowly over the words and even singing hymns in her heart. While mentally going through the song she was supposed to play in church on Sunday morning, her fingers moving over imaginary keys, she must have fallen asleep. She hadn't planned to do that, but the door was suddenly opening again and she'd heard no footsteps.

"I have to take care of this now," her jailer began by saying. "I won't have your death on my mind."

Liberty stared at him as he set a basket, presumably of food, and a jug beside her.

"You'll have to eat sparingly, but you won't starve."

"You can't be serious!" Liberty said in outrage, coming awake in a hurry. "You can't leave me in here."

"I don't think it will be long. Aunt likes her home too much. She should be back any day now."

Liberty had come to her feet, causing Davis to back away a little.

"If I die," she said fiercely, "it'll be on your head. Don't try to tell yourself anything else!"

"You'll be fine," he said with an irritating confidence, the door starting to close. "And don't forget," he immediately opened it again to say, "I will tie you up if you make a single noise."

Liberty had never known such frustration. To be this helpless was maddening. She made herself sit back down and take slow, even breaths. Bumping the jug, she realized she was thirsty. She'd missed lunch, but as soon as she'd had a drink, her mind went back to obtaining her freedom. It might take some time, but she *would* come up with a plan.

🥀 🥀 🥀

"And then Mam fell asleep during her sandwich," Laura told Griffin. Knowing he would have to work late, he had stopped by the house and found her home with Tess. "She was tired."

"What did you do?"

"I just sat there beside her."

"That was nice of you. Did Libby get you the milk you wanted?"

"Libby wasn't home. She's been at Mrs. Tobler's all day getting a new dress. She didn't even come home for lunch or to help Mam start dinner."

Griffin's entire frame stiffened. Mr. Saint, Mrs. Mills, and Mrs. Tobler had been on his mind since he'd started making plans for that night. But this news about Liberty could not wait that long.

"I need to head out for a little bit," Griffin rose and said. "I'll check back with you, Tess." He gave her a swift kiss.

"All right," Tess said calmly, thinking of the little girl next to her. But she knew something was wrong and began to pray.

"'Bye, Laura," he said as he kissed the top of her head.

"'Bye."

Griffin tried not to run. He debated going all the way to the Hathaways' to get Slater but decided to swing by the office instead. His heart slowed with relief to see Arrow out front.

"I need you" was all he said, his head going swiftly inside and back out again. Slater was fast to respond, and on the way to the Mills', Griffin gave him the news.

"I hope it's just an uncomfortable hunch that doesn't pan out."

"You and me both," Slater agreed. Hunch or not, it needed to be checked. If Liberty was there and they didn't follow this lead, they would never forgive themselves.

In the next few seconds Griffin told Slater what he wanted to do. They had given Davis Mills the benefit of the doubt earlier that day and knocked on the front door. Griffin was not going to make that mistake again.

☙ ☙ ☙

Liberty listened to the noise of doors opening or furniture moving, she couldn't decide which. She did know one thing, however—if he was moving furniture, that meant that the hole was covered and he was getting ready to leave. Even if he had the gun with him again, Liberty was not going to take this lying down. The pointed-heel shoes in her hands, she launched her assault against the door with a vengeance.

"Let me out! Do you hear me? I said, GET ME OUT OF HERE!"

Liberty continued to shout, kick, and beat against the door until her hair flew in her face and her throat felt raw. She screamed for all she was worth, and when the door was opened, she attacked the man with the shoes, her arms swinging in a desperate attempt to gain the upper hand.

She found herself subdued, arms locked at her sides in a tight grasp. It happened so swiftly that for a moment she couldn't breathe. When she did find her breath, she looked up into Slater Rawlings' face.

"Oh, Slater," Liberty whispered. "Did I hurt you?"

Slater smiled, but the answer was clear: His cheek was bleeding and one eyelid was already beginning to swell.

"Are you all right?" was all he wanted to know.

"Yes. Oh, Slater," she cried again.

"What happened here, Libby?"

It was Griffin. Liberty hadn't even seen him. For the first time in her life, Liberty began to babble. Both Griffin and Slater listened to words like "dirt mounds, money sacks, water jug, derringer, front door, key, shoes," and so on. They both tried to take in the sequence, but she kept changing directions on them, all the time gesturing to the room and pointing out the dust that lay in thick layers on the furniture.

"Take her home," Griffin said. "I'll make a final check here and with Mr. Saint, then see if the neighbors spotted anyone."

Liberty told herself to offer her services, but Griffin had looked at her strangely. It was then that she realized this had been more upsetting than she first thought.

"I'm sorry," she heard herself say.

Griffin hugged her. "We're just glad you're all right."

"I should be helping you."

Griffin shook his head. "I'll be by later and we'll talk about it, okay?"

Liberty nodded, and Slater took her by the arm. She was shocked to see it was almost dark out. Why had she thought that just a few hours had passed? And when had she left Mrs. Tobler's to head home?

"Here we go," Slater said, and Liberty looked up to see that he'd brought his horse close to the step and was reaching for her. Liberty automatically lifted her arms, and a moment later she was sitting across the front of Arrow's saddle. Slater's arms came around her to hold the reins, and Liberty let herself relax against him. Actually, she gave no thought to what she was doing. She just didn't have the strength right now to sit up straight.

"Slater?"

"Yeah?"

"He took the floor apart and had bags of money buried in the dirt."

"In the living room?"

"Yes. He wouldn't let me out of the closet." She sighed a little. "I thought about you."

"Good thoughts?"

She nodded against him, and Slater had everything he could do not to tip her head back and kiss her. It was so nice to have her close.

Liberty's full weight was leaning against Slater by the time they arrived at the house, and for an instant he wondered if she might have fallen asleep. She wasn't asleep, but he had to steady her on her feet once they dismounted.

"Well, Libby," her mother said as soon as they both walked in the kitchen door, "Mrs. Tobler must have been sewing with a vengeance."

Liberty shrugged a little as her mother got a better look at her.

"Is Duffy here, Kate?" Slater asked.

"In the living room reading with Zach," she answered while taking in the marks on his face. "What's happened?"

The next hour was spent explaining and checking wounds. Liberty changed clothes and ate with the family, but her disappointment over Slater not staying was keen. He'd gone back to check on Griffin.

When Griffin learned that no one had seen a thing, he'd gone back to the office, searched through the wanted circulars, and filled out a report, readying it completely to be mailed the next day. He'd also gone back to the house and checked out what Liberty had told Slater about the living room floor, but there was nothing else he could do. Davis Mills had to be miles out of town by now, and Shotgun's sheriff had to leave it at that. He only hoped that Mrs. Mills would return soon and not be buried under her own living room floor.

🌿 🌿 🌿

"All this time, Duff—" Kate said after they were in bed that night. "All this time I thought if Libby wasn't in law enforcement, she'd be safe, and here she gets grabbed just trying to check on Mrs. Mills. I can't help but wonder what things are coming to."

"It's like we've talked about before, Kate. Don't expect things to get better. It won't happen."

Kate nodded. Sometimes Duffy's logical mind infuriated her, but not now. She needed to think clearly, or she would never let Liberty out of the house again.

"I'm so glad Griffin and Slater were there, Duffy, so very glad. I don't know if I could lose my Libby. I don't think I can."

Kate's first tears flowed. She had wanted to cry when she heard what happened but held herself in check, trying to be strong for her daughter, who still looked a little shocked and confused during dinner.

"She's always been the calm one, Duffy," Kate sobbed. "She looked just like a lost child, and then I saw Slater's face. I know he loves her. I know it killed him to have to leave before she came back downstairs."

Duffy held her and thought about God's promises. Never did He tell His children that this life would be safe and pain free. Indeed, every book in the Bible indicated otherwise. Nevertheless, God did promise never to desert His loved ones or give them more than they could handle. Picturing Liberty in that closet was a sickening thing. The man could have done anything, but they all had to choose to take God at His Word, which meant Liberty wasn't alone. The all-powerful God of the universe had been right there beside her at every moment.

"I have to sleep now," Kate said, her voice slurred with fatigue.

"Okay. I'm going to check on the kids one more time. I'll see you in the morning."

"I love you, Duffy."

"I love you too, Kate," he said before kissing her cheek.

The doctor slipped quietly from the room, heading down the hall to see Laura and Zach, and finally to knock gently before opening Liberty's door a crack. There was no light on, but the moonlight coming from the window told him Liberty was standing at the glass looking out.

"Are you all right?" her stepfather asked.

"Just a little restless," Liberty told him as she turned and let the curtain fall back into place. "I can't stop thinking about everything he said and trying to decipher if he gave any clues as to where he was headed."

"Will you take some advice?"

"Certainly."

"Stop being an officer of the law and try to sleep. All of this will still be here in the morning."

"All right," Liberty agreed and even thanked Duffy as he shut the door, but his words took her off in another direction. *Stop being an officer of the law.* Why did that one simple sentence hurt so much? Right now Liberty didn't have a clue, and the prospect of finding out made her feel pretty helpless.

Seeing no other option, she climbed into bed, willing herself to sleep. It took some time and some confessing, since she'd started to worry, but by the time she drifted off to sleep, she was ready to leave the whole affair in God's capable hands.

🌹 🌹 🌹

Three mornings after the uproar at Mrs. Mills' house, a newcomer walked from the hotel, his eyes taking in the neat, even streets of Shotgun's small community. He'd arrived rather late the night before and opted to bunk at the hotel for that night. The room had been comfortable and warm, and he felt rested as he started up the street.

He hadn't gone far when he spotted Shotgun's deputy. Slater stood in front of the general store with a mountain of a man and a tiny, enraged woman.

"I tell you it's robbery!" Mrs. Swenson insisted, her whole frame vibrating in irritation. "And I want this man arrested."

"Mrs. Swenson." Slater's voice was remarkably patient. "Price and Amy may charge whatever they want. It's their store."

"Nonsense! Why, only last year I paid half that much for a tin of peaches. I tell you it's against the law."

Price tried to reason with her, but she would have none of it. She ended up storming down the boardwalk, muttering all the way.

"She'll cool down," Amy said as she came on the scene. "My guess is she'll be back in the morning and pay without a whimper."

Slater nodded as the couple thanked him and went back inside. Slater turned up the street, only then seeing the tall, slim man with the dark red hair who had come from the hotel. He'd leaned against the side of the building, watching the whole scene with great interest. Slater thought he had the warmest brown eyes in Texas. It wasn't hard to figure that Dakota must have headed straight home. Slater began to smile. Cash Rawlings had come to town.

Sixteen

As SOON AS THE BROTHERS were back at the sheriff's office, they embraced for a long time.

"I've missed you, Cash," Slater said, feeling strangely choked up as they drew back.

"You could have come home," the oldest Rawlings said, not unkindly.

"I planned on it but found it wasn't so easy." Cash smiled. "Dak says her name is Libby."

Slater laughed. "She's not the only reason, but she's a good one."

"What's she like?"

"Oh, Cash," Slater sighed. "How much time have you got?"

Cash smiled again; somehow he'd always known that softhearted Slater would be the first to fall.

"Does she know?" he asked next.

"Not directly, but we're getting there."

"So she loves you in return?"

"I hope so."

For a moment they were silent.

"Grandma sends her love."

"How is she?"

"Doing well. Surprisingly enough, she's getting a little more independent. She cut her visit short this last time and headed home. Said she had things to do."

Slater laughed, wishing he could see their father's mother, who, although her son and daughter-in-law had returned to St. Louis, had stayed in Texas.

"I take it Dak came home?" Slater asked.

"On the verge of apoplexy. Said you needed straightening out."

Slater's look was telling.

"I knew it was probably the other way around," Cash confessed, knowing which of his brothers needed more guidance at the moment. "What happened?"

Slater gave his brother a detailed account of the bank shooting, the death of Desna Frank, and Desna's funeral service. Cash had no trouble catching on.

"I wonder how long he's going to fight this."

"I don't know, but this is the most riled up I've ever seen him. He's still angry with me over leaving the Rangers, and it's not like him to carry things around. He left here in a huff. I hated to have him go like that. With our jobs, it could be the last time we ever lay eyes on each other, but he didn't give me much choice."

"No, he didn't, but you did the right thing by letting him go. Dak is a big boy—too old to be leaving in a rage—but to beg him to stay wouldn't have been wise. He needs to see that you're man enough to make this choice and not just his kid brother anymore."

"He's certainly protective. If I hadn't met Libby's family, he probably would have trussed me up, thrown me over his saddle, and carried me off."

"So he has at least seen that you've made a life here?"

"Yes. In fact, I think he was on his way to accepting that, but the service set him off. He'd even been coming to church with me, and he's threatened me if I let Libby get away."

Cash suddenly frowned. "He also mumbled something about her arresting you."

Slater took some time to explain the way he'd met Liberty, and then said, "You can pray for us, Cash, because her acting as deputy is something I can't live with."

"I will pray, and although I'm not an expert, I will tell you: You're doing well to remember that you can't marry her and expect to change her."

They suddenly smiled at each other, remembering that their mother had learned this the hard way. Charles Rawlings Sr. was as independent a man as any they'd ever known. He raised his boys to be the same way. As much as he loved Virginia Rawlings, Charles was not going to be slowed down. If he wanted to travel, he traveled. Virginia was welcome to go along, but if she didn't want to go, he went without her. He was as faithful as any husband could be, but having a wife and children was not going to alter his lifestyle. Following in the wake of her vagabond husband, Virginia had seen much of the countryside.

"So when can I meet her?" Cash wanted to know.

"It just happens that I'm invited to dinner tonight. I can't stay long since I'll be on duty, but I'm sure they would welcome you with open arms."

"All right. Should I leave my gear at the hotel?"

"Not if you don't mind sharing a bed. It's fairly wide, and as I recall, you don't snore too loudly."

Cash only snorted in disbelief and asked, "By the way, what happened to your eye and cheek?"

"I was attacked by a pair of shoes."

Cash's right brow winged upward. "I think I need to hear about this."

"You will," Slater decided swiftly, "but only *after* you meet Libby."

Cash smiled again. It was so good to see his brother, but seeing him also reminded him of how little time they'd spent together in the last few years. For his part, Cash didn't care if Slater snored all night. The day, however, had the possibilities of dragging. He was most anxious to meet this woman named Libby.

🌿 🌿 🌿

"When Mam has her baby, I'll help her because I'm the big sister. Even if the baby is a boy, I'll still be the big sister."

"I'm sure you'll do a fine job," Cash said seriously. He was being welcomed as his brothers had, by witnessing Laura firsthand and falling just as swiftly in love with her.

"Do you have a baby?" Laura wished to know.

"No. I'm not married."

Laura nodded seriously. "You can share ours when you come to town."

"Thank you very much."

Liberty took that moment to slip into the room. She sat next to Zach and whispered, "What is Laura sharing?"

"The baby."

Liberty's eyes became hysterically round, and Zach had to cover his mouth to muffle laughter. Cash chose that moment to look up at them.

"Cash Rawlings," Slater began, having been waiting for this moment, "please meet Liberty Drake."

"The pleasure is all mine," Cash said as he rose, moving to shake Liberty's hand and bending slightly over her, his eyes alight with pleasure.

"You're tall," Liberty told him.

"Yes. Dakota got the strength; Slater got the manners; and I'm just tall."

Looking at those broad shoulders and the way he bent to catch her eye, Liberty wasn't fooled. She was still smiling at him when Duffy called them to the table.

"Your brother's nice," Liberty had a chance to say softly to Slater as he seated her at the table.

"I was hoping you would think so."

"I can't remember—are any more of you going to show up?"

Slater smiled. "No. Just the three of us. Had enough?"

"Since I haven't figured *you* out—yes."

"What's to figure out?"

Liberty's look was pointed, but Slater had no time to question her.

"So tell us, Cash," Kate began, "how large is your ranch?"

That started the conversation ball rolling, and in seemingly no time at all, Slater said he had to get to work, thanked his host and hostess, and stood.

"I'll walk you out," Liberty offered after Cash told him he would see him that night at the Hathaways'.

Slater stopped on the porch, turning to Liberty as she came out and shut the door.

"So what's to figure out?"

"What?" Liberty questioned right back.

"That's right. What?"

Liberty laughed. "I think next time I'll keep my mouth shut."

"Don't do that. I'll never find out."

Liberty could hear the smile in his voice. There was so much she wanted to say but found her mouth empty.

"Griff will be looking for me," Slater spoke when she didn't. "I'd better scoot."

"Okay. Thanks for coming."

"Thank *you*. Take care of Cash for me."

"We'll do that."

Slater hesitated. There had been one advantage about working construction: Come darkness, you had to quit. Seeing no hope for it, he bid Liberty goodnight and went on his way, asking himself when he was going to have time to get to know this woman better.

🌿 🌿 🌿

"It was nice of you to show me the way, Libby," Cash said as they walked toward the Hathaways'. "It's too bad Slater couldn't be with us."

When Liberty didn't answer, Cash pressed her a little more.

"You do wish Slater could join us, don't you, Libby?"

"I wouldn't have believed it!" she exclaimed suddenly.

"What?" Cash asked from some distance over her head, his voice indicating true confusion.

"Your Texas Ranger brother was something of a matchmaker too. I wouldn't have thought it could run in the family."

Cash hooted with laughter, but just as soon as he found his breath, he tried again.

"What did Dak learn?"

"No more than you're going to."

"Come on, Libby," he coaxed, having swiftly fallen into easy familiarity with her. "Just a hint."

Liberty stopped in the street and looked up at him, dark as it was.

"What is it you want to know?"

"Just how you feel about Shotgun's deputy. Nothing more."

"Is that all? Well, if I had known that..."

Liberty began walking again, and Cash fell into step beside her.

"In case you haven't noticed, Dak and I think a lot of Slater," he said after half a block. "Watching him with you makes us care about you as well."

Liberty stopped suddenly, her heart coming to her throat.

"What do you see when he's with me?"

"Ah, Libby," Cash replied, his voice gentle. "He'll have to tell you that."

Cash heard her sigh in the dark.

"Going to finish walking me to the house now?"

"I already did. That's the Hathaways' right there."

Cash looked toward the trim two-story and back to his companion. "Well, thank you, Libby. I appreciate your showing me."

"You're welcome, Cash. I'm glad you can stay a few days. It should be fun."

"Indeed."

"Goodnight," Liberty said and started away, coming to a stop only when Cash fell into step beside her. "Where are you going?"

"I'm going to walk you back," Cash said simply. "I can't let a lady walk all the way home after dark. And besides," he added outrageously, "I just might get some information out of you yet."

They started back toward the Peterson house to the sound of Liberty's laughter.

☙ ☙ ☙

"Oh, you're cold. Have you been outside?" Tess asked as Griffin climbed into bed late Friday night.

"Yes. We had to check out a disturbance at the Potters'—one that turned out to be nothing at all—and Maddie Flowers kept us standing on her porch until she was completely dressed."

"And all for nothing."

"Yes. The Potters must have started early in the day, because everyone but Rush was passed-out drunk."

"What had Mrs. Flowers wanted?"

"She said she heard noises, and this time we thought we'd catch them in the act. It was dead quiet by the time we arrived, and she was ready for bed."

Tess laughed at his disgruntled tone. Griffin kissed her.

"Your man is freezing in the cold, and all you can do is laugh."

Tess chuckled again.

"If I wasn't so tired, I'd kiss you again," he threatened.

Tess only snuggled close. "There's always the morning."

Griffin sighed and talked to himself. "It's like you've known for some time now, Griff, you should have married the woman the moment you laid eyes on her."

Tess chuckled softly this time, thanking God as she often did that He had brought her husband home safely one more time.

❦ ❦ ❦

"Okay," Liberty said to her small charges the next morning, "we're going into the general store next. Josie, you stick close to Laura, and both of you remember to look with your eyes, not your hands."

Little heads bobbed in agreement, and Liberty watched as her sister, an old pro at shopping, led Josie down the aisle that displayed the toys. When she saw that they were safely ensconced, she began on her list. So much had been on her mind lately. She could still feel herself in that closet; Desna Frank's funeral often came to mind; the Lord was showing her new things in the book of Romans; she was still trying to sort out Slater's feelings on her wearing a badge—and then there was Slater himself. It was a relief for her mother to ask her to shop.

"We've got to stop meeting like this," a soft voice whispered in her ear.

Liberty couldn't stop her smile as she turned to see Slater at her shoulder.

"How are you?" he asked warmly.

"I'm fine. How about yourself?"

"Better all the time."

Liberty smiled into his eyes, her thoughts very loving, and then caught herself.

"We had fun with Cash last night," she said, pretending to be interested in the set of bowls on the shelf.

"He said he enjoyed it too," Slater answered as he studied her profile. He thought her nose turned up in the most adorable way. "He said a very pretty lady escorted him home."

Liberty laughed. "Did he tell you he escorted her right back?"

"He didn't have to. I would have been surprised if he'd done anything else."

Liberty shook her head. "I think the mold was broken after the Rawlings boys were born. I've never known such manners."

"I'll tell Mother next time I write."

"How often do you hear from her?" Liberty wondered aloud.

"Every few months."

"Are they pleased with what you're doing here? I mean, do they wish you'd settled closer to them or the ranch?"

"They know that we're Texans through and through, but my mother would like to see us more often."

"Not your father?"

Slater smiled. "He loves us, but that man is an adventurer. As long as we write and tell him what we're doing and what we've seen, he's happy."

The thought crossed Liberty's mind that his father's feelings might change if there were grandchildren involved. She thought about saying so and then realized how embarrassing that would be.

"Are you blushing?" Slater asked without thinking, causing Liberty to turn even redder.

Slater's manners kicked in at that point and he turned away, only to see Laura and Josie coming toward him.

"Hello, girls," he said quietly. Much as he wanted to question her, he turned away to give Liberty a chance to compose herself. "How are you today?"

"This is my friend Josie. She likes toys too."

"I think toys are pretty fun. Did you have a favorite, Josie?"

"Is the deputy in here?" a man's voice called from the door, and Slater turned away to answer. The three females didn't hear why he was needed. Liberty was tempted to follow and see if she could help, but she would not leave the girls in anyone else's care, not with Josie along. They went on with their shopping before heading to Duffy's office for a visit. Liberty, never knowing where her sister's mind would head, was glad that Laura waited to talk to her until they were gone from the general store, their purchases wrapped in neat brown paper.

"I want to tell you something but not have you be shocked," Laura said as they neared Duffy's office door, Josie going in ahead of them.

"I'll do my best not to be shocked," Liberty told her, already wanting to laugh.

"I hope you marry Slater."

"Why do you hope that?"

"So you can protect each other with your guns."

Liberty only smiled, leaned close, and kissed her soft cheek.

"Now, can I tell you something?"

Laura nodded yes.

"Thank you for not saying anything in front of Slater or anyone else. As long as you always talk quietly to me about Slater, without everyone listening, I won't be shocked. Deal?"

"Deal."

The two joined Josie in Duffy's office, and he was delighted to have them. Liberty, on the other hand, spent some time looking out the window that gave a view of Main Street. She could hear the girls' chatter and Duffy's soothing replies, but her mind was elsewhere; namely, on why Slater had been called away. It was all Liberty could do not to head home, change, and go to his aid. That he wouldn't thank her for this did not enter her mind. She only knew she wanted to protect and be with that man.

Slater and Cash made their way up to the Petersons' front door. Ready as they were for Sunday dinner, they moved slowly. They had the rest of the day together, but

Cash was leaving in the morning, and they didn't know when they would see each other again.

"I knew from your letter, Slate, that you were growing in your church, but it was good to be here and see it first-hand. Pastor Caron does a fine job."

"He's taught me a lot. Griffin has too and probably doesn't even know it."

"It will be great to give such a good report to Grandma, but I know that Dakota is not going to be happy with me. He'll want to have heard that I came here and straightened you out."

"Tess Drake said something to me one day that was a big help with that. She said that Dakota might run into the same man that led me to Christ. I haven't forgotten that. I had had some contact with Des, but never did I dream he would have such an impact on me. I need to be reminded that I'm not the only person who could talk to Dakota or who prays that he'll see the truth. By the time you see him again, Cash, it could be that he'll have done some real soul-searching."

Cash looked at his youngest sibling.

"When did you grow up, Slater?"

Slater smiled a little, but his eyes were thoughtful. "Funny, but some days I find I have so much to learn that I think I'm still a child."

Cash reached to put an arm around his shoulders.

"When I forget how good God has been to me, Slate, I have only to remind myself of the way He reached down and saved Grandma, me, and then you. Considering how self-centered we all were, I call that a miracle."

"I'll miss you, Cash," Slater said, his eyes having to look up a little.

"I'll miss you too. Don't be a stranger."

The men went inside then, Cash so glad that he'd come and Slater having a sudden daydream. He'd like to go home, he'd like it very much, but he wanted to go with a certain woman on his arm; God willing, his wife.

Seventeen

THE GUNSHOTS STARTED AT DAWN, just 24 hours after Cash left town. The house sat off a piece, but the nearest structure was the schoolhouse. Had it been a weekend, Griffin might have let her get it out of her system, but not on a school day. And because it was Bernie, he had to have Liberty. Not even noticing the tightening of Slater's mouth when he told him, he mounted his horse and rode for his mother's, Slater right behind him. And all the time the shots could be heard.

"I need Libby, Mam," he said as he met her in the kitchen.

"I heard the shots, so I think Libby must have too. I'll go up and check."

Kate slipped away, and some time later Liberty arrived on the scene, dressed in work clothes. She looked as calm and confident as ever.

"Bernie?" she asked, strapping on her gun belt.

"Yes. She's a little early this year."

"Too bad she couldn't wait for the weekend."

Slater didn't question any of this but understood that Bernie must be a regular.

The three rode out as soon as Morton had been saddled, Slater stepping forward to do this against his better judgment. The sky was lighting fast, always a help. They rode toward Bernice Shambles' house, coming in on the barn side. She never shot that way. Every year they confiscated her gun, but she always managed to come up with another one. Daryl Shambles had left Bernie more than ten years before, but she had never gotten over it. Every winter she took shots at the tree he'd planted, the main problem being that the tree sat between Bernice's and the school-house.

"We'll have to get around, Lib, or she'll never hear us. The side we tried last year didn't work. Let's go to the other side this time."

"That will give me a better view of the windows," Liberty said. "Let's hope she stops firing long enough to listen."

The horses had been tied, and the three now made their way along the far side of the barn, their steps punctuated by gunshots.

"What is she shooting at?" Slater finally asked.

"The huge tree on the west side of the house."

"Right toward the school," Slater muttered.

"She would be crushed if she hit anyone," Liberty filled in, "but she never thinks of that ahead of time."

"How often does she do this?"

"Once a year too often," Liberty said.

They were in position now, and Griffin tried to holler up at her. He waited for the shots to stop and then began.

"Bernie, put the weapon down!"

More shots were his answer, so the next time they slowed, Liberty gave it a try.

"I want to come in and talk to you, Bernie, but you have to put the gun..."

There was no point in going on.

They were patient. They tried calling to her for close to 20 minutes, but it was no use. Liberty finally got disgusted enough to take the upper hand. Stepping out just enough, she systematically took out four of Bernie's windows.

Dead silence followed and then a small voice.

"Libby? Is that you?"

"I'm out here," she called back.

"Why didn't you say so?"

"I've been trying, but you just kept shooting. Are you hurt?"

"No, but I'm sad."

Liberty started forward but suddenly found herself hauled backward.

"Don't even think about it," Slater said in a voice not to be argued with. He had taken Liberty by the waist and pulled her back until she was against his chest in a no-nonsense hold.

"She'll be calm now," Griffin explained. "We can all go. The only person she'll ever put her gun down for is Libby."

"Then I'll go first," Slater said, moving Liberty behind him and leading the way, knowing he could die in the next instant. Every town had its regulars, but no one could predict everything. As it was, not another shot was fired. The three moved to the door, and Bernie was even there to let them in.

"This is the day," Bernie said, but Liberty didn't comment. Bernie always said the same thing, but over the years the date had fluctuated. Liberty believed that when a person hung onto grief, he or she changed.

"We'll come in and talk to you for a while," Liberty said as she took the gun from her hand.

"You're welcome to talk to Bernie, Lib, but it will have to be at the jailhouse."

This said, Griffin took the cuffs from his belt and handcuffed Bernie's hands behind her back. "This has to stop, Bernie," he went on. "I don't know how else to get through to you. I've been dealing with you since I became sheriff, and how many years had it gone on before that?"

Both Bernie and Liberty stared at him in shock. Griffin ignored his sister and continued to address his prisoner.

"Too long, I'll be bound. Maybe a little time in jail and a hefty fine will make you think about someone other than yourself next year."

"But I miss him," Bernie whined pitifully, but Griffin was not moved.

"You think you miss him? How do you think the parents of the child you shoot will feel? Daryl left here of his own free will. The child or schoolmarm you hit will be a victim."

Liberty was still in shock when Griffin began to lead Bernie away, Slater falling in behind him. Since none of them climbed back onto their horses, they had a bit of a walk as they headed toward town. Bernie was very subdued, and Liberty was angry. She had never seen Griffin act like this toward a woman. What had changed? Slater was an incredible gentleman, but could he have had a hand in this action?

"In you go," Griffin said to Bernie as he opened the cell door. He removed her cuffs but shut and locked the door without looking back. Slater had put Bernie's gun on the desk, and Griffin now tagged it and locked it up.

"Could I see you a moment, Griffin?" Liberty asked, her voice tight.

Griffin had been expecting as much, but not quite so soon.

"Can it wait a few hours, Lib?"

Liberty nodded, but she was not happy. Knowing that her job was done, she told Griffin she'd see him later and bid Slater goodbye, but she didn't go right home. She was so overcome with fury that she didn't think she could be civil even to her own family. She completely disagreed with the way Griffin had handled Bernie, and she never remembered a time when her brother wouldn't allow her to speak to him.

"I don't even know him anymore," Liberty muttered to herself in rage. She wasn't even watching where she was headed and suddenly realized she was on the way back to Bernie's. Another angry spark lit inside of her.

Take a woman off without even letting her gather some things! Well, I'll just do it myself. I'll take things to Bernie and make her the most comfortable prisoner we've ever had. Leave it to a man not to understand.

Liberty all but stomped into the house and began searching for things Bernie might want. Her emotions spiraling completely out of control, she carried on in a fury. The few times she let her mind tell her she was wrong, she pushed the thought away. At the moment she thought she might never speak to her brother, or any man, ever again.

🌿 🌿 🌿

"The sheriff asked me to come by and tell you to ring the school bell right on time, Miss Winters. The shooting's over."

"Oh, thank you, Deputy Rawlings. I appreciate your stopping."

The couple was standing on the school steps. Slater had knocked and been ready to go in, but Miss Winters had suddenly come out and nearly run into him.

"I've got coffee on," she said. "It's a cold morning; may I bring you a cup?"

"Yes, please," Slater said sincerely. He was cold—very cold. They had been out early and then stood in the cold. Then, just after he'd gotten back inside the jailhouse, Griffin had sent him out to the school.

"Here you go," Miss Winters came with two mugs; she had also slipped into her coat.

"Thank you. This is good," Slater told her as he took a sip. "I just remembered that you were coming out to do something. I should drink this and let you get back to work."

"Oh, I just have to hang a sign. I shouldn't have come out without my coat in the first place."

"Do you want some help?"

"I'd love some," she admitted, looking very young and in need of a rescue. "The last time I tried to pound a nail, I hit my hand."

"We can't have that." Slater put his mug aside. "Just show me where you want it."

The next few minutes were filled with hilarity as Slater's cold hands fumbled with the nails, dropping two of them and moving too slowly to catch them before they disappeared into the spaces between the boards. He and Miss Winters were laughing so hard at one point that they couldn't even work. Slater ended up leaning against the building to catch his breath, laughing once again when the schoolteacher commented that it didn't feel that cold anymore.

Across the field, just coming out of Bernie's house, Liberty took in this scene and froze in her steps. She had gathered two bags of items for Bernie, but in the process her anger had cooled. Now, watching the man she loved as he laughed and enjoyed the company of another woman, all anger left her.

There's probably a perfectly good explanation for what I'm seeing, Liberty thought, reason having once again returned. *And if I hadn't been so het up about coming here, I wouldn't have seen them together at all.*

Turning slowly back inside, Liberty replaced the items. By the time she came out the front door again, the steps of the schoolhouse were empty and all was quiet. Liberty climbed into Morton's saddle and turned toward home, wishing she'd repented sooner and was already back in the warmth of that house. She also hoped that Griffin would forget that she wanted to talk to him. She had changed her mind.

❧ ❧ ❧

"Hi," Griffin said kindly as he came to the house just before lunch. "Did you still want to see me, Lib?"

"No," his sister said honestly.

Griffin stared at her as she sat at the kitchen table and calmly frosted a batch of molasses cookies. She had never been secretive with her feelings, but something wasn't right.

"Are you sure?" he tried again, but Laura came into the room.

"Hi, Griff!" she greeted him with a huge smile. Griffin swung her up into his arms for a hug. He could see that she wanted to talk, and most of the time he let her, but not today.

"I need to see Libby. You go find Mam."

"All right," she agreed with such a wistful little face that Griffin had to harden his heart, but he felt compelled to get back to Liberty. He was ready to launch into a discussion the moment he sat at the table with her, but Liberty started first.

"Tell me, Griff. Have you ever known women who control the people around them, even their husbands, by pouting or getting angry?"

"Lots of them."

"Me too," Liberty nodded. "I was upset with you when you put Bernie in jail. I even went to her house to get some of her things so she would be more comfortable, but then I realized where I was. I was at Bernie's house: the woman who shoots at a tree every year because a man left her. I've never known Bernie to say she was wrong or do anything more than whine about how miserable she is. It suddenly became very clear to me why Daryl left."

Griffin studied her. Unless he missed his guess, she'd had a hard morning but was doing better now.

"You're not like Bernie, Lib. I hope you know that."

"But I could be," Liberty said quietly, her eyes on the cookie in her hand. "I didn't see it until today. I've always had things my way, Griff, so there's never been a need to fight you, but today I wanted to argue and interfere. That's not the same as covering for you."

Griffin's heart swelled with love for her. "You're one in a million, Libby."

Liberty smiled over the compliment, her own heart swelling a bit. She was very content right now that she had not made a scene. It had taken several hours for her to calm down completely, but she didn't have to apologize to Griffin or Slater over anything she said.

In the next few minutes, Griffin explained to Liberty why he'd locked Bernie up, and Liberty thought his views were very sound. She returned the kiss he placed on her cheek when he went to find Laura and Mam, thanked him, and went on with the frosting.

She was very glad she didn't have to repent to Slater, but her heart was not quite as settled where that man was concerned. Liberty was finding that not knowing exactly where she stood was terribly unsettling. Each day was filled with thinking of him, praying for him, and wondering where he was, what he was doing, and if he thought of her in return. Today's thoughts, however, were also full of Shotgun's pretty young schoolteacher.

❧ ❧ ❧

"I'm so sorry, Libby," Mrs. Mills said for the fifth time, tears coming to her eyes. "How awful for you. I'm surprised you even want to set foot in here again."

Liberty smiled at her and said honestly, "Nothing has changed, Mrs. Mills."

The living room looked remarkably different than it had a week ago. Everything was spotlessly clean, but it wasn't hard for Liberty to picture the way it had been.

"He was really quite devious, wasn't he, Mrs. Mills?" Liberty said thoughtfully.

"Yes. I haven't been comfortable with him for the last few visits, so I began to travel when he came. It was just a month back when I returned to find things covered with dust. Davis had a reason, but I was so put off with the mess that I didn't listen very well." The woman looked at the floor. "I wouldn't have guessed what he was up to in a hundred years."

"Griffin told me he's had a meeting with all the neighbors and that you've had secure locks put on all the doors."

"Indeed, I have. I don't care if he is family, I'll not have him use my home to store stolen money—or come again for that matter."

Liberty nodded, thinking about the few facts they had. Mrs. Mills had told them where Davis lived, and Griffin had been in touch with the law there, but they hadn't heard of any significant bank robberies. The bags of money Liberty had seen had been part of a large job.

"Griffin told me that dozens of cases go unsolved every year," Mrs. Mills said. "I fear this might be one we'll have to live with."

"Will it make things awkward for you when you see your husband's family?" Liberty asked.

"No. We're so spread out these days, and in truth, my brother-in-law and I are not on good terms. He doesn't like the way I've never settled down. As if every woman must be dominated and ruled by a husband. Well, some of us just won't be!" These last words were said with an indignant sniff, and Liberty had all she could do not to ask Mrs. Mills how she'd become a Mrs. when she felt that way. Or maybe that was it: She had been ruled and dominated in her marriage and was glad to have the man gone. Liberty wondered if the older woman might explain, but someone knocked on the door just then. Liberty was sitting with a perfect view of that portal and couldn't stop the thundering of her heart when she saw that it was Slater.

"Why, Mr. Rawlings," Mrs. Mills nearly gushed. "Come in."

"Thank you, Mrs. Mills. I hope I'm not disturbing you."

"Not at all. Libby is here visiting me. Come right in."

Slater's hat had come off, and he gave Liberty a smile as he took the chair his hostess indicated.

"What can we do for you, Mr. Rawlings?" Mrs. Mills asked.

"Actually, I just came by to ask Libby if I could see her home."

For all her seemingly negative ideas about marriage and men, Mrs. Mills beamed at them.

"Of course, what a wonderful idea. Libby and I were just visiting—something we can do anytime."

Liberty didn't remember too much more as she found herself embarrassed, not only by Mrs. Mills' obvious efforts to put them together, but by her own thoughts about Slater and Miss Winters. But she did suddenly find herself outside with Slater, that man taking the reins of both horses in one hand and leading the way.

"I hope that was all right, Libby. I hope I didn't interrupt."

"Not at all. How did you know I was there?"

"I have the rest of the day off, so I went to your house and your mother told me where to find you."

"Were you looking for me for a reason?"

"Do I need a reason?" he asked softly, and Liberty gave him a sideways glance but didn't answer.

"How was your day?" he now tried. They had seen each other so briefly that morning, and he had known she was upset over Griffin's treatment of Bernice. Slater wondered if Griffin had told Liberty how Bernice had taken it. That woman had curled up on the bunk and gone sound asleep for the next four hours.

"Enlightening," she said cryptically.

"Oh!" was all Slater could think to say.

They walked in silence for a time.

"Are you going to enlighten *me*?" Slater finally ventured.

Liberty laughed. "Not exactly. Let's just say I learned some things about myself that were very helpful."

Slater studied her profile and waited for her to look at him. When she did, she couldn't look away from his eyes. She even stumbled in the road a little, but that only caused Slater to take her hand. He held it all the way to the small barn at the back of the Petersons' house.

Without a word of conversation, Slater tied Arrow to the hitching post outside the barn and went inside to stable Morton. Liberty followed, pulling hay from the rack so the horse could reach it, applying the water bucket, and then standing back against the wall, out of the way, until Slater was done. Slater eventually turned to see where she'd disappeared to and found her in the shadows. Like a powerful magnet, he went to her, his hands going to the wall around her, as he leaned close.

"I thought about you all day," he admitted.

"Oh, Slater."

"Tell me that means you thought of me too."

"It does."

Slater sighed and didn't even try to fight the temptation. Not rushing or hesitating, his head lowered. His lips caught Liberty's in a kiss that sent both their senses staggering. Not content to keep his arms free of her, with hands to her waist, he pulled her close. Liberty needed no other prompting. Her own arms went around his neck, and she kissed him back.

They were both gasping when Slater broke away, only to study Liberty's face and kiss her again. She was a wonderful fit in his arms, and for long moments she was his only thought.

"I have to go inside!" Zach's young voice suddenly shouted. He was up by the house but must have been calling to the boys who'd walked with him from school. The sound was just enough to bring Slater back to earth. He began to move away, but Liberty caught his arm; she was still in a fog of sensation.

"Slater?"

"Yes?"

"Will you come to dinner tonight? Are you free?"

He nodded, his eyes still on her face and then her mouth. "The usual time?"

"Yes," Liberty said softly. She had never been kissed before, and now she'd been kissed by the man she loved.

The thought of being separated from him made her anxious.

"I'll see you then."

"Okay."

Liberty wasn't sure why she didn't invite him inside right then, but with a final look into his eyes, she made her way across the backyard and to the house. Slater watched her go, his arms still aching to hold her, but his heart telling him how wrong he'd been.

"What a mess," he said softly, causing Morton's ears to twitch. It was a good thing that he had some time before dinner; he had a good deal of thinking to do and a fair measure of confessing. He wasn't playing games where Liberty Drake was concerned, but she was not his to hold and kiss as he'd just done.

"And it's time you remember that," he said, pulling himself into Arrow's saddle and going for a long ride.

❧ ❧ ❧

"Maybe I shouldn't have invited Slater," Liberty said to her mother as she checked on her in her room.

"Not at all, Libby," Kate said genuinely, but she was too tired to rise. "I'm glad you did, but I'm not feeling the best, so I think I'll stay right here."

"All right. I'll bring something up for you. Do you want it before we eat or later?"

Liberty felt alarmed when her mother didn't answer but then realized she'd fallen asleep that fast. She was glad, however, that as she was leaving the room, Duffy was coming down the hall.

"Zach told me she's not feeling well."

"That's what she told me. She fell asleep almost in midsentence."

"I'll check on her and be down soon."

"We'll wait for you."

Duffy thanked her, and Liberty continued on downstairs, only to find Slater in the kitchen with her brother and sister.

"May I see you a moment, Libby?" he asked without preamble.

"Certainly."

Liberty was on the verge of asking where, when Slater turned toward the door. Liberty followed him.

"I had no right to kiss you," Slater began as soon as the door was shut. They stood facing each other on the step. "I've confessed to the Lord, and now I'm repenting to you. I'm sorry I did that."

"I started feeling pretty awful about 30 minutes after you left. I'm sorry too, Slater."

"Liberty," Slater said, moving so close and bending over her that had Liberty not known better, she might have thought she would be kissed again. "I'm not playing games here. I want you to understand that. With whom do I talk? Do I go to Griffin or Duffy and tell him I want to court you? Just tell me, and I'll take care of it as soon as I can."

"Duffy," Liberty barely managed, wanting to kiss him all over again.

Slater nodded and worked to study her face in the dusky light.

"You do things to my heart, Liberty Kathleen. I want you to know that."

Liberty thought that if he could feel her own heart, he'd know he wasn't alone, but no words would come.

"Libby?" Laura called through the door. "Are you out there?"

Slater reached to squeeze Liberty's hand and then opened the back door for her to go in. He didn't know how he would manage the waiting. He wanted to be married right now. He wanted to move fast, but the only way they would be sure not to make a mistake was to go slowly.

Slater joined the family for dinner that night, his heart light with the knowledge that Liberty was open to his suit.

It would be some days before he remembered the issue that was not settled between them, and hoping it would go away was not going to make it happen.

Eighteen

"WELL, HELLO, SLATER," Duffy said the following day. He'd only just arrived at his office and was not expecting anyone for almost an hour.

"Is this bad timing, Duffy?"

"Not at all."

This was normally the time Duffy read his Bible, but he could see that Slater had something on his mind.

"How is Kate?" the younger man asked. His eyes showed that he cared, but his stance carried a good deal of tension.

"Much better. We think she was just tired. She was up early this morning and ready to go."

"Good," Slater said and then fell quiet. This was so much easier when it was just he and Liberty. With Duffy looking at him, kind as he was, Slater felt oddly tongue-tied. When he didn't say anything, Duffy caught on and also saw a way to have a little fun at Slater's expense.

"Are you not feeling well, Slater?"

"No, I'm fine," Slater assured him.

"There are colds going around. You're sure you haven't caught something?"

"I'm sure not."

"Old Mrs. Featherpenny—" Duffy went on expansively, making up a name, "she was in recently with a horrible rash. Itched and itched. Thought she would go mad. I gave her some ointment, but sometimes these things take a while. You don't have a rash, do you?"

Slater shook his head, now looking at Duffy as though the man had lost his senses.

"This is only mid-February, but you know we do have our fair share of fevers in the spring, people fancying themselves in love and mooning about with their heads in the clouds."

Catching the glint in the doctor's eyes, Slater finally smiled.

"And can a doctor help with that?"

"Well, it depends on the doctor. I might be a bit of help in Libby or Laura's case, but I wasn't much help to Tess."

"Now that you've mentioned Libby..." Slater, seeing his opportunity, eased in. "She said I should talk to you."

"About a rash?" Duffy teased one more time.

Slater laughed.

"Sometimes I think that would be easier."

"What's hard about Libby?"

"Going slow."

Duffy nodded wisely. He well-remembered that he was ready to marry Kate long before the date arrived.

"Are you here today to tell me you love my girl, Slater?"

"That just about sums it up. You can see how little I have. I don't even have my own place. But I'd like to visit with Libby with the intent of finding out what we have here."

"My blessing doesn't hinge on the answer to this question, but do you plan to stay in Shotgun?"

"I do, yes. I love the church here, and I can easily see myself settled down in this town."

"Liberty would be glad to know that. She loves Shotgun."

"It's a fine town. People care."

"Indeed, they do. Well, Slater, I think I can speak for both Kate and myself. You're free in our eyes to see Libby and to court her. You did say that she told you to talk to me?"

"Yes."

"Then I assume you have her consent."

"It certainly looks that way."

"How long have you been living here?" Duffy could not remember.

"A little over four months. It seems longer, maybe because Libby and I have seen each other a lot during that time."

"That'll do it."

Both men were thankful that Dr. Peterson's first patient waited until that moment to come through the door. Entering any sooner might have made it awkward all around. Slater was able to leave knowing he'd done what he set out to do. The only problem that remained the rest of the day was keeping his mind on the job. Liberty seemed to be crowding in more than she ever had before.

🌻 🌻 🌻

"He asked whom he should talk to, Griffin or Duffy," Liberty told Tess that same morning. "He told me he's not playing games."

Tess gave Liberty a squeeze, wanting to holler with delight.

"What did you say?" Tess asked as she dragged Liberty into the living room.

"That he should go to Duffy. I don't know when he will, but he said he'd take care of it soon."

Tess sighed. "He's wonderful, Libby. Griff thinks so much of him."

"He is wonderful. Even the way his family has come into town and liked us all so much seems like more evidence that we're to be together."

"And how do you feel, Lib? Would you say you're in love, or are you still thinking on it?"

"I think I'm in love. I feel something for Slater that I've never felt for anyone. I know we have to be careful not to just follow our hearts, but feelings do play a part, don't they, Tess?"

"Yes, they do, but you're right, we can only go on emotions when every thought and action is biblical."

Liberty blinked. "I think I want you to explain that to me."

"Well, when I met Griff, I was instantly attracted. Had my family not liked him, or had he proven to be a nonbeliever or someone who said he believed but didn't live it, then I would have to have taken a step back, no matter what my heart said.

"If at any point I had started to feel that I couldn't live without him, then I would have had to examine my own heart and see that as sin. The only Person I can't live without is Christ."

"That's why you felt such a peace about marrying Griff, even in his line of work?"

"Yes. Don't misunderstand me, Libby. I want Griffin with me forever, but if God has a better plan, I have to be open to that."

Liberty nodded, and for a moment Tess hesitated in indecision. It was on her heart to ask Liberty if she and Slater had ever worked out the issue of Liberty's acting as deputy. Tess didn't know why, but she was afraid to open the subject.

"I told Mam I would help her with the laundry," Liberty said, rising slowly. She wanted to sit and dream with Tess all day.

"I'd better get to work too," Tess said, feeling guilty. "My mother asked us to dinner, and I said I would make dessert."

"Thanks for letting me come over and share."

"Anytime," Tess said lightly, her heart telling her that she was letting an opportunity slip away.

Liberty waved and went on her way, completely unsuspecting. Her heart still in a quandary, Tess stood for a time after she left, planning to ask Griffin about it as soon as he got home.

❦ ❦ ❦

Slater wondered how many times Liberty had done this. Moving slowly on his way to the Brass Spittoon, he thought this had to be much like her first encounter with him. Having seen Griffin's way of handling these situations, Slater went right to the bar and spoke with Gordie. That man nodded in the direction of a corner table. Slater turned. Even with his back to the main room, there was no missing Dakota Rawlings.

Slater went toward him, his sense of danger draining away. He walked until he stood beside him, but Dakota didn't look up.

"Hand it over," Slater ordered, wasting no time.

Dakota, on the other hand, tipped his hat back and looked slowly up at Slater as though he had all the time in the world.

"Something wrong, deputy?"

Slater put his hand out.

Looking rather amused, Dakota put the pistol in Slater's hand.

"I would think you'd have other things to do," Slater muttered and turned away. Dakota rose and stayed right with him. Slater was well aware of Dakota behind him, but remembering the way the older Rawlings had left things, he was suddenly angry. They were half a block down the street before Slater gave vent to it.

"And if you think," Slater suddenly turned and said with quiet fierceness, "that everything is fine between us after you left here like a spoiled child, you can think again!"

Dakota was not given time to answer, so he slowly followed Slater down the street. The deputy headed to the office and took a seat behind the desk. Dakota came through the door in time to see him unload the gun, tag it, and put it on one corner of the desk. Slater then looked at him, and as stern as Slater appeared, Dakota took a seat and spoke.

"I'm sorry, Slate. I did leave here like a child, and I wasn't ten miles down the trail before I was regretting it."

"Why didn't you return?" Slater asked, his voice having calmed completely.

"Because I still don't agree. I'd have paid dearly if anything had happened to you before I returned, but I still don't agree."

"Tell me, Dak. Exactly what is it that you find so impossible to accept?"

Dakota looked at him. "Maybe it's the change. I didn't think you needed saving from anything, but you are different. I think I'm all right, and I'm happy with that belief. I don't feel I need more."

Slater nodded but still said, "Do you remember the fights Mother used to have with Father? They never ended without Father saying, 'Your mother and I can agree, just as long as I don't confuse her with the facts.' We used to laugh about that, but sometimes I think it's very true. The facts are staring you in the face, Dak, but you're happy with what you have." Slater shook his head in wonder. "No man knows how long he's going to live. I hope you won't take too long deciding if what you have will take you through eternity."

"Maybe there is no eternity," Dakota stated. "Preachers have been spooking people with that line for years."

"I guess you used the operative word, Dak—*maybe*. I believe with all my heart that we are eternal beings. You're not sure. It sounds to me as though you need to be as prepared as I am when death knocks on your door."

Dakota would not have said so at the moment, but Slater had given him something to think about. He was quiet while he digested all of this, unaware of the way Slater watched him.

"How long are you in town for?" Slater asked.

"That depends on you."

"Meaning?"

"If you want me to leave, I'll go."

"Don't be ridiculous, Dak. I didn't want you to leave the first time."

Dakota took the olive branch that Slater offered him. He would have to head back out on the trail soon—he hated the thought of doing that, something he'd never experienced before. He knew it was because of the way he'd left.

"Griffin ever get married?"

"Indeed," Slater told him and went on to say where he was living and that Dakota would be welcomed at the Hathaways'. They talked for a time before Slater headed out to walk the streets and keep an eye on things. Dakota accompanied him, the conversation turning to Cash's visit. For right now the younger brother knew he had to let the other subject go. It didn't stop his praying though—something he did fervently—asking God for another chance to share his faith.

🌸 🌸 🌸

"Anybody here?"

The afternoon was slipping away fast, and the temperature was dropping as Tess stepped into Kate's kitchen and called to her.

"In the living room, Tess," her mother-in-law answered.

Tess went through the house and found Kate and Liberty rehanging curtains.

"Hi, Tess," Kate greeted her. "Be prepared to get dusty."

Tess laughed. "That's fine. As long as I don't have to sit by myself, I can stand a little dust."

Both women were instantly alert.

"Bad news?" Liberty asked.

"It's hard to say. Griffin stopped for an extra gun. Mrs. Flowers was in again. He and Slater are headed to confront the Potters. It doesn't sound as though he'll give them any quarter this time."

"Oh, Tess," Kate began, but Liberty cut her off.

"I've got to go," she said softly and moved toward the door.

Tess watched Kate as she went utterly still. She waited for the older woman to say something to stop Liberty, but it didn't happen. Tess felt torn inside. Another gun would be so helpful, but she also knew that Slater would not find it worth the risk. Neither woman spoke, and in almost record time, Liberty was back downstairs, clothes changed, gun belt in place.

"Please be careful," her mother finally managed.

"Yes, Libby, do," Tess was able to add.

Liberty called her assurance back to them, and moments later they heard Morton's hooves. The swiftness of her actions caused Tess' heart to sink with dread. She didn't like rushed things. Too often one was left to repent for a long time to follow.

"Let's pray," Kate suggested.

Tess had no argument with that. She didn't know if she would see her husband again, but Kate had more on the line: Half of her children were riding into battle. No, Tess didn't need to be asked twice. She sat with her mother-in-law, content to pray for as long as she wanted.

🌹 🌹 🌹

The men were on their horses, their faces grim. Both had known it would come to this, but neither man looked forward to it. Maddie Flowers had just come and said that the Potters had caroused all night. Griffin felt he'd given them enough time. Slater wished that Dakota hadn't left to run an errand, but he hoped he wouldn't be gone long and would find the note he left.

"What in the world?" Griffin exclaimed. Slater looked up to follow his gaze. Coming toward them, her face full of determination, was Liberty. Slater didn't waste any time. His mouth tight with equal resolve, he turned back to the sheriff.

"I'll handle this," he told Griffin as soon as their eyes met, and from the look in his deputy's eyes, Griffin wouldn't have argued for the world.

Slater was already off his horse when Liberty arrived, and just as soon as she slid off Morton's back, ready to ask about the plan, Slater took her hand. He led her into the office and spoke with his face just inches from her own.

"I don't want you to do this."

"Slater," Liberty returned, ready to explain, "you don't know the Potters like I do. You and Griffin need me."

"I don't want you to do this, Libby, and I mean it."

Liberty began to shake her head, so Slater placed his hands gently on either side of her face and held it still.

"No, Liberty."

Her look was nothing short of longsuffering.

"I'll ask Griff," she said, and would have moved toward the door if Slater hadn't caught her hand.

Giving her no time to anticipate his next move, he led her into one of the cells. Bending once again to catch her eye, he said, "I can't put you at risk." Slater then exited, locked the door, and hung the key out of reach.

"Slater," Liberty said on a laugh, sure he could not be serious. "Stop fooling around."

Slater only shook his head. How could he have let this go unsettled? Now was not the time to speculate, but that didn't change his actions. She was not coming to the Potters'.

"I don't want you hurt," he said gently. "I think it would kill me."

"The Potters will probably do that for you."

She'd said it with such conviction that Slater sadly shook his head. "You really are arrogant, Libby. You don't think anyone else can do this."

She was getting ready to argue with him again, but he turned away. He glanced back just as he went out the door. She wasn't happy with him, but neither was she ready to panic. Something wasn't right, but right now he couldn't put his finger on it. Slater felt he had no choice but to shut the door and walk away.

      🍃 🍃 🍃

Never before had Liberty Drake been tempted to pinch herself. She thought she must be in a dream. Had Slater just locked her in jail? Had he really taken it that far? Liberty thought the man was amazing.

You'd think I was a criminal, and here I am trying to help.

With a shake of her head, she turned away from the bars. Griffin Drake was no fool. Every lawman had heard stories of getting locked in his own jail. Griffin had never been one to take chances. Liberty was in front of the bunk now, getting ready to count the bricks, climb up, and fetch the hidden key. Whether Slater Rawlings thought so or not, Liberty knew she was needed.

The opening of the door stopped all movement. With as casual a shift as she could muster, Liberty turned to see who had come in.

"Dakota!"

"Hi, Libby." His voice held just the right amount of amusement and surprise. "I can't say as I expected to find you in there."

"Would you let me out?" she asked sweetly.

Dakota paused. "Why are you in there?"

Liberty thought fast. "You know Slater. He can be such a joker."

Dakota watched her.

"In fact," she lied again, "you just missed him. If you'll let me out, I'll take you to him."

Dakota was amused again but not swayed. She looked awfully cute behind bars, those hazel eyes making their appeal, but his brother had given him strict orders.

"How have you been?" Dakota asked, causing Liberty to blink. Her mind raced as she studied his expression and knew she'd been set up.

"Dakota," she began, all trace of congeniality gone. "I want out of here."

"Can't do that, Lib."

"Why not?"

"Slater's orders were very clear."

"But they need me."

"Slater doesn't seem to think so."

"Did you ask Griffin?"

"I didn't have to. My brother knows what he wants, and he wants you safe."

Liberty knew very real frustration for the first time. She knew she would have to keep calm to get out, but that was taking an effort.

"Why don't you go," she now tried. "They went to the Potters', and they're going to need all the help they can get."

"I can't do that either."

"Why not?" Liberty asked, although she believed she knew the answer.

"Because Slater thinks you know a way out of here."

Liberty was stunned. How had Slater figured that out? Surely Griffin wouldn't have told. Liberty's frustration rose yet again. She was suddenly so angry that tears filled her eyes.

Dakota had been headed to the desk chair to sit down but saw Libby's brimming eyes and approached.

"Libby?"

Thinking fast, Liberty played the tears for all they were worth.

"I really think they need me, Dak," she managed in a quivery voice.

"Libby." Dakota's voice was most tender. "If you could just trust that—"

Liberty waited only until he drew close. In a move he wouldn't have believed if he hadn't seen it, Liberty lifted his gun from the holster. For a second he was stunned. Then he smiled.

"What are you going to do with that?"

"Let me out of here, Dakota," she said, her voice level.

"No."

"I'm not going to say it again."

Dakota was in the act of turning away, seeing no point in arguing, when a shot was fired and his hat flew off. He whirled back to face Liberty with blazing eyes.

"I don't like to be shot at, Miss Drake!"

Liberty didn't appear to have heard. With the gun still aimed at him, she spoke in that same measured tone.

"Now the next one is going to hurt. You won't die, but you'll be in pain and probably bleed all over your clothes."

Dakota was so angry he could have spit. When he'd come upon Slater and Griffin leaving, having just been joined by Price who drove a huge wagon, he thought his brother's idea for keeping an eye on Liberty sounded fun. He hadn't bargained on how badly she wanted out of that cell. He didn't honestly think she would shoot him, but knowing how much she wanted her freedom, he could not deny her.

He went for the key, just barely keeping his temper. He didn't know what was worse, having to face his brother when he found that Liberty had gotten around him, or having to face a woman who was upset enough to take shots at him to gain her release. None too happy with himself or anyone else, Dakota fetched the key, wishing he'd stayed out of town one more day.

Nineteen

THE POTTERS WERE NOT PREPARED for a visit from the sheriff. Indeed, the drinking in the barn had started a little early this day. It put Rush and Possum in a good mood, but both Ned and Critter were none too happy to see Shotgun's law enforcement arriving.

"Let me do the talkin'!" the father of the clan snapped at his boys.

"I think this should do the talkin'," Critter proclaimed, a shotgun in his hand.

"Gimme that!" Ned ordered, but Critter was having none of it. They scuffled around a bit, all four hands on the weapon, and froze when the gun went off.

Four sets of eyes rounded in fear, just as the first shots came from without. The Potters hit the dirt. From behind a small outcropping of rocks, Griffin and Slater let off a steady stream of bullets as the four inside scrambled for cover. The barn being ancient, daylight could be seen from every crack and crevice, with new holes appearing all the time and wood splintering around them. Ned thought he would kill Critter himself if he could get close enough.

"Ned!" The firing finally stopped, and that man heard his name being called. "Do you hear me?"

It was Griffin.

"Yeah, I—" Ned began, but Critter jumped in.

"We hear ya, Sheriff, and all you're gonna hear is this!"

Critter fired one shot, and the bullets started up again. For what seemed like many minutes, the Potters hid in the barn and waited yet again for silence, each one wondering how many guns the law had brought.

At last it was quiet, but Griffin did not shout toward the barn. From next to him, Slater held his peace as well.

"Going to let them sweat a little," Griffin said, almost to himself.

"Something tells me Ned would talk to you."

"I think you're right. He'll do anything to stay out of jail, but he hasn't learned to control Critter in all these years, and now he's going to pay."

"My guess is Critter won't be able to last much longer."

As though on cue, Critter let off two shots, and both Slater and Griffin went at it again. This went on for much longer than either man would have cared for, the youngest Potter shooting one or two bullets, and the lawmen answering with a round. Things happened to be quiet when they heard the voices.

"Knock it off!" one of the Potters thundered.

"Shut up! Get away from me."

Not surprisingly, a few shots came outside, and for the last time Griffin and Slater went into action, staying well back since Critter was firing on them as well. It took a little more time at this point, but at last the guns fell quiet. The barn was quiet too.

"If you've had enough," Griffin tried again, "throw the guns out ahead of you and come out of there with your hands up!"

Slater and Griffin were both peeking out when the barn door slowly swung open, creaking like the stays in a tight corset. A moment later a shotgun was tossed far from the door, and out walked Ned. Behind him came Rush and Possum, Critter between them. That they had landed a few blows in his direction was obvious. He was staggering a bit and the men on either side of him were clearly keeping him on his feet. When Griffin, Slater, and now Price, who had come into position, stepped out with guns drawn, they dropped Critter on his face to put their hands in the air.

"Very nice, boys," Griffin congratulated them. "Just step apart a little, not too close to the gun, and keep those hands right where we can see them. Easy now, Critter," Griffin said to him as he came to his hands and knees.

There wasn't a single argument at this point, mostly due to the fact that Critter's mouth was too swollen for talking. The three men moved in on them, and in fairly short order, the four Potters were cuffed and loaded into the wagon. That was when Slater spotted him.

To the side of a small outcropping of rocks stood Dakota. Slater told himself to stay calm, but even as he thought it, he felt his temper rising. It didn't help to suddenly spot Liberty's horse.

Seeing that he'd been spotted, Dakota started toward him. The men met halfway.

"Where is she?"

"Sitting behind the rocks."

Slater's mouth tightened. "What happened?"

"She got my gun away from me. I don't think she would have hurt me, but knowing how much she wanted out, Slate, I let her go. I'm sorry."

"It's not you who needs to apologize," Slater gritted, coming around Dakota to head to the rock. He didn't know when he'd been so disappointed and angry. They should have had this out a long time ago, but even at that, Liberty should have known he just wanted her to be safe. Slater walked until he stood just a few feet from her. She was sitting quite still, her back against the rock, and finally looked up at him.

"I can't believe you've done this," he said quietly. "I thought I knew you, Libby. I thought you were the one."

"Slater," she began softly, but he cut her off with a downward slash of his hand.

"Don't talk to me." Slater uttered the very words he believed he would never say. "I don't want to hear any excuses right now. I wanted to marry you, Libby, but you don't trust anyone but yourself. You're a law unto yourself. I'm just now seeing that."

Liberty sat very still as he turned and walked away. She didn't know when she'd been in such pain. In a haze of misery, she heard the wagon start into motion and couldn't be sure if her brother and Slater's horses had left as well. She didn't even hear Dakota come up, but he was suddenly there.

"I'll ride back with you, Libby," he said.

"You don't have to, Dakota."

"I want to."

Liberty nodded. In reality she wanted to be alone, but she saw that Dakota was offering his friendship. Liberty came slowly to her feet and moved toward Morton. She had little interest in doing anything right now but made herself climb into the saddle and turn the horse toward home.

Riding quietly beside her, Dakota took in her white features and searched for something to say. He hadn't actually heard Slater's words, but it wasn't hard to guess that they hadn't been too welcoming. It was on Dakota's mind to ask Liberty why coming had been so important, but she looked like a fragile piece of crystal to him right now. One move and she might break into a million tiny bits.

"Dakota?" Liberty suddenly spoke, surprising him just as they hit the edge of town.

"Yeah?"

"I think I'll stop by and see Duffy."

"Okay."

"Thank you for riding back with me."

"Anytime."

Liberty pulled off a little then and moved Morton to the right side of the street. Dakota watched her stop in front of the office and even as she sat for a moment and then slid out of the saddle. He wanted to leave her some privacy, so he forced himself to turn away. Not knowing quite what to do with himself, he went ahead to the jailhouse, thinking he might be a help. He also thought his brother might need someone to talk to.

🌿 🌿 🌿

Duffy heard the door open, but no one answered his greeting. He had his hands full of bottles at the moment, and then he needed to wash, so it took a minute for him to move into the other room. The last person he expected to see was his daughter.

"Well, Libby. What's up?"

Liberty didn't look directly at him, and Duffy, ever the kind and sensitive parent, came and sat down on one of the chairs across from her. Only then did Liberty's eyes meet his.

"I've done it this time, Duffy," she began.

"Okay," Duffy said simply, wanting her to know he was listening.

"I went someplace I shouldn't have, and I've ruined everything."

Duffy didn't believe that but told himself not to be too hasty. "Can you tell me about it?" he asked gently.

"I suppose I should explain everything, but for right now I just need you to know that I've been shot."

"Where, Libby?" Duffy forced himself to remain calm, even as he took in her bloodless lips and glazed eyes with new understanding.

"In the side. I think the bullet must have ricocheted off a rock, but even at that, it burns something fierce. I never knew it would hurt like this." Duffy watched in amazement as she stood. "I'm going to head home now—I just wanted you to know."

"This way, Libby," Duffy said softly, also having come to his feet. Letting the doctor in him completely take over, he continued, "I need you to come back here and lie down on the table."

"I should help Mam with dinner," Liberty said in a strange voice, and Duffy knew that shock was setting in. She did as she was told, however, and a minute later Duffy was pushing aside her jacket and cutting away the blood-stained shirt at her left side. He worked to tamp down every emotion as he labored over her injury. That this had happened to one of his own—his precious Liberty—was turning out to be very hard.

"Oh, Duffy," Liberty gasped as he cleansed the wound. The bullet had passed through, but it had made a mess.

Duffy didn't answer her. He was a surgeon at work now, having to turn his emotions off almost to the point of indifference. He cleansed and stitched, not letting himself think about the possible infections that could set in and what they could do, and especially not letting himself think about who had let this happen, not letting his mind stray to the woman he loved above all others or the child within her and the way this was going to affect them both.

Almost an hour passed before the bleeding stopped. It was not an effusive wound, but loss of blood from someone as petite as Liberty scared him a little. She was silent now, her eyes staring blankly at the ceiling. In all this time she hadn't fainted or even closed her eyes. He had known she was strong but had not expected her to be able to speak so coherently.

"Are you wrapping it?"

"Yes."

"So you're almost done?"

"Yes."

"I want to go home and lie in my own bed, Duffy."

"You shouldn't move. I've got the bleeding stopped, but you need to lie still."

Liberty shook her head. "I want you to help me home. I ache with things I haven't told you yet, Duffy. I can't tell you how much I need to go home."

It was the first time he'd heard emotion in her voice, and for some reason it scared him more than the wound.

She was crushed about something that brought her more pain than a bullet wound. Duffy found himself unable to argue with her.

"Give me a few minutes," he said. "I'll help you, but stay put for right now."

Waiting for her to nod, Duffy went out back to hitch Cotton to the buggy. This all set, he slipped around to the front, grabbed Morton's reins, and took him to the back. By the time he came in the back door, Liberty was rising from the table. She stood, her hands leaning on the surface, her mouth open as she gasped for air.

"All right," Duffy said, thinking to save the lecture for later. It was probably too late anyway; she most surely had started bleeding again.

With an arm supporting her, he led her to the back door. Not until he maneuvered her into the buggy did he go back for his bag and to get the lamps.

❧ ❧ ❧

The ride home was a complete loss for Liberty. For the next several minutes she didn't know where she was or what was going on around her. The pain had intensified, and when Slater's face moved through her mind, she wanted to be sick. She didn't remember the buggy jostling her much or even the walk up the steps, but she was suddenly in the kitchen, her mother's concerned face coming into view.

"I just want to go to bed, Mam," Liberty said.

Biting her lip to keep from speaking, Kate moved into Zach's view when she saw the blood on her daughter's coat.

"Up you go," Duffy now said, not giving anything more than a swift glance at his wife. He would explain it all to her, but not until Liberty was in bed and his youngest children were out of earshot.

Not surprisingly—with a word to Zach and Laura—Kate followed her husband and daughter. She told the children to stay in the kitchen and went to help Liberty settle in.

"I want you to know," Kate said, not looking at anyone as she eased Liberty's jacket from her shoulders and started on the buttons on her shirt, "that I've spent the entire afternoon and evening giving my children to the Lord. I won't say that I'm not upset, but I feel that God prepared me for this." Kate turned and stared into her husband's eyes. "All of this to say, I'm all right, and I don't want to be told to go lie down."

In the process of pulling the covers down on the bed, Duffy calmly met her gaze but did not comment. He found Liberty's nightgown hanging on the back of the door and brought it to the end of the bed.

"Sit down," he commanded his daughter, removing her boots after she'd lowered herself onto the mattress. He did not slip out of the room as the rest of Liberty's things were removed but stayed to recheck her wound, which had started to bleed again, and keep track of Kate's reaction when she saw that her daughter had actually been shot. None of this took an extreme amount of time, and after padding the wound some more and laying an extra sheet on the bed, Liberty was finally lying with the covers close around her.

"I should spank you," Kate whispered as she sat on the edge and held Liberty's hand, her eyes just now filling with tears. "Getting yourself shot. Of all things."

Liberty only looked at her, and for a moment Kate was alarmed.

"Liberty? I didn't mean that."

"It's all right, Mam," Liberty said as she shut her eyes. "It's all right."

Kate looked to Duffy, her expression fearful.

"Sleep now, Lib," Duffy said, having just checked her side one more time. "And try to lie still."

Liberty nodded against the pillow, and Duffy, with an arm around Kate, took her from the room. The lantern was still burning, but Duffy left it, knowing he would be back to check on her again soon, and probably all through the night.

"We need to go back down, Kate, and tell Zach and Laura what's happened. We can't leave them sitting frightened in the kitchen."

Kate could only nod. She had said she was all right but found herself shaking and very glad that her husband was in charge. They arrived in the kitchen to see Zach getting a glass of water for Laura. Kate went to help him. After she'd kissed his cheek and thanked him, they sat at the table where Laura was watching them with serious eyes.

"Is Libby sick?" she asked.

"Yes," Duffy told her.

"She went to help Griffin today and got hurt," Kate filled in. Duffy had not heard the specifics but was not surprised.

Zach's little face paled. "Is she shot?"

"Yes, Zach," Duffy said. "And she hurts quite a bit, but I think she's going to be fine."

"Does she need water?" Laura wanted to know. "I could give her mine."

"That's very kind of you, honey, but right now she just needs to rest."

"Where was she shot?" Zach now asked.

"In the side. The bullet is out, and I think she'll heal quickly, but she's going to need lots of rest."

Their little faces were so sober. Kate could see that they were not going to eat another bite.

"Why don't we go into the living room and read," she suggested.

The children were still nodding solemnly when Duffy suggested, "I think we should go up and take a peek at Libby. She might be awake, and you can tell her you're praying for her and love her."

266 • Lori Wick

Not for the first time, Kate thanked God for her husband's wisdom. The children's faces brightened instantly, and they were swift to accompany Duffy upstairs. Kate brought up the rear and found herself fighting tears as Laura talked with her sister.

"We're here, Libby. You don't need to be worried anymore. Zach and I are here to pray for you."

Liberty's eyes, which had opened at the sound of their coming, now closed, but she smiled and moved her fingers in a little wave.

"I love you, Libby," tenderhearted Zach said, his little hand coming up to touch hers.

"I love you too, Zach. You too, Laura."

"Okay," Duffy said now. "Why don't you go back down with Mam, and I'll join you in just a bit."

The children left with a final glance at their sister. It was so hard to see her in bed. She was always the strong one.

"Here we go," Kate said, keeping her voice as normal as possible.

As their footsteps receded in the hall and Duffy touched her forehead, Libby opened her eyes.

"Duffy?"

"I'm right here."

"I've been so selfish. Please don't let Mam be upset. Tell her to take it easy. If the baby doesn't make it because of me, I'll never forgive myself."

Duffy was checking Liberty's side for bleeding, which seemed to have stopped, and didn't immediately speak.

"We'll have to get a garment that opens on the side, Lib. This long nightgown ends up all bunched under you."

"Duffy, didn't you hear what I said?"

"I heard," he said quietly, as he settled the bedcovers back in place and a placed a hand on either side of her to look directly into her eyes. "But just as I want your mother to look after herself right now, I want you to concentrate on getting better. You've lost a good deal of blood, and you're not going to be jumping out of that bed in the morning."

Liberty looked up at him but didn't comment.

"I'm going to go down now and spend some time with the kids and then put them to bed. Sleep if you can and lie still. I could give you something."

Liberty shook her head no.

"All right."

Duffy kissed Liberty's brow and slipped from the room, this time turning the lantern down a bit on his way out. He wanted to sit with her. He wanted to keep an eye on how much she moved in her sleep. But he knew that would have to wait until Zach and Laura were in bed. He found them flanking Kate on the davenport and listening as she read. He did not interrupt but sat on Zach's other side and listened as well.

"Libby will be all right," Laura leaned around her mother to tell the doctor.

"You're interrupting Mam, Laura," he told her.

Laura looked up at her mother. "She wants Libby to be all right too."

Duffy didn't try to correct her, and Kate stopped reading. Maybe it was best to talk about what had happened and not try to distract the children with a story. Maybe the time would be better spent in prayer.

"I think that Libby will be all right too, Laura, but tell me why you think so."

"Well, she's always been all right before, and we're going to pray for her," she offered, her little heart speaking with great confidence.

Duffy thought about how confident believers could be in God, even if things didn't turn out exactly as they hoped for, and for this reason he only smiled at his daughter, thanked her, and suggested they turn in a little early. Kate finished reading the story she was on, and Duffy said it was time to head up.

"Kiss Mam," he ordered, not wanting her to move from her seat.

The children embraced her warmly, and Kate held them tight, but she was nothing short of relieved that Duffy was putting them to bed. Her first thought was to run to Liberty's side and be with her, but she tried to act as normally as possible.

Rising and putting the book away, she went to the kitchen. She had not eaten but still wasn't hungry. She filled a plate for her husband and put it on the stove to stay warm. Then she started the cleanup, something so routine that it gave her a chance to pray continuously. She was just finishing the dirty dishes when the back door opened and Griffin walked in.

"Hi, Mam," he said, kissing her cheek when he saw how drained she looked.

"Hello, dear."

"How's Libby?" Griffin asked innocently. She was the reason he'd come, but not for the reason his mother thought.

"The bleeding has stopped, and she's resting quietly. Duffy thinks she'll be fine, but she's awfully—" Kate stumbled to a halt as she watched her son's face. "Griffin, what is it?"

"Why is Libby bleeding?"

Kate was stunned. No wonder he hadn't come earlier, or for that matter, taken her to Duffy's office.

"She was shot today, Griffin. I had no idea you didn't know."

"Where is she?" he asked, already moving toward the door.

"In her room, but Griff—" his mother stopped him, "Duffy just put the kids down; please don't go rushing up there and frighten them if they're still awake."

Griffin put his hand up in understanding. He nodded and took some deep breaths, this time moving slowly to the stairs. Kate didn't go with him but could tell that he was walking at a more controlled pace. And indeed she was right. Griffin's pace was slow, giving complete lie to the way his heart nearly pounded through his chest.

Oh, Father in heaven, Libby's been hit. I didn't know, Lord, I didn't know. My sister, who I love so much. I can't believe it. I've wrestled with this whole issue, not really wanting to face it, and now this has happened. Please help her. Please touch her and heal her.

Griffin was at the doorway of Liberty's room now and found Duffy in the rocking chair by the bed, his Bible open in his hand and his head turned to catch the soft light of the lantern. Griffin spoke when the older man looked up.

"I didn't know."

Duffy nodded. He had wondered why Griffin and Slater had not been around, but his main thought was Liberty.

Griffin came in, his eyes glued to Liberty's colorless cheeks. He came to the side of the bed and just stood looking down at her.

"How bad?" he whispered to Duffy without shifting his gaze.

"It passed clear through. She thought it might have ricocheted."

"Where was she hit?"

"Her left side."

Griffin licked his lips, wishing she would wake up so he could talk to her. He could count on one hand the amount of times he had been this upset. His father's death came to mind, as did the night Liberty told him that Tess thought he might as well be dead. Now his sister lay hurt and vulnerable, and something deep inside Griffin told him he could have prevented it. His father's death was beyond his control. When he learned of Tess' feelings, he had instantly acted. Not so with Liberty. He had been thinking about her involvement for a long time, and now he'd waited too long.

Griffin broke from his reverie when he heard movement at the door. He turned to see his mother enter. The fullness under her apron was another reminder of the many people who were affected. He watched his mother as she stepped up and joined him. If Liberty's even breathing was any indication, she was deeply asleep; nevertheless, they whispered.

"Tell me, Griffin," Kate commented, having recovered enough to question him, "if you didn't know Libby was hurt, why did you come?"

He shook his head. "Slater was not at all happy that Libby came out to the Potters'. He was pretty hard on her."

The words were no more out of his mouth than a thunderstruck look crossed his face.

"Slater!" he whispered in soft dismay.

"He doesn't know?"

"No."

Kate was relieved. She had worried that Slater was deliberately staying away.

Griffin, still watching Liberty's face, put his hat back on. He knew how he would feel if he'd been hard on Tess and she was harmed before he'd made it right. Maybe Liberty had needed to hear what Slater said, but that wouldn't change the way he felt when he learned she was hurt and he'd just ridden away. Much as he knew his deputy would be upset, Griffin had to tell him. Telling his family he would be back as soon as he could and to tell Liberty he'd been there, he left the room, intent on finding Slater and explaining as gently as he could.

Twenty

LIBERTY THOUGHT SHE MIGHT BE FLOATING. She was warm, almost hot, and for some time she couldn't tell where she was. She saw flowers along the creek bank, little yellow ones. They were so pretty and so early for this time of year. Reaching out with her arm, she bent to pick one but found herself gasping in pain. Her eyes flew open, and after a moment, she found herself staring at the ceiling in her own bedroom. Her sigh was very soft as memory returned.

I never believed it would come to this, Lord. I never thought I would not be able to let go. Giving up the job has been hurting and bothering me for a long time, but I didn't think I was capable of doing what I did today.

Liberty shuddered with shame as she remembered. It was as if she had taken leave of her senses, but that hadn't happened. Completely in her right mind, she'd been desperate to be involved, sure that no one else could handle it. Arrogant. Just as Slater had said.

Liberty's whole frame shook for a moment. She couldn't think of Slater—not now—not ever. He was sure to be gone soon. *I thought you were the one. I wanted to marry you.* Both statements in the past tense. He might stay until Griffin could find a replacement, but he'd only come through town on a whim in the first place. It would just be a matter of time before he went on his way. Liberty knew she mustn't do anything to stop him. She would make sure she apologized and thanked him for taking her measure so correctly, but she must never make him feel that he must stay.

But first, she had to see Dakota. Liberty prayed even now that he was still in town. There was no excuse for the way she'd treated him, but she would still ask for his forgiveness and hope that he didn't despise her.

A noise at the door just then carried Liberty's eyes that way. Duffy came in quietly even when he saw that she was awake. He laid a hand on her cheek. She was getting warm, but that might be the covers.

"Are you too warm?" he asked.

"No. My feet are cold."

Duffy took the quilt from the brass footboard and laid it across her feet and lower legs. He then came back to the rocking chair and pulled it even closer so he could talk with her.

"Griff was here."

"Was I asleep?"

"Yeah. He was pretty shaken."

Liberty looked away.

"What happened out there, Libby, that no one knew of this?"

Liberty did not answer. She was ashamed of her actions, but it was more than that. She didn't feel she could explain yet how blameless the men had been. She thought that whatever she said, Duffy would think they should have come to her aid.

"Oh, Libby," Duffy whispered softly. "What's happened to hurt you so much?"

Liberty's heart broke over the caring in his voice.

"My own sin, mostly, a complete lack of trust. And I think that's the reason it's so hard for me to talk about it."

"Have you confessed it?"

"Yes."

"Then there's no reason for you to be ashamed in front of me."

Liberty felt as though she had been released. Going slowly, working to gather her thoughts and remember the details, she filled Duffy in, not surprised that his eyes were full of compassion even when she admitted to what she considered reprehensible actions toward the Rawlings brothers, especially Dakota.

"Slater will want to see you, honey," Duffy said when she had finished.

Liberty smiled sadly. "I guess he probably will. I'll have to find a way to tell him he did the right thing."

Duffy knew this was not the time to argue, but Slater should have let Liberty speak. The doctor somehow knew that he would regret that more than anything else.

"I'm going to pray for Slater," Duffy said. "I think he'll need it."

Liberty nodded. It was just like Duffy to be willing to walk in the other man's shoes. Had Liberty seen Griffin just then, she'd have also known how timely her stepfather's prayers would be.

🌢 🌢 🌢

"Could I see you both a moment?" Griffin asked Slater and Dakota the moment he stepped into the Hathaways' living room. The men were buried in the newspaper, Mr. Hathaway as well. Mrs. Hathaway had opened the front door, looking delighted that "her boys" had company.

"If you need privacy," Mrs. Hathaway said as she joined them, "feel free to talk in the kitchen."

"Thank you," Griffin replied as she handed him a lantern. He went in the direction she pointed and waited until Slater and Dakota were both inside the door.

"Dakota," Griffin wasted no time in asking, "did you ride back with Libby today?"

"Yes. She went to Duffy's as soon as she got to town."

Griffin nodded. "She was shot out there today."

Not surprisingly, both men looked thunderstruck.

"Where?" Slater asked, his voice hoarse.

"In the side. It's clean, but she's lost some blood. Duffy says she'll be all right."

Slater began to move away and turned back. "Is she home?"

"Yes."

There was no need for other words. Dakota went through to tell their hosts that they would be out for a while, and by the time he got back, Slater had already jumped onto Arrow's bare back and started down the street.

Slater had never felt like this. He had not lost anyone he loved, unusual for a man in his position, and although he'd been saddened by death many times, his heart had never been deeply involved. Knowing that Liberty was hurt and realizing that he hadn't been there for her were the most painful things he could ever recall.

Arriving on the Petersons' street, Slater rode between the two houses. Not bothering to tie Arrow's reins, he entered the kitchen without knocking. Kate and Tess were talking at the table. Slater looked between them and then toward the door.

"Duffy's up there, Slater," Kate said kindly. "I'm sure it will be fine if you go up."

"Thank you." The words came automatically as he moved through the kitchen.

Realizing he wasn't going to know the way, Kate followed him. She directed him toward the light spilling into the dark hall and stood back as he filled the doorway.

"I was just thinking of you, Slater," Duffy said. His gaze swung to Liberty for a moment. "She just fell back to sleep."

Slater tried to speak, but there was no moisture in his mouth. He moved toward the bed, his heart frozen with fear. She might not get up again. She might die before he could tell her how sorry he was and how much he loved her. They might never have a life together, and he wanted that so much.

"Duffy?" Liberty said with her eyes closed.

"I'm right here."

"I have to see Dakota. I have to make it right."

"Okay. If he comes, I'll tell him. Would you like to see Slater?"

Liberty sighed. "He'll just feel bad," she said, her voice fading. "He shouldn't feel bad."

"Libby," Slater tried her name, having drawn close, but Liberty only mumbled and fell back to sleep.

Slater stared at her face, her dark hair in a riot around her head and on the pillow. She was the prettiest little thing he'd ever seen. Her dark lashes, always so thick and long, made little fans on her pale cheeks. Slater felt his breath catch in his throat. Never had anyone been so precious to him. It was as if she were already his. It felt as though she'd been his for all time.

"Sit down," Duffy directed softly, having given up his chair.

Slater obeyed without thought. He stared at Liberty a time longer and then turned to her stepfather.

"Did she tell you what happened?"

"Just that one of Critter's bullets must have ricocheted."

Slater nodded. "Did she tell you she tried to speak to me and I wouldn't let her?"

"Yes."

"Was she going to tell me she was hurt or something else?"

Duffy's silence was answer enough. It was almost more than the tall blond cowboy could take. His eyes went upward as they filled with tears.

You left her! You wouldn't even let her speak!

Noise at the door brought both men's heads around. Griffin was there, Dakota just behind him. They were on their way into the room when Liberty spoke, her eyes still closed.

"Mam?"

"I'm here," Kate said as she came in behind the men, followed by Tess.

For a moment she didn't say anything, so Duffy spoke. "You have quite a bit of company here, Libby."

"Do any of them have any candy? I wish I had a peppermint."

Griffin didn't even try to hold his laughter. Liberty smiled when she heard it and opened her eyes.

"Here we are," Griffin began, "scared to death, and you want candy."

Liberty smiled a little, but her eyes found Dakota, and her face grew sad.

"I'm sorry," she said to him, her eyes filling. "I was such a fool. Everyone misses, and if I had missed when I shot at you, I might have hurt or killed you. Please forgive me, Dakota."

"It's all right, Libby," he said, barely able to speak. She might not believe him, but he really did understand.

Movement out of the corner of her eye caused her to look that way. Not until that moment had she seen Slater, who was by her side near her pillow.

"I'm sorry, Libby," were the first words out of his mouth. "I should have let you talk."

Liberty's hand went up and he took it.

"I shouldn't have been there. I've never been so foolish, Slate. I just hope you can forgive me."

He kissed the back of her hand and tenderly held onto it.

Griffin had gone to the far side of the bed, as had Tess, and when they'd all caught her eye long enough to smile or speak to her, Duffy ushered them from the room. Kate stayed a moment longer to kiss her cheek, but the last one to be seen out by the doctor was Slater.

"I'll see you tomorrow," he said quietly to Libby. "Sleep well."

Liberty nodded and watched him leave. She didn't speak until his steps told her he was down the hall.

"Tell him he doesn't have to come," Liberty told Duffy.

"I can't do that."

"Why not?"

"Because he does have to come."

Liberty blinked. "Says who?"

"Says me." Duffy bent and kissed her brow. "Go to sleep. I'll check on you later."

Liberty didn't have much choice; she was already sleepy. But not at any time before she dropped off did she understand what he meant.

🌸 🌸 🌸

"And then the little horse said he didn't like his hay," Laura said from the foot of Liberty's bed almost a week after the shooting. The patient was sitting up against the headboard, swathed with quilts and bolstered with pillows. There had been a slight fever, but the wound was healing fast. Weakness from the loss of blood, however, was still apparent.

"What did his mother do?"

"I don't know," she said, her little brow perplexed. "I'm still figuring that part of the story out."

Liberty would have laughed, but she'd learned her lesson about laughing too much when Laura had come in to talk to her every day.

"Maybe she should take the hay away from him because he isn't thankful."

Laura looked amazed. "That's good, Libby," she said intently. "We should write that down."

Liberty had to laugh then, even though it caused her to gasp. And as her little nurse had started to do, she came close, careful not to bump Liberty's side, and took her sister's hand in both of hers, praying that the pain would go away soon. Liberty thought that if her feelings for Laura were any more tender, she would melt into a puddle.

"Hey, Libby," Zach announced as he joined them, "I have to go to school."

"Okay. Thanks for coming in to say goodbye."

"I'll have a new book to read you when I get home today."

"Great. I'll look forward to it."

The little boy came over to kiss her, Liberty leaning toward him as best she could. The kiss usually landed in midair, but they always caught each other's smiles, and Liberty thought about him all day once he was gone.

Zach hadn't been gone from the room five minutes when Kate came in. She shooed Laura downstairs to eat, pulled Liberty's curtains open, cracked the window, and made sure Libby could reach the cup of coffee she'd just brought in. She then took Laura's place at the foot of the bed.

"How'd you sleep?"

"Not so well. I kept waking up and wanting to turn on my bad side. Did I keep you awake?"

"A little."

"I do wonder when I'm going to feel like getting out of this bed."

"It'll come. It would seem that everyone will still be here, so take your time."

Liberty found that comment odd, even as she realized her mother had said it the day before.

"What do you mean 'everyone will still be here'?"

"Your brother, Tess, and the Rawlings have just about moved in. I thought you knew that."

Liberty's mouth opened. "Mam, you can't do that! You can't be entertaining all these people and still be taking it slow."

"Liberty, they haven't let me do a thing. If the church family isn't bringing something, Tess is cooking. Dakota walks Zach to and from school every day, and unless Slater is working or sleeping, he's here cleaning something, trying to cook, or seeing to the kids."

Liberty was flabbergasted. She had done a lot of sleeping, that was certainly true, but that life was being lived below stairs in such a surprising way was a little hard to take in.

"Why?" was the only word she could find.

Kate looked very sympathetic. "How else are they going to be near you, Lib? Slater especially. He can't exactly sit around your bedroom."

Sadness overwhelmed Liberty. She didn't want Slater hanging around because he felt guilty. She was glad that everyone had come and taken the burden from her mother, but Liberty had reconciled herself to not having the life she'd envisioned. For a moment she thought she might be selling both God and Slater short, but that didn't seem likely.

"How about some breakfast?" Kate asked.

"That sounds good."

Kate was gone for a long time, and when she returned with a breakfast tray, it was also to explain that Dakota had just been there.

"He said to tell you goodbye and that he'd come back through as soon as he could."

"I take it he has to go back to work?"

"Yes. He wished he could see you, but I told him you'd understand."

"Yes, I do. I appreciate how gracious he's been."

"Yes. As special as he is right now, it's wonderful to think of who he would be if he came to Christ."

"Slater and I have talked about that very thing."

Kate took in the wistful expression that came into her daughter's eyes and knew that it was about more than Dakota's need for salvation. With a word about checking on her soon, Kate made sure Libby had the Bible, pencil, and paper she'd asked for and slipped from the room. Liberty had not asked to be alone, but it wasn't hard to see that this was just what she needed.

❧ ❧ ❧

"We have to talk to you," Griffin said the next day, coming into her room one week to the day after Liberty had been hurt.

Liberty looked into Tess and Griffin's faces. They would certainly be more happy if a baby was on the way, but she hoped that their news was good.

"We owe you an apology, Lib," Tess began. "I feel very much at fault for waiting so long. Griffin said he's to blame, but I've been very cowardly."

Liberty still looked between them, her face open.

"Libby," Griffin sad down in the rocker and leaned close. "It's been on my mind for some time now, especially knowing how Slater feels, that I shouldn't be using you to back me up. I felt the Lord speaking to my heart, but it was easier to depend on you. I called on you for help with Bernie and then thought afterward that maybe she lets herself go just to get you to come.

"And I can't help but wonder if I had put in my vote of disapproval about your coming last week and not left the whole thing in Slater's hands you might have listened. I'm sorry, Libby. I'm sorry I didn't obey the Lord and prevent this from happening in the first place."

"And I didn't speak to you as a friend, Libby," Tess now put in. "I knew the way Slater felt but never asked you about it. I'm sorry."

Liberty nodded and said quietly, "I must admit that I've always taken the family's support as a positive sign, but Slater's strong feelings have certainly made me think."

They fell silent for a moment before Tess said, "Are you all right, Libby?"

Liberty's thoughts had turned to Slater, causing the region around her heart to ache, but she forced herself to nod and smile. Griffin rescued her by turning the conversation to business.

"The circuit judge will be through in about two weeks. The Potters are back on the farm, but they've stayed very quiet, especially because I told them one of their bullets hit and could have killed someone."

"Slater and Griffin went out to Maddie Flowers' too," Tess added. "Her still is gone as well."

"I can guess how she took that," Liberty said dryly.

Griffin chuckled. "I thought she would faint, but she was quiet even when we smashed her *medicinal* bottles."

Liberty now laughed a little too. "And what of Davis Mills? Any word yet?"

Griffin shook his head. "Only that the law in Austin thinks he must have pulled a lot of little jobs and been storing the money under his aunt's floor, since there's been no report of a large bank holdup. He's left almost no trail, but I plan to keep my eyes and ears open."

Liberty smiled at him, thinking he was the man to do it. Hard as her own situation was, Liberty believed with all her heart that her brother was a fine lawman. Shotgun was blessed to have him.

Griffin and Tess didn't stay much longer, something for which Liberty was grateful. She had some more thinking to do and that, along with their visit, seemed to wear her out. She settled against her pillow, knowing that if she had it to do over again, out of her love for Slater, she would do whatever he asked.

It wouldn't come easily to me, Father. Not only am I comfortable with a gun, I'm also too quick to want to do Your job, but I would try. I would try with all my heart. I can see now that Slater only wanted to protect and take care of me. I wish he still did.

Liberty fell asleep while telling God that she didn't think she'd ever get over him.

☙ ☙ ☙

"You're certainly in a good mood," Griffin commented to his deputy on the first day of March.

"I am," Slater agreed.

"Going to tell me why?"

"Well," he drew the word out, clearly having a fine time. "As a matter of fact, a little bird told me that a certain lady was out of bed yesterday for the first time. I'm hoping I'll find her downstairs when I go by at lunch."

Griffin tried not to smile when he said, "I don't suppose I'll get another moment of work out of you until you see her."

"Probably not," Slater said unrepentantly, looking out the window, hands behind his back as he rocked on his heels.

"Someone could probably be holding up Price and Amy, and you would just smile."

"Now, that I wouldn't do," Slater turned and said with mischievous eyes. "It might keep me from seeing your sister."

Griffin could only laugh. "Get out of here, Slate. I don't want to see your face until Libby smiles at you and you're ready to work."

Slater was not going to argue. With hat in place and a certain Drake on his mind, he made a beeline for the door. It was a little early for lunch, but Liberty still might be downstairs.

The separation had been torture. Slater found himself able to be downstairs with Tess, the children, or Kate, people he cared for very much but didn't feel desperate to see. When he asked after Liberty's health, he knew they told him the truth, but he had a natural need to see her for himself; and not just see her, but be close, talk to her, and watch her face for signs of the old Liberty.

"Well, Slater," Kate said when he knocked and slipped in the kitchen door, "this is a surprise."

Slater smiled. Not until he'd gotten very close to Liberty's mother had he discovered that she had a very subtle sense of humor. You had to spend a great amount of time with her to see it, but it was there.

"I just thought you might need me to sweep the floor or burn some trash."

Kate could barely keep from smiling. "Actually," she began, turning back to the pudding she was stirring in order to hide her gleaming eyes, "I was hoping you could dust the living room."

"I'll do it," he said, hoping she was only kidding but ready to do as she asked.

"Just go on through. I think you'll know what to do when you get there."

Slater did not waste any time. He left his hat by the door, smoothing his hair and trying to keep his pace normal as he went. Still, he must have been heard because Liberty's and Laura's faces were turned to him as soon as he stepped across the threshold.

"Slater!" Laura cried, launching herself in his direction.

Slater swung her up into his arms for a hug and kissed her small cheek.

"How are you today?"

"I'm very good. Libby and I are very good."

Slater finally let his eyes swing to where Liberty sat quietly on the sofa. She wore a black and white checked dress with tiny pink flowers running over the fabric. Her feet were on the footstool, and she had a thick quilt over her legs and lap. Slater moved toward her now, sitting in the chair closest to the sofa and fighting the urge to sit right beside her. He settled Laura in his lap and spoke.

"Do you agree with Laura's diagnosis? Are you very good?"

Liberty smiled. "Yes, I would say I am. I don't care to pull myself into a buggy or throw a ball, but I'm doing fine."

"You look wonderful," Slater said softly, his eyes not missing a thing, not even when her cheeks turned a little pink and she shifted her gaze to the window.

"Are you working today?" Liberty asked, her eyes and hands busy with the quilt now.

"Yes, I'm just taking a long lunch."

Liberty nodded. "How's Griff?"

"Doing fine. He had a meeting with the town council this morning. They've voted to hire more men. Griff is thinking about putting ads in the Austin papers to get a little more exposure."

Liberty smiled. "My mother still has the newspaper clipping from San Antonio that my father answered to get the job here."

"I'd like to see that."

"I can ask her," Laura volunteered, startling both adults. They had been so preoccupied with one another that Laura had been momentarily forgotten.

"That would be nice of you, Laura," Liberty said with a smile, not realizing the little girl meant to go right then. Not until she moved from the room did Liberty realize her mistake. She didn't feel emotionally ready to be alone with this man she still loved, but it was too late. She looked over to find his eyes on her and knew he was ready to speak.

Twenty-One

"I WANT TO THANK YOU," Liberty blurted before Slater could utter a word.

"Thank me?"

"Yes," Liberty nodded, still embarrassed and having a hard time meeting his eyes. "I never saw my actions for what they were. I was arrogant and untrusting. You helped me to see that. If I had it to do over again, I would do it differently. That's why I'm thanking you."

"When you were still laid up, my mind wandered and I had some moments when I feared you might hate me," Slater admitted. "All I ever wanted to do was protect you, but I think I came across as overbearing and stubborn."

"You were overbearing and stubborn at times, Slater, but it was over something you believed in. That makes complete sense to me now."

Slater had so much he wanted to say, but fell rather silent for a moment. The silence allowed Slater to hear Kate and Laura in the kitchen. It reminded him of how hard it was to find time alone with Liberty. For this reason, Slater moved forward a little bit in his chair, his forearms resting on the top of his thighs as he leaned closer.

"Every little thing about you fascinates me, "Slater surprised Liberty by saying. "I've never known a woman with such a wide range of talents, Libby, and I mean that. I can't tell you how my thoughts whirled to find the woman who'd pulled a gun on me in a saloon walking up the aisle

286 • Lori Wick

to play the piano at church. And playing beautifully, I might add. Then at lunch, I see you helping with the meal.

"Added to that, you're a marvelous care giver. You love and take care of others so naturally. You take food to folks in need, you check on the older women in town like a loving daughter, you're like another pair of hands for your mother, and you cherish Laura and Zach as if they were your own.

"And each time I think of them losing you, I die a little inside. That's what I wrestle with every time you put on that gun. I want to take care of you, but with that gun you don't need me." Saying this, Slater saw Liberty go pale and wished he'd waited to speak of this.

"Libby," Slater said urgently, taking in her stricken face. "I'm sorry to have said this to you now. You've been hurt, and I shouldn't have tried—"

Liberty put her hand out to stop him, and Slater took it. She shook her head, and he held her hand in both of his and waited. He also prayed, hoping she would tell him her thoughts so he could make it right.

"I've always protected the people and the town I love, but you've given me much to think about, Slater. Don't ever apologize for that."

Did that mean...? Slater found himself thinking, but was afraid to hope or ask the question aloud. It didn't, however, change the strong urge to gently take this woman in his arms and tell her he loved her. The thought was so powerful within him that his face flushed. He could only stare at her, which caused Liberty's own cheeks to redden before she looked away, gently reclaiming her hand just as Laura shot into the room.

"Libby, Mam wants to know if you want lunch in here or in the kitchen. We're having pudding," she added, as if this might be the deciding factor.

"I'll come to the table," Liberty told her, already moving the quilt from her lap.

Slater stood, ready to help, but other than moving very slowly, Liberty seemed totally normal. Slater wrestled with the things he'd said. Had it been too soon? Her words and actions would not indicate so, but he was still tempted to worry. What Slater didn't know was how good it had been for Liberty to be able to thank him. She didn't honestly believe that they would end up married, but she wanted him to know that he'd been a help in showing her how untrusting she'd been.

"Slater," Kate asked once they were seated, "will you pray for us?"

"Certainly. Father in heaven, we thank You for Your love and grace to us, for Your protecting hand and mercy. Thank You that Libby is able to be in the kitchen, moving on her own. Thank You for Kate, Laura, and the baby, and the special family You've put in this place. Thank You for this wonderful food. I pray all this in Christ's holy name. Amen."

"You didn't thank God for yourself, Slater," Laura noted as soon as her eyes were open.

"Didn't I?" Slater asked as he took a roll and passed the basket to Liberty.

"No. Don't you thank God for you?"

"Well," Slater replied as he thought about this, "I thank God for everything He's done for me. Does that help?"

"I think so," she said, her brow lowered in that intense way he loved.

"You could thank God for Slater," Kate suggested.

Laura nodded, her mouth moving as she chewed but again looking very thoughtful. She swallowed, opened her mouth to say something about being thankful if Liberty and Slater got married, but suddenly caught her big sister's eye.

"Oh," she said softly, shutting her mouth.

"Oh, what?" Kate asked innocently.

Laura looked so uncertain that her mother dropped it. Not having to think long before understanding dawned,

Kate went back to her plate without looking at Slater or Liberty.

Liberty cast a sidelong look at her sister and one at Slater. If he suspected anything, he was hiding it very well.

Suddenly Libby was tired. It was enough for her body to work on healing without adding emotions to the mix. But what else could she feel when Slater was in the room? Her sigh was more internal than anything else, but heartfelt nonetheless. She continued to eat, listening to what Kate had to say about plans for the day but also asking God to help her survive the emotions running through her. Right now she didn't think she would.

🌿 🌿 🌿

"You're grinning again today like you did yesterday," Griffin commented the next morning. "Are you planning another long lunch?"

"No, I won't need much time," Slater said, still looking like the cat with the cream.

"Going back to talk to her?"

"*Talk to her?*" Slater replied, looking surprised. "I'm not going to talk, I'm going to tell her she has to marry me and that's the end of it."

Griffin laughed. "I take it Dakota was on your trail before he left."

"As if I needed him," Slater said with a shake of his head. "But he did threaten to ask for me if I didn't do the job soon. I wanted to ask her yesterday if she'll marry me and let me take care of her."

"She's sure healing fast. Duff is very pleased."

"She looks wonderful," Slater said quietly, his eyes on nothing in particular. Griffin couldn't stop his smile as he studied the other man. He felt as though he'd waited a long time for a Slater Rawlings to walk in the door. Slater was a man who would love his sister and appreciate the woman she was. Griffin understood now why Slater had never wanted Liberty to pack a gun. His own relationship with Tess had been a big help to him on that too, and they were both thankful that Slater had never stopped loving Liberty.

Both men were needed before Slater could get away for lunch, but that didn't change Slater's thoughts, or Griffin's for that matter. Just as soon as there was a break and Griffin told Slater he could spare him, Slater went to the Petersons', his mind on what he intended to say. Griffin watched him go, somehow feeling a burden to pray for his sister. She'd been through quite a bit since Slater Rawlings rode into town. Griffin only hoped she was still thinking clearly enough to know a good man when he was standing in front of her.

🌹 🌹 🌹

Slater found Liberty in the living room again, this time alone. She appeared to be hemming a dress. She did look up to greet him but immediately bent back over her work. This time he sat right next to her.

"What's this?" Slater asked, lifting the fabric a little.

"A dress of Laura's. Mam was smart enough to make it big, but now the hem has to come down."

"She's growing fast. I can just see her in school this fall."

"It'll be awfully quiet around here."

Slater didn't comment. His eyes were on her profile, and he stared until she looked at him.

Liberty was so surprised by the warm look in his eyes that she didn't look away.

"Marry me," he ordered softly.

Surprised as she was, Liberty shook her head. "You don't have to do this, Slater."

It took Slater a moment to figure out what she meant, and when he did, he said, "Let me get this straight. I feel guilty about the way I handled things at the Potters', so now I'm proposing to make up for it?"

"Something like that," Liberty admitted.

"So you don't love me?" he asked, putting everything on the line.

"I didn't say that," Liberty said swiftly before going back to her needle.

Silence hung heavily between them, and Liberty had all she could do not to howl when she shoved the needle into her thumb. Finally, she chanced a look in his direction and found him still watching her, a tender smile on his face.

"So your answer is no?" he clarified.

"That's right."

A large smile crossed his features.

"What does that mean?" Liberty had to ask.

"If you're talking about the smile, I was just thinking of how fun it's going to be to convince you." He leaned close before adding in a whisper, "And don't forget, Liberty Kathleen, I'm a very patient man."

Liberty's mouth swung open as he pushed to his feet, bent to kiss her cheek, put his hat on, told her he would see her later, and walked from the room. No one looking at Slater Rawlings as he made his way back to the sheriff's office would have believed that his proposal had been turned down—least of all Griffin—who stood in anticipation when he was back so soon.

"She must have said yes," Griffin began.

"On the contrary—she turned me down flat."

Griffin hesitated. The smile on the blond man's face belied those words, but something told Griffin they were true.

"Why did she say no?"

"Because she thinks I only asked out of guilt."

"Guilt about what?"

"The way I treated her at the Potter place."

Griffin was so stunned that he sat back down. He thought for a moment and then offered, "Do you want me to talk to her?"

"There's no need," Slater said calmly. "I'll talk her around."

Griffin could see that he meant it and decided to leave well enough alone. Not long after, he went home for his own lunch, prayers for Slater and his sister filling his heart.

Slater, not at all sorry to be on his own, also thought of Liberty and prayed for her. He could tell that her mind was made up, but that didn't daunt him in the least. Indeed, he smiled again now and rocked back on his heels, just thinking about how swiftly she went back to her sewing when he asked if she loved him.

"Oh, yes, Libby," Slater said to the empty office as he sat down at the desk to get back to work. "I'll get around you. Just see if I don't."

🌸 🌸 🌸

"You're awfully quiet tonight, Lib," Duffy said that evening. The children were in bed, and the three adults sat in the living room. "How are you feeling?"

"All right. I moved a little suddenly today and regretted that, but other than the itching, it's not bad."

"I noticed that when Slater was here today," Kate put in, her head bent over some needlework, "he looked like a man with a mission."

"He wants to marry me," Liberty informed them.

Both Duffy, who had been reading the paper, and Kate froze and then looked at her.

"You don't seem too excited," Duffy mentioned carefully.

"I turned him down."

Kate could not control herself. Tears filled her eyes, and she looked across at Liberty.

"I'm sorry, Mam," Liberty whispered. "I didn't know it would hurt you."

"It's not me, Libby." Kate's voice was just as hushed. "I thought you loved Slater."

"I do. I love him like I've never loved anyone, but I think he just feels bad about what happened. I can't have him thinking he's in love when all he feels is guilt."

Liberty's face held an expression her parents had never seen before. She seemed so vulnerable that it shook them terribly. Not for anything would they scold her or try to convince her that Slater did in fact love her. They both believed he did, but this had to come from her heart, not theirs.

"Follow your heart," Duffy said, needing to voice the words. "We think Slater is a fine man, but if you're doubting, Libby girl, don't let anyone rush you anywhere."

"Thank you, Duffy."

Kate smiled at her. Her eyes were still suspiciously moist, but she was able to agree with her spouse. "It's a big step, Libby. A woman would be a fool to start out with doubts."

Liberty nodded, but even as her mother said the word *doubts*, she began to struggle with her own. Maybe she was being too hard on Slater. After all, he'd showed her that he cared long before the Potter incident.

"I think I'll head up," Liberty said, not needing to feign exhaustion in an effort to be alone. She was remarkably weary. As she readied for bed, Slater came to mind again. Liberty thought how nice it would be to have him there, talking to her or maybe helping with the buttons on her dress or the pins in her hair. Tears poured down her face as she changed clothes and climbed beneath the covers. She was too tired to do anything more than cry and ask the Lord if she would ever survive this.

❧ ❧ ❧

"Did you say painting the fence out by the barn?" Slater asked Kate just two days later.

"Yes."

Slater stared at the woman, waiting for her to laugh in jest. That didn't happen.

"Why is she doing that?" Slater asked.

Kate looked hesitant but eventually admitted, "I think she needs to keep busy right now."

Again Slater thought. "Is that your way of saying she's having second thoughts about saying no to me?"

Kate bit her lip. "I don't know that for certain, Slater, but I think she prefers to be shot again rather than hurt you or be hurt by you. She's going to have to keep busy to pull that off."

Slater's eyes narrowed. He looked so much like Dakota just then that Kate missed the older Rawlings terribly and prayed for him wherever he was.

"I think I'll go out to see her."

"All right. Send Laura in if you need to."

The deputy nodded, thanked her, and moved out the door. While he was still a way off, he spotted them, both with their backs to the house, Liberty in an old dress, her right arm moving slowly with the brush, Laura talking sixteen to the dozen beside her. Slater could see how easy it would be to keep her back to him, so he circled the barn and came up opposite Liberty, looking at her over the top of the fence.

"Hi," he said, startling her a little.

"Hello," she said and smiled some, but the greeting appeared strained.

"What made you decide to paint?"

"The fence has needed it for a while," Laura put in, and Liberty smiled down at her.

"Does this hurt your side, Libby?" Slater asked.

"No. I couldn't do it if I was left-handed, but it's not bad."

He wanted to ask what Duffy thought of the idea but chose not to baby her.

"Laura," Kate called from the house, "Josie Frank is here to see you."

"Oh, Libby! Oh, Libby," the little girl flapped, "I have to go."

"That's all right. I'll just keep painting."

Laura took off then, and Slater smiled as he watched her dress and hair fly.

"She takes good care of you."

"Yes, she does."

They fell quiet then, Slater leaning against the fence as though he had all day, his whole head showing over the top as he watched Liberty work. She was starting to grow nervous under his gaze and finally frowned, wishing she could think of some snappy thing to say. Slater went first.

"I never thought about how cute you would look with paint on your eyelashes and cheek."

Liberty shot a look at him and said, "Did you come by for some special reason, Slater?"

"Only to tell you that I love you."

Liberty nearly dropped the brush.

"It's the silliest thing," Slater went on conversationally. "You know I want to marry you and take care of you, but not how much I love you. I get things switched around sometimes."

Liberty began to paint as though she were under the gun. She told herself not to look up but to get the job done and get inside. She worked along steadily for some time and finally chanced a glance at Slater. He was gone.

Liberty's head whipped around, but he was not in sight. It was time to paint the lower half of the section she was in, so Liberty dropped to her knees. However, the brush didn't move for quite some time, and Liberty got more paint on her face attempting to wipe away the tears that she couldn't seem to stop.

❧ ❧ ❧

Liberty told herself to breathe. She had survived not being able to play the piano in church the day before and hadn't broken down, even when Slater came to sit by her. She told herself that if she could just keep busy, she would make it. Then Monday came, and she went to get the mail. Why she opened Dakota's letter just outside the building, she didn't know, but she had, and now she must find Slater.

The jailhouse was empty. She thought about heading to Hathaways' house but was fairly certain he wouldn't still be there. She had just decided to go ask Tess if she knew where Griffin was so, she could ask him about Slater, when the door opened and the man she loved stepped in.

"Hi," he said warmly, a smile coming to his face the moment he saw her. He came close but didn't try to speak. Liberty's face looked strained, and he thought she might cry if he touched her.

"You see, it's like this," Liberty began with no warning. "I just like you so much, Slater." Tears came to her eyes, but she kept on. "I have from the start. I don't know when that turned to love, but it did, and it just won't go away. But all my love, Slater, doesn't change the fear, this horrible terror inside of me, that you only feel obligated."

"I don't Libby," Slater clarified. "I promise you."

"That's what Dakota said," she told him as she handed him the letter.

Slater read, *Dear Libby, nothing would induce Slater to marry a woman out of guilt. He's always loved you. Never forget that. Dakota.*

Slater looked down at her, his heart in his eyes. "I can't tell you how true this is, Libby. I love you so much. I ache with what I feel. I wish I could have done things differently at the Potters', if only to convince you that for weeks now, I've known you were the one."

"Oh, Slater." Liberty wanted to stop crying but couldn't. "Please ask me again."

Slater's arms were around her before she saw him coming.

"Marry me?"

"Yes."

He held her gently, so very careful of her side. Liberty would have raised both arms to hold him close but could only manage one. Slater kissed her sweetly, first her soft cheek and then her mouth.

"I love you, Libby. Don't you ever forget it."

"I won't, Slater, but you can remind me anytime you want."

Slater had to laugh. The only thing fuller than his arms right now was his heart, and that was fair to bursting.

You did it, Lord, his heart cried in joy as he held Liberty with the utmost care. *I didn't know how and I didn't know when. I only knew You would. I'll spend the rest of my days thanking You for this miracle You performed on my behalf.*

Epilogue

June 1882

THE TELEGRAM READ: *Dakota hurt. Come swiftly. D. Curtis.* Slater had left for Desmond's house within the hour. Now, a week later, he moved swiftly toward Duffy and Kate's, one thought on his mind: seeing his wife.

It was getting late. Darkness was falling fast, but Slater took little notice. He heeled Arrow to just short of a run as he moved toward the home his in-laws were sharing with them until he and his wife could find a place, his heart hoping he would find Liberty on her own.

Slater took Arrow back to the barn, stabled him as swiftly as he could, and walked in ground-eating strides toward the kitchen door. All he could do was smile and lean against the door when he found Liberty at the kitchen table, a recipe book open in front of her. She was bent over reading something and took a moment to look up to see who had entered. An instant later she flew into his arms.

"I missed you," she said as soon as she could breathe.

Slater wanted only to kiss her again.

"How's Dakota?" she finally got out.

"Hurt bad," Slater said as he led her to a chair, sat in it, and invited her to sit in his lap. "He's lost a lot of blood, and he'll be at Desmond's place for a while, but he's strong. And the best news of all, Libby," Slater added, "he came to Christ."

"Oh, Slater!"

"It's true. Cash was there too. Dakota told us he's never been so scared. The bullets just kept coming, and he knew he couldn't do a thing. He said that he's never before seen how lost he was, and at that moment was completely terrified of dying. He talked to Desmond as soon as he woke up, but not until Cash and I got there did he tell anyone he was ready to talk to the Lord."

"Oh, Slater." Liberty hugged him tightly. "I've been praying and praying. I must admit that I thought the Lord might use this injury in Dakota's life, but I didn't know how completely."

Slater's sigh was heartfelt. "You should have seen his face, Lib. He looked so at peace. He's a shot-up mess, but all the fear and defensiveness are gone." Slater couldn't go on. He was suddenly too choked up to speak. He and Liberty sat quietly together until Slater heard a noise. It sounded like a tiny baby's cry.

"What was that?" Slater asked, wondering if Zach and Laura had gotten a kitten.

Liberty grinned hugely. "That's my baby sister."

Slater's mouth fell open. "Your mother had her baby?"

Liberty still grinned. "Last night, just before midnight. Come see her."

Slater was in a state of shock as Liberty led him to the living room. It was empty, save for the small person in the cradle, who was just starting to make noise.

"Well, now," she said tenderly as she scooped up the light bundle, "did you think we'd all forgotten you? You have to wake up and meet your big brother-in-law." Liberty bounced her a little and coaxed, "Come on, Jeanette, wake up and talk to us."

Liberty and Slater laughed when the baby would have none of it. She turned her face toward Liberty and went back to sleep. The three of them sat on the sofa then, and Slater took Jeanette in his arms.

"I've never seen anything so perfect," he said as he lifted her tiny hand and examined each finger. Jeanette's tiny head was beautifully shaped and covered with soft, dark fuzz. She was feather-light to hold, and for a time Slater was transfixed with this precious infant.

"How's your mother?" he suddenly remembered to ask.

"Doing great. Up and around already and feeling strong. Duffy's plan is for her to take it easy on the stairs—only two trips down a day—so I'll be bringing Jeanette down here with me so Mam can sleep and not think she's hearing the baby cry all the time."

Their eyes went back to the baby then, and for a time they just watched her. Jeanette's next cry was a real one. In no time at all, she was awake and howling, obviously ready to be fed. Liberty took her upstairs to Kate and then rejoined her husband on the sofa. They had not been apart since they'd been married in April. They spent some time catching up, both glad for a little time alone.

"We could have one of our own," Slater offered, his arms holding Liberty tightly.

"Indeed. I'm all for it," Liberty said with a smile.

Slater moved to kiss her, accidently bumping her nose.

"I'm sorry," he apologized.

Liberty shrugged it off, saying, "My aim has always been better."

Slater couldn't hold his laughter. Indeed, he was still laughing when Liberty kissed him, and as he expected, her aim was perfect.

About the Author

🌹 🌹 🌹

LORI WICK is one of the most
versatile Christian fiction writers
in the market today. Her works
include pioneer fiction, a series
set in Victorian England, and
contemporary novels. Lori's
books (over 1.5 million copies
in print) continue to delight
readers and top the Christian
bestselling fiction list.
Lori and her husband, Bob,
live in Wisconsin with
"the coolest kids
in the world."